movement from the standpoint of inquiry. He examines the pragmatic logic of consequences and its relations to positivism and operationalism.

The importance of pragmatism is usually held to lie in its logic, which attempts to relate the earlier notions of structure and process. The thesis of the author, however, is that its real significance is its conception of existence in terms of the present. This conception calls for a new form of inquiry, the nature of which is suggested briefly in the conclusion.

It is the conviction of the author that the vitality of philosophy depends on two factors: its persistence as an independent form of inquiry into reality and its close relations with significant movements and events of the times. He believes that philosophy recently has been conceived too much in terms of scientific methodology, and he attempts to show its significance as an autonomous mode of inquiry.

> *After graduating from the University of Minnesota in 1924,* OTIS LEE *studied at Oxford as a Rhodes Scholar. He then taught at the University of Michigan, Harvard University, and Pomona College and, until his recent death, was Professor of Philosophy at Vassar.*

EXISTENCE
and INQUIRY

EXISTENCE
and INQUIRY

A STUDY OF THOUGHT
in the MODERN WORLD

BY OTIS LEE

THE UNIVERSITY OF CHICAGO PRESS
CHICAGO, ILLINOIS

THE UNIVERSITY OF CHICAGO PRESS, CHICAGO 37
Cambridge University Press, London, N.W. 1, England
W. J. Gage & Co., Limited, Toronto 2B, Canada

Copyright 1949 by The University of Chicago. All rights reserved. Published 1949. Composed and printed by THE UNIVERSITY OF CHICAGO PRESS, *Chicago, Illinois, U.S.A.*

To
DOROTHY
who supplied the perspective

ACKNOWLEDGMENTS

THE writing of this book was begun during the tenure of a Guggenheim Fellowship and was continued through aid from Vassar College, including a grant from the Salmon Fund. I am grateful to the John Simon Guggenheim Memorial Foundation and to Vassar College for their assistance and for the confidence of which it was the expression. Without their support, both the thinking and the writing of the book would still be far from completion.

But, without aid of another sort, it could scarcely have been commenced at all. I am glad to acknowledge a great debt to A. N. Whitehead and Richard Kroner, from whom I first learned to understand something of the history of thought.

The analysis of the dialectical theory of negation and parts of the interpretation of pragmatism have appeared in the *Review of Metaphysics* and are reprinted with the kind permission of the editors.

TABLE OF CONTENTS

INTRODUCTION: On the Relation of History to Present Problems . 1

I. ANALYSIS 17
   1. Experience and Understanding 18
   2. The Search for Primary Truths 22
   3. Self-evidence 33
   4. Reconstruction of Familiar Facts 52
   5. Decline 66
   6. Clarity and Existence 80

II. DIALECTIC 91
   1. Opposites 94
   2. Negation 109
   3. The Course of Inquiry 129
   4. Idealism, Materialism, and Process 146
   5. Logic and Process 161
   6. Dialectic and Empiricism 184

III. PRAGMATISM 189
   1. The Origins of Pragmatism 189
   2. The Genetic and Experimental Methods 198
   3. The Notion of Consequences 216
   4. Logical Consequences 228
   5. Psychological Consequences 254
   6. Instrumentalism 267
   7. Truth, Value, and the Present 280

EXISTENCE AND INQUIRY 297

INDEX 315

INTRODUCTION: ON THE RELATION OF HISTORY TO PRESENT PROBLEMS

THE aims of this book are to describe how philosophy came to be where it is today, to evaluate its present state, and to offer some suggestions for the future. The program is ambitious. However, the book itself is modest in scope, for the argument is focused on a single topic, which defines the standpoint for selection of material and problems. That topic is "inquiry."

The subject of inquiry takes on interest at times when the foundations of knowledge are being examined. In periods of stability, we use assumptions and methods without questioning or even being aware of them. Success and habit guard them from our attention. But, when difficulties arise within inquiry itself or when the interpretation and use of its results come to be challenged from some other quarter, inquiry itself becomes a subject of examination. Our own is such a time; and both conditions for a study of inquiry are present today—the internal difficulties and the external challenge. The widespread discussion of language is a sure indication that the traditional meanings of important terms are changing or have disappeared under the impact of recent discoveries and theories. Our fundamental presuppositions, concepts, and values have been disturbed, in connection with the critical changes that are under way all through our culture, as well as within the sciences. And the uses made of scientific knowledge in technology, industry, warfare, and social control have given rise to questions concerning its place in the community and its relation to other kinds of human experience.

This condition, however, is not really new. Methods of investigation, language, the nature of knowledge, and the limitations of the human mind have been under discussion almost continuously since the beginning of the modern era. The original stimulus was supplied by the relations and conflicts between theology, philosophy, the sciences, and the arts. Theological and philosophical terms, for instance, were inadvertently employed in science; somewhat later the reverse process occurred. Discussion continued in the effort to clarify these various relations and, in particular, to define the character of a rigorously empirical study of nature. The importance of theology in the controversies gradually lessened; but that of the arts and, more recently, of human relations and the social sciences has increased. Thus the study of inquiry has been pursued almost continuously for the last three hundred years or more. The reason is that our society has continued the struggle against tradition through all that period; and its efforts have, for the most part, been in one direction. However, the tone of the discussion has gradually changed.

I use the term "inquiry" deliberately, rather than the narrower term, "method." Inquiry has a number of different aspects. First of all, it is an activity or process. But, to be more than random guessing, to be carried on effectively, it must be pursued by some definite method or by more than one; and, if a method proves inadequate, it must be modified and improved. Thus we speak of the "analytic method" and of the "historical method." The use of a method, in turn, involves subsidiary techniques. There are techniques involved in using laboratory apparatus and in weighing the authenticity and importance of historical documents; and there are techniques in reasoning, too—ways, for example, of reformulating statements of ordinary discourse in a standard language of argument and of throwing an argument into deductive form. Moreover, every inquiry has a subject matter, on which it is directed. It also has an aim or end, toward which it proceeds. Finally, as a form of rational activity, it has presuppositions, and its pursuit involves the acceptance of certain values. Thus inquiry is a complex activity.

As we proceed from the earlier part of the modern era toward the present, discussion of inquiry tends to narrow, or, at any rate, the emphasis changes. There is more stress on methods and tech-

INTRODUCTION

niques and less on object and aim. Earlier writers did publish treatises on "method," it is true; but they meant by the term something much broader than what we understand today. Nowadays, talk of method may be carried on almost to the exclusion of object and end. At any rate, this is the case in philosophy, which here seems to reflect the spirit of the time.

Discussion of method in the abstract is artificial, if not futile. In the sciences, methods are developed in relation to specific problems and subject matter. Or, if we wish to speak generally of an empirical method—it would better be called an "attitude"—it acquires specific, concrete significance in connection with each of the various branches in which it is employed. Yet abstract discussions of method are prevalent today, and they range from abstruse treatises to popular instruction on how to think clearly. They are the end-product of a historical development which has tended steadily toward the restatement of the world in terms of human experience. With reference to knowledge, this means a definition of objects in terms of the experiences of the knower. From there, one slips easily into a substitution of how we know for what we know. But, whether the transition is actually made or not, the result is a tendency to translate possible discovery into terms of actual experience and to reduce the object of inquiry to that of knowledge.

There is need, therefore, amid the general examination of assumptions now under way in our society, for a consideration of the nature of inquiry. And the need is unusually great in philosophy; for, while the crisis of our time is readily admitted in the spheres of economic, political, and social institutions, there is a tendency to assume that our conceptions of knowledge and how to attain it are fundamentally correct and that any revisions which may be necessary will be made as required, almost automatically, in the course of future investigation. We hear of a crisis of belief, but seldom of a crisis in knowledge. Yet it seems unlikely that, in a culture based on knowledge and reason as largely as our own is, the basic difficulties should be unrelated to knowledge. Either knowledge is not so important in the life of Western society as has been supposed, or what we call knowledge is not so adequate a guide to living as is often asserted.

The question therefore suggests itself, What is wrong, and what can be done? First, we must try to discover what is wrong. To know what needs to be done, it is necessary to know how the present has come to be what it is. No significant change can be effected without a study of the past; lacking that, our efforts at change are fumbling and ineffective. The first step is to come to terms with history. Every age must do this; and the sharper the break we attempt to make, the greater is the need of historical analysis. The following essays attempt to make a contribution to such analysis and evaluation in philosophy. Their content is largely historical. It is therefore perhaps appropriate at this point to consider briefly the place of historical studies in philosophy.

In general, the importance of history lies in the contribution that it makes to the knowledge of ourselves which is essential for intelligent conduct. History, understood in a broad sense, takes the place of common tradition to some extent, in modern society. For many informed and reflective people, it is a substitute for those religious, educational, and other practices by which men in other societies assimilate their common social heritage. Since our heritage has been disintegrating under the impact of individualism, we tend to learn about it, instead. But we cannot know what we are without knowing what we are not; for the metaphysical principle that being and not-being are inseparable applies to human life as it does to everything else. This, apart from other grounds of use and self-gratulation, explains the fascination which strange customs have always had for men. For this reason, the study of significant material, if intelligently pursued, is always relevant to the present and never sinks to the level of a merely antiquarian interest. The theory of the eighteenth century, that man is everywhere and at all times the same, is mistaken. The theory which has gradually displaced it, that everything is in flux and therefore human nature is always and fundamentally changing, is also mistaken. Other

INTRODUCTION

people are of interest to us because there exist both sameness and significant differences.

But the material of history is endless, and so are the alternatives to any one way of life or thought. The common complaint that historians never "explain" anything, because they are always qualifying and adding to their accounts as they discover more "causes," has some justification—though both the complaint and the writing against which it is directed often rest on misconceptions of what history should do. If we are to achieve any real results, we must limit ourselves and make a selection. It might be made according to either of two useful principles. We might choose ways of life and thought very widely divergent from our own, in order that the sharp contrasts should throw the latter into sharp relief and enable us to perceive aspects and limitations in our own point of view which we should otherwise overlook. Or we might choose periods and movements which are very close to our own and which have strongly influenced and shaped our own attitudes, presuppositions, and values.

The latter is the principle governing the choice of materials in the present volume. However, the two principles are not so different as might appear at first glance. What superficially appears to be very different from ourselves may turn out, upon examination, to have underlying similarities. And, on the other hand, it is a commonplace that nothing is so out of date as the recent past. We are often irritated by people very like ourselves, because we see in them the traits we find it hard to admit as our own. In much the same way we tend to repudiate the recent past, although we are, in fact, unconsciously influenced by it, and to swing in our thinking to an opposite extreme. Thus in examining ideas and trends of thinking in the modern world, we shall be studying both the roots of our own thought and the concepts against which the present age has reacted violently.

The past, of course, is still with us. Forms and forces deriving from other times are still exemplified and active in the present. This suggests the question: Why should we trouble to study anything at all other than ourselves? If the past still persists in the present, let us find it there; if it does not, it is gone and does not concern us. The answer is correct. In the last analysis the only valid reason for such study is the discovery of contrasts which help free us from the bonds of the familiar. If we could get them from the present, or, rather, so far as we can get from the present, there is no need to look further. But they are more difficult to discover, as well as more important, than is often supposed. That is why we need to go beyond our own experience and problems, in order fully to have the one and deal with the other.

Apart from the creation and discovery of novelties, the present is a constant selection, evaluation, and reorganization of materials at hand, which we have largely inherited. This is as true of ideas as it is of institutions. But our use of materials is never quite the same as that made in the past; just because the present is different, the use to which we put them is also somewhat different. We wish to give the materials full value, so utilize them that they may make as significant a contribution as possible to our own experience and outlook. It is therefore important to know, as well as we can, the significance that the materials had and the part that they played in the lives of our predecessors. In some cases these will be pretty much the same for us, and we shall find in the past the meaning of vital traditions. In this way, the study of history will discover to the present the value of attitudes and concepts which otherwise might be discarded as mere survivals from another age. In other instances we find that our problems, or the form in which they present themselves to us, are so different that elements which at first appear thoroughly modern have, in reality, lost the significance they once had and so deserve to be forgotten. Thus we study history not only to discover what we are but also to learn what to do.

There are two ways of studying the past. We may aim at a complete reconstruction in order to gain sympathetic insight into a way of life and an experience other than our own. Such may be the purpose not only of the study of a period in social history but also of the interpretation of a work of art or a philosophical text.

INTRODUCTION

Such interpretation involves mastery of the language in which the work was written and of usage at the time when it was written. This, in turn, requires a knowledge of the beliefs, attitudes, and ways of thought of the day, which find their expression in the language. It is necessary also to analyze the social institutions and forces of the time and the relation of the writer to them, for his place in society influences his outlook. But society is never entirely static, and the views of a man are also conditioned by the direction in which his society is moving. It is therefore important to understand the intellectual and social history of the period. This kind of study is endless, for the concrete is infinitely complex, and we can never exhaust it in description. It might be called "pure history," not because it is divorced from application, for that is not so, but because it is the effort to see the past as it was. It is an attempt to portray the concrete in its concreteness.

On the other hand, we may go to the past directly for the solution of our own specific problems. In this case, we shall take what we can use and leave the rest; and we shall select on the basis of our own needs. We shall not attempt a reconstruction. This is always a matter of degree in any case, for human energy is limited. It has become a truism that knowledge involves selection, and what better principle of selection could we find than our own needs and interests? What other principle can we possibly use, for that matter? And if history does not talk our language in this sense— if it does not touch our needs—what can it have to say to us? But if the first approach to the past is inconclusive in its results, this one is dangerous. How can we understand anything that has happened, out of its context? And if we do not have the original context, we will supply our own and thus surely misread the past in terms of the present.

The second approach, nevertheless, is the one taken in this book. There is need today for a reorientation in philosophy; and this requires a radical change in our conceptions of inquiry and truth. An analysis of the movements of thought which led up to the present will show how philosophy came to be where it is now and why. This knowledge, in turn, will help us in effecting the change that is necessary if we are to achieve a sound and healthy attitude toward philosophical questions. The analysis is undertaken solely for the aid that it may supply in dealing with the contemporary problem. The subject of the book is what is usually called "modern philosophy"—that is to say, the philosophy of the period since the rise of experimental science, the Protestant Reformation, a certain phase of capitalism, nationalism, individualism, and other movements and attitudes characteristic of our society. It is, moreover, restricted to the analysis of one philosophical problem in that period. I make no attempt to trace the history of philosophy as a whole during the period or to relate the ideas to the life and times in which they were formulated.

However, I have tried to follow one maxim throughout: Examine every point of view on its own terms and allow it to show its own standards and limitations. This might be called the "principle of internal criticism." It forbids us to impose our own assumptions on the past and commands us, instead, to find the postulates, in some part unformulated and implicit, of the outlook that we are examining. It assumes that we can actually do this, progressively, if we make the effort. And it also assumes that other periods may have been as coherent in their outlook as our own, and possibly even more so; that they had their own sets of presuppositions, aims, values, and criteria of knowledge, all more or less closely related. The degree of the coherence can be determined only by the evidence that we find. This maxim is the connecting link between the two approaches to history just mentioned; and if it can really be followed, it resolves the dilemma of choosing between them; for, if the past really will make evident its own presuppositions, standards, and aims, it is not necessary for us to impose ours on it; and if this can happen in the course of studying a restricted problem, it is not necessary to attempt a complete reconstruction. The alternatives present a false antithesis. The important question is not how far the past is like or unlike the present but how we can learn from it; and we do that by extracting its essence. And it is not true that, to understand it, we should have to reconstruct it in every detail, as though we were restoring a monument for a museum.

Here, then, are two presuppositions of the present work: First, that there is such identity in human nature at different times and places and such continuity between present and past that it is not necessary to interpret the past in terms of the present. We are capable of understanding the past. Second, that it is possible to grasp the essence of some aspects of the past without attempting anything like a complete reconstruction. Finite knowledge is possible.

The application of the principle, however, requires some understanding of those aspects of the past which are closely relevant to the subject of study. If we are to understand what any philosopher or era meant by "inquiry," for instance, we must know something of the values of the time, since, as we have seen, these or some of them are involved in the pursuit of knowledge. We must know something of how people thought, their presuppositions and their processes of reasoning. And, above all, we must know how they thought of reality, for this is the ultimate object of inquiry. How far such reconstruction must go, in order to achieve the purposes of a limited study, and how the selection is to be made, in order to present a true picture, are problems which must be dealt with individually in every undertaking. Whether they have been solved in the following essays, the reader will judge for himself.

It is my purpose to consider the significant conceptions of inquiry which have been developed in modern thought. Such a statement, of course, implies a judgment, the defense of which must be the argument itself. However, an outline will indicate the course of its development.

During the first great period of modern thought, the universe was conceived in terms of an intelligible system or structure of related elements. It had a real and basic unity; and it was not regarded as a compound, made out of elements and relations as parts. But to know anything is to grasp it in terms of them, and this can be done without falsification. The structure is the universe, as seen by the human mind. Knowledge, accordingly, is analytic in character. We understand by reducing the unknown to the known, the confused and obscure to the clear and distinct, and, for the most part, the complex to the simple. Elements or "simple natures," including relations, are the objects most easily kown to us. And, as they are elements in a totality, understanding involves a reconstruction of the whole in terms of them.

The analytic theory of inquiry has two branches. One is logical, strongly influenced by mathematics, and based on such formal principles as the laws of contradiction and identity. The other is psychological. It presupposes the formal principles, for the most part, and applies them to the sensuous content of experience, the raw material of knowledge. For both branches, analysis is directly concerned with the world as it presents itself; existence is its object. Logical reasoning is not the manipulation of postulated entities according to conventional rules; and psychological experience is not the association of private sensations into patterns, according to simple laws, which it later became. It is characteristic of the thought of this period that the critical and negative phase of inquiry, which dissolves beliefs, opinions, and the facts of common sense, is inseparable from the positive construction of rational beliefs about intelligible objects. Philosophy is a unified, double process of criticizing and reconstructing beliefs. The reason for the unity is, that, whatever the state of mind may be, it is always directed toward the world; and this direction relates its various activities.

The notion that reason is primarily criticism did not seriously influence philosophy until the conviction that we are directly in contact with things faded away. But the era of criticism which followed when that happened did not produce any important new idea about inquiry. It only stripped from the theory of analysis its essential relation to existence and employed what was left as a means of destroying superstitions. Its weakness was the failure to see that a philosophy which destroys prejudices and then stops leaves man even more helpless and vulnerable than he was before,

INTRODUCTION

shivering, so to speak, in his intellectual nakedness. His only remedy then is the romantic belief that we are naturally good and wise and so do not need to think.

The next great period was marked by the discovery of process. The first period had thought of change largely as motion in space; it also had a concept of activity somewhat like the old Greek notion of "energizing." But process is something different from both of these. It was first discovered through the study of history and then spread with the development of the biological and social sciences and with increased awareness of the inner life of man in some of its aspects. Because the world seen as process was very different from what it had been before, a new theory of inquiry was needed to deal with it. Dialectic was the answer first proposed—a logic of process. It is framed in terms of opposites, because existence itself is a process of conflicting opposites. Dialectical idealism and materialism agree on this point; but they differ in their interpretation of opposites. Idealism develops a theory of their generation and relation, while materialism assumes them as a datum and describes their interactions. In its interpretation of the history of inquiry, however, dialectic confused the superficial logic of the age of reason with the very different concept of analysis which had preceded it. In reacting against the first, it also rejected the second, and so it fails to account for structure and order—a fatal weakness. Thus, while dialectic saw the problem for knowledge which the new concept of reality involved, it could not solve it.

Dialectic has been more widely misunderstood than any other movement in modern philosophy. It has been interpreted to the English-speaking world through a British tradition committed to a point of view which makes it nonsense. The result has been the myth of the "block-universe" and the arid controversies over internal and external relations. The initial mistake was to regard idealism primarily as a theory of knowledge instead of as a theory of reality. The result was that the theory of knowledge had to be related to a concept of existence which dialectic begins by repudiating. And, since philosophy has not yet come to take society and the social sciences seriously, dialectical materialism, which so largely stems from an analysis of society, has been practically ignored.

Contemporary philosophy is still occupied with the problem of logic and process. There is need, on the one hand, for a theory of concepts and method capable of describing the traits of existence and, on the other, for some account of the relation of man himself to the process in which he is involved. The movement today which is perhaps most characteristic in these respects and which has advanced farthest toward a solution is pragmatism. It has both elaborated a logic and developed an account of its existential setting. In many ways it combines the notions of structure and process. Thinking elaborates a conceptual structure, which is then applied in experiment to the immediately experienced flow of events. The application is implied both in the structure itself, which refers to the empirical content of future events, and in the psychological habits and attitudes in which it is embodied. The pragmatic theory of inquiry is the subject of the third part of the book. No attempt is made to discuss other contemporary movements. But the contemporary predicament is a common one; all points of view are faced by the same problems and have at their disposal pretty much the same alternatives. Moreover, the other important theories of inquiry are represented in pragmatism at one point or another, just as it is to be found in them. Here, again, no attempt is made to consider systematically any other aspect of pragmatism than its doctrine of inquiry, although it is a comprehensive and many-sided movement; and this doctrine itself is chiefly a method. We shall consider pragmatism only so far as it bears on our problem. This is the justification for an emphasis which otherwise would be both arbitrary and misleading.

The examination of pragmatism is somewhat more negative in tone than is that of either analysis or dialectic. The reason is that, following the characteristic shift already mentioned, pragmatism fails to give an adequate account of the object on which its method is directed. It has a view of existence; but it has not related this

INTRODUCTION

to its theory of inquiry. There are two questions which arise in this connection. Does the pragmatic method account, or make a place, for the object of inquiry? Is the method of consequences appropriate for philosophy? I shall urge that the primary significance of pragmatism lies in its notion of present existence rather than in the method of consequences but that, to understand the present, we need another theory of inquiry than what is offered. Description of the present involves, but is not the same as, prediction of the future.

Discussion of these questions will entail some consideration of the definition of the term "consequences," which is central to the pragmatic theory of meaning and of truth. It will also necessitate some consideration of the relations between philosophy and the sciences. For a long time discussion of this matter has been colored by the opposition of positivism and transcendentalism. But there are signs that the question is now reshaping itself in more fruitful terms and that both philosophy and science are moving to positions which will lead to greater mutual respect, understanding, and aid. The question as to whether or not philosophy is scientific is futile when it is asked without further explanation. The answer depends on how science and philosophy are defined and what aspects of each are taken into account. We shall not consider all the bearings of the question. The real issue at present is this: What are the nature and assumptions of the experimental method, operationalism, or the predictive theory of knowledge, as these are understood in philosophy today; and are these concepts appropriate to serve either as instruments or as criteria of philosophical inquiry?

I have used the term "existence" rather than "reality" in the title of this book, because existence is the point of departure and the initial object of inquiry. I use the term to refer to unanalyzed experience, perceived fact, and the objects of unreflective opinion, because these all have to do with sensible, spatiotemporal entities and processes. Whether existence exhausts all that is or whether (as I believe) its examination discloses something more is a question that need not be raised here. We are primarily concerned with the starting-point; and, if inquiry should show that reality is wider than existence, the evidence will be found in existence itself. Understood in the sense explained here, existence has always been considered by philosophers to be the object of reflection and analysis. The simplest definition of reality is: that which is independent of our opinions and inquiries. I employ the term in a somewhat more restricted sense, however: either in a neutral manner (as in the next paragraph), to refer to whatever is, without either implying or denying its limitation to existence, or, more positively (as in discussing certain philosophical ideas), when the object of inquiry is held to be wider than existence. However, the meaning of this term must be partly read from the context, and I have not attempted to adhere to a single, precise definition. I have also sometimes referred to nature as the object of inquiry, using the term not as a synonym for either of the other two but rather to imply the unity or relatedness of all that is; because this is a condition of intelligibility in philosophy, the denial of which (or, more often, the mistakenly imputed denial of which) has worked much harm.

There is an element of circularity involved in thinking. Inquiry is an attempt to understand reality. Therefore, its methods, if they are to succeed, must conform to reality, in the sense of being relevant and suitable to their object. But what is reality? It is the purpose of method to discover the answer to that question; a method is needed to investigate what reality is. Yet, unless the method is in harmony with reality from the beginning, it will not be useful. With the aid of a powerful method, the process of knowing may be self-corrective; but it can hardly be maintained that the method itself will possess this characteristic, unless it is substantially correct to begin with. There is, however, nothing paradoxical in the situation. A problem arises only if we assume that the two factors are separable; it disappears when they are seen to be interdependent. The method and object of inquiry presuppose each other.

INTRODUCTION

This contention, or proposition, defines the approach of the present discussion. Inquiry has often been treated in terms of the origin and criteria of knowledge; and the result has been a classification of theories under the headings "rationalism" and "empiricism." Knowledge originates in and is tested by either reason or the experience of the senses. Other accounts have stressed the methods employed in thinking; they have given us theories of deduction, induction, and hypothesis. Of these, the first two have obvious affinities with reason and the senses, respectively; while the third was developed when this neat contrast broke down. We now recognize that empirical reasoning involves all three. I shall consider inquiry, rather, in terms of its object and shall describe its forms as functions of their objects.

It follows from the interdependence of the elements of inquiry that any method is deficient so far as it fails to include implicit reference to a correlative object and that a changed conception of reality will generate its own conception of inquiry. There does not yet exist, however, a theory of inquiry corresponding to our contemporary view of reality. It may be that a study of the circumstances out of which this situation arose will provide clues toward the construction of such a theory. To discover them is the purpose of this book.

PART I
Analysis

WE FIND ourselves in a world that is complex, obscure, urgent, and often blurred in outline. And when we begin to reflect, we find that we have prejudices, beliefs, opinions, illusions, hopes, and fears about that world. The objects we experience, then, are objects not of knowledge but of belief and faith. When we reach this point, we find that we want to get beyond our ill-defined and often untrustworthy beliefs to knowledge.

To state the same thing in different terms, experience as it comes to us is not clear, but thick and obscure; it does not have sharp edges or allow of many clean-cut distinctions. Experience in this sense includes everything; it is an all-embracing descriptive term and is equivalent to "the facts," whatever they may be. But experience has another meaning for us. There is the truism that we "learn from experience," and it implies that knowledge originates in experience rather than being identical with it. It is possible to learn from experience because the latter is a criterion or norm, by which beliefs, hypotheses, and preconceptions are tested. We bring ideas, as we say, to the test of experience. Here the term "experience" has a narrower denotation; there are some ways of experiencing and some objects of experience which exhibit certain characteristics entitling them to special consideration: they are particularly trustworthy. Thus there arises the contrast between mere experience and true experience. Common speech often combines the two. We speak of a man of wide experience or of an experienced mechanic, farmer, administrator. And we mean a person who has both done or undergone many things and also profited by them. It is important for our purpose to distinguish the two meanings very carefully. The problem of understanding the world may be stated as that of passing from the former to the latter—from the disorderly, obscure experience that is constantly surging in upon our awareness, to the orderly, clear experience which results from the application of thinking in the widest sense of that term.

1. Experience and Understanding

At this point two questions arise. First, What is it to understand? And, second, How is it possible for human beings to achieve understanding? One answer to the first question has just been suggested. It is the answer of a great, double tradition of modern philosophy: To understand is to reduce things to terms of clear and orderly experience. Or, as this school of thought expressed it, to understand is to see things in terms of indubitable, self-evident facts and truths.

We shall presently consider the meaning of the term "self-evident" at some length; but for the moment rough illustrations may suffice. Some things are intelligible in themselves, or relatively so; others are intelligible only when seen in relation to something else. The former are the self-evident—let us say "the evident," for the sake of brevity. Bad weather is not evident but, rather, an unreasonable and unpleasant surprise; its meteorological explanation is closer to being evident. The conclusion of an argument is not evident, when taken by itself; the whole of the argument or perhaps its premises are more nearly so. An act of murder is not evident; the total state of the murderer, which from one point of view might be called the cause, is more so—is more nearly intelligible. A chemical compound is not evident, but its formula might be held to be nearly so. When the mind is unimpeded in its functioning by prejudice or custom or some other cause, it grasps the evident; this is what is apprehended when the act of intellectual apprehension is unobstructed. And to understand things is either to reduce them to what is evident or to see them as following from what is evident, almost in a mathematical sense. So far as things cannot be seen in these ways, they cannot be understood.

I say that this is the answer of a double tradition in philosophy because the evident had two main interpretations. Some held that it is what is apprehended by reason; others, that it is what is apprehended by the senses. But, although the philosophies based on reason and on the senses differ in many ways, they are in agreement with respect to the criterion of truth. The true is the clear and distinct, or the intrinsically intelligible; and it is the object of contemplation rather than of action.

The second question arises because at the outset of his reflections man appears to be bound by custom, authority, and preconceptions of various sorts. And, what is even more significant, he seems to receive and register his experiences passively. How, in this initial condition, can he overcome his inertia, shake off his prejudices, and ask questions about the world, to which he does not already have his own half-unconscious answers? He needs to apply a generally valid criterion to mere experience, in order to discover whether it is true experience; he needs to measure the objects that present themselves to him by some yardstick, such as self-evidence. But where is he to find the criterion? He needs a method in order to deal with his world, to judge concerning the true and the false. But this involves general rules or general procedures. Where will he get them? He first needs the general, in order to deal with particular facts; but what he has to begin with is the particular facts and not the general at all. To get above his initial confusion, it appears that he must lift himself by his own bootstraps.

To this second question the answer of the tradition is that he does lift himself by his bootstraps. The mind possesses an inherent activity and power, and its initial passivity in the face of experience is only relative. The process of self-correction is possible only by virtue of this initial impetus, supplied by the mind itself. As the classical philosophers said, the mind has a native strength and rude native tools, by means of which it acquires some crude knowledge; with the aid of its own tools, it makes for itself more effective instruments of knowing and then uses them to make still better ones. There is such a thing as unreflective, natural knowledge of particular things, too, without which the strength of the mind would have nothing against which to exert itself. But in natural knowledge the true and the false are mixed together; and the task is to separate them—to formulate the true and eliminate the false. Improvements in the instruments of the mind are accompanied by the gradual development of the body of knowledge; the two growths are interdependent.

The procedure which the mind employs, then, in its attempts to understand the world is a developing thing and is only more or less explicit and articulate at any given time. But the steps which thinking will trace, under the guidance of the notion of self-evidence, can be outlined in a general way. The guiding idea determines a certain pattern of inquiry, which is clearly discernible in the work of all the philosophers who accepted it, although the degree of explicitness and the elements which are stressed differ from one formulation to another. There are two main processes which thinking must undertake. First, it must find self-evident facts or truths; and, second, it must reinterpret the common-sense world—the world of thick experience—in terms of them. The first of these processes might be called "analysis," the second, "synthesis." But it would be more accurate to call them two halves of a single movement, for they are not really separate or even separable. The problem of thinking is to understand the world as it is given; and they are simply the two stages in its solution.

The first stage has two parts. On the one hand, the mind must be purified of those prejudices, illusions, passions, and nonrational elements in general which prevent its apprehending what is intrinsically intelligible. This is a process of self-criticism, correction, and preparation for knowledge. It is methodological or provisional skepticism. Just as a telescope must be clean or a knife sharp, to be effective, so the mind must be cleared of debris, if it is to do its work properly. On the other hand, the complex and obscure objects of experience must be analyzed, in order to uncover the simple,

ANALYSIS

indubitable elements that are imbedded in them. This process is also one of abstraction, for, to be seen, the simple elements must be abstracted or separated from the concrete complexity in which they occur. The outcome of this double process of mental purification and analysis of data will be the acquisition by the mind of evident truths of reason or indubitable facts of sense experience. They constitute the material or foundation for all remaining knowledge.

The second stage is the reinterpretation of the world as it originally presented itself, in terms of these first principles of knowledge. This stage also has two parts. On the one hand, it is a reconstruction of the world out of certified materials. At least ideally, this reconstruction is deductive in character; for, if we knew all the simple elements and relations contained in an object or group of objects, we should be able to give a systematic account of them as they really are. The nature of an object follows from its self-evident foundation. On the other hand, reinterpretation is a process of criticism, testing, and—since the world is, after all, not a single, rational system—rejection of whatever cannot be transformed into the evident. The clear and evident aspects of things are prior for knowledge or are logically original; common-sense things, so far as they are intelligible, are derivative from and dependent on these. So far as common-sense things cannot be accounted for in such terms, they must be rejected as illusory, unreal, or fictitious. They are found to have been objects of false belief and cannot become objects of knowledge. Thus the reconstruction of the world by reason involves an element of systematic, in contrast with provisional, skepticism.

Such, in brief outline, are understanding and the way it is to be achieved, according to those thinkers who took the self-evident for the true. It is a composite picture and represents the views of no single philosopher in every detail. Yet it is the conception of inquiry and of knowledge which, though never completely formulated, dominated an important period in the history of thought. And just as, according to the thinkers of that time, general truths can be abstracted from the confused particulars in which they are embodied, so this dominant conception can be abstracted from the various theories formed under its influence. It is a point of view which we easily criticize on many grounds; but it is as important as it is difficult for us to understand.

The analysis conveniently falls into three parts. First, the process of seeking primary truths. It includes purification of the mind and analysis of the rough objects of experience. Second, the criterion of truth. We shall have to consider what self-evidence is, what reasons there may be for adopting it as a standard, and what sorts of things may be evident. This is the most difficult part of the discussion and the most important. Third, the application of primary truths to the interpretation of the world as it is crudely given to unreflective experience. This involves the attempt to reconstruct the world in rational terms and the rejection of those objects which do not admit of such reconstruction as pseudo-objects. Let us take up the topics in this order.

2. The Search for Primary Truths

Philosophy, it is often said, tries to discover the final "Why?" of things. Most of the answers that we give to this question are relative or provisional but are adequate for our purposes. Why is this man ambitious? Because of his beliefs, because of his early family relationships, because of his glands or his natural abundance of energy, because he lives in a competitive society. Why did the automobile stop? Why was the battle won or the election lost? We can quickly supply several answers to such questions, but we know that they are incomplete. When they are given, we may ask for a further explanation and repeat the same question. Is there a final "Why?" If so, it must contain its own answer, so that no further questions can, or need be, asked. This final "Why?" would be self-evident; it would contain its own explanation. But it is not necessarily philosophy that seeks final answers. If the human mind sometimes wants an explanation and not merely practical solutions for its problems, then it may look for that explanation whenever it thinks, whether in philosophy, science, or somewhere else. Such, at least, was the view of the period we are considering, which did not believe in a sharp division of intellectual labor and regarded self-evidence as the universal ideal of reason.

But, if there are evident truths and realities, a search is necessary before we can find them. We are certainly not aware of them in ordinary experience. The search has two parts, as has already been said. First, it is a struggle from the darkness of the natural mind to a state where the light of reason can shine unobstructed. Second, it is a movement from the complex and confused facts of unreflective experience to the relatively simple, primary truths which constitute the basis of all real knowledge.

These primary truths are not evident to everyone, or to anyone without a preliminary effort, because the rational activity of the mind is at first hindered by various nonrational factors. It is overlaid with ill-founded opinions and prejudices of all sorts and is distorted by the influence of custom, authority, imagination, will, and the passions. If it is the nature of man to know, this original state of the mind is unnatural. But the truth is that man has always been nonrational as well as rational; his natural rationality is as much or even more a capacity than it is a developed activity. So we need not ask, it seems, how the natural receptivity of the mind to truth became lost or impaired. It is obvious to everyone that unreflective man is sunk in prejudice, false opinion, and superstition; and these must be removed before he can apprehend truth. Whatever it may once have been, the mind is not an empty wax tablet now. The question is, rather, how it can wipe itself clean, purify itself of the extraneous influences which are already present in it. And the answer is that it purifies itself by a procedure of methodological skepticism, doubt, and criticism—a process by which the accretions of foreign matter covering the mind are scraped away.

The skepticism is only methodological because it is part of the search for truth and not a state in which the mind rests. It is brought to an end when something indubitable is reached or when opinions once rejected as unfounded are seen to have a solid foundation after all and are thus converted into knowledge. But provisionally the attempt must be made to doubt everything; and that means that the common attitudes of the mind, such as believing, imagining, opining, inferring, hoping, and fearing, must be discarded. The result of this process, when it is carried through, is that the natural light of reason is uncovered; the mind is made clean and ready to take the impression of clear and distinct ideas.

But what is it that carries out the purification? How can the mind correct its own shortcomings and heal its own diseases? If we lack not only truth but even the attitude that will lead us to it, how can we save ourselves by our own unaided efforts? Yet these are all we have. There is no doctor, no divine grace, and no human authority to whom we can turn.

These questions the philosophy of evidence never answered satisfactorily. To see why it failed to do so, we must first note an ambiguity in the notion of the deficient state of the natural mind. This state might be one in which the mind is overlaid with prejudices, the light of reason covered up but still shining, so to speak. Or it might be a state in which the native power of the mind is actually corrupted by the effect of prejudice within it. Either the operation of the mind is hampered from without, or it is impaired from within. If the first, the mind can itself correct the imagination, judgment, will, or whatever is responsible for prejudice. But in that case, why does the mind not always apprehend the truth? Why is a search necessary at all? If the second, there is a difficulty in seeing how self-correction is possible at all. We might perhaps say that there are two kinds of reason, a fallible judgment which is corrupted and another reasoning power which is not. Or we might say that there is a negative, critical reason which dissolves prejudice, as well as a positive and contemplative reason which apprehends truth and that the second is powerless until the first has done its work. But these suggestions raise questions as to the relation between the two and what they have in common, that entitles both to be called "reason." Their greatest weakness is that they attempt to explain the criticism of limited activities of the

ANALYSIS

mind, such as imagining, opining, and judging, in terms of another activity which is no less limited than those it criticizes; but one limited mental activity is not likely to come nearer to truth than is another on the same level.

There seem to be at least two possible answers to the question of how fallible man can improve his knowledge. The methodological skeptics wavered between them because they never resolved the ambiguity which we have described. One possibility is that there is a single reason which inquires as well as apprehends and that the second activity presupposes the first, which would explain why doubt must precede the grasp of truth. In this case mind is not limited, as imagination, judgment, and the rest are. The other possibility is that, while reason grasps truth, it is the whole individual who doubts and inquires rather than any special part of his nature; although mind is less restricted than are other activities, such as imagination, it is still limited enough to be unable to correct its own deficiencies. The methodological skeptics could never choose between these alternatives because, while they conceived of man as rational and were thus inclined to say that inquiry is a rational activity, at the same time, their contemplative notions of mind and truth inclined them to say that all mental processes are at least partly nonrational and aim at a mental apprehension which is not a process at all. They tended to think of reason as an activity which is not a process. They wanted to hold that the mind inquires as well as apprehends; but an inability to explain how mind, being contemplative, can inquire weakened their position. A conception of mind as process developed only later, when difficulties inherent in the theory of mind as contemplative had emerged. But failure to resolve this difficulty did not weaken their strong conviction that self-examination is a prerequisite to knowledge.

The search for primary truths is also an analysis of the confused objects of thick experience into clear and distinct elements or of complexes into their relatively simple constituents. We analyze a piece of music in this sense, when we distinguish the notes, themes, key, rhythm, and other elements in it. However, it must not be assumed that the objects of thick experience are capable of such analysis or reduction without remainder; they may contain factors which never can be made clear. Nor is it implied that such constituents as may be found are in some sense prior to the total complex from which they are derived; this is another question. The process is perhaps better described as "abstraction," which is one kind of analysis. We abstract circularity from a plate or wheel when we attend to this property and ignore the others; or it is sometimes said that we abstract from the others when we pick out the shape. The act is the same, whichever way it is stated. Descartes refers to his procedure in the *Meditations* as "analysis," but the term does not fit, if it implies a complete translation of the confused and complex into the clear and simple; for, although he begins by partially analyzing crude experience, he then discards rather than analyzes further most of what he finds. It is really abstraction, for, in rejecting unfounded opinions and eliminating the influence of the imagination, passions, senses, and will, he is abstracting from them all and from their objects, leaving behind a residue of truth. The search that we are considering is an abstractive analysis.

It has a number of different aspects, which were not always clearly distinguished. In the first place, as we have seen, it is a movement from the confused and obscure to the clear and distinct. But it is also a movement from the complex to the simple. Here we are describing aspects of experience. If we turn to their objects, we find a corresponding relation of dependence. The music itself is conditioned by the notes, just as our clear idea of it is conditioned by our ideas of them. A material object composed of atoms is conditioned by them, and they might even be described as its "cause." So we have a movement in the object, from conditioned to condition or from effect to cause. If the condition is an infinite reality, of which conditioned objects are finite manifestations, the movement is also from part to whole (though in this case it can hardly be described as an abstractive analysis). God as infinite

ANALYSIS

being may be identified with the whole of things; and in that case the natural objects which are effects of his activity are at least analogous to parts. To understand them is to see them in relation to the whole, the primary truth on which they depend. Sometimes, however, analysis is from whole to parts, as when an object of sense-perception is analyzed into those dimensions, aspects, or properties which science describes. As a transition from non-evident to evident, the movement is also from opinion to knowledge and from unknown to known. This last is close to the mathematical meaning of the analytic method at the time.

Of all these aspects the two most prominent were the first: the search is for the clear and distinct, and it is for the simple. These are not necessarily the same; a simple color may be obscurely seen in a dim light, and a complex mathematical proof may be clear and distinct. But it is easy to understand why they tended to be identified. A color or a shape is certainly simpler than the physical object that is colored and shaped; and these properties are also clearer or sharper, when we discriminate them. The law of contradiction is both simpler and clearer to the mind than is the argument in which it is employed. Though not identical, the two aspects obviously have some relation. But the first is the most important, for our starting-point is the crude world of common sense, and that world as we experience it is conspicuously characterized by confusion and obscurity; in what respects it is simple and in what complex, on the other hand, is not easy to say. Of course, it cannot be known in advance that the inquiring mind will find any object that is perfectly clear and distinct or absolutely simple. All we can say is that, if the world is to be understood, such objects must be found, for they are the basis of all explanation; and as they are more closely approximated, the world is better known.

It might also be said that the search for first principles is a quest for the origins of knowledge. The empiricists maintained that no idea or word is understood until its origins in sense experience are discovered. Thus our idea of infinity is essentially the imagined sensation of going on endlessly in space or time. But, while this aspect was, no doubt, a factor in empiricism, it was certainly subordinate. To any philosophy which finds its principles of explanation in the self-evident, the question of origins is secondary; the difference between what came earlier and what later in experience is unimportant. So long as ideas really are evident, they are true; and to ask whether they appeared early or late in the history of the individual is irrelevant to the problem of knowledge. If there is any reason for mistrusting the derivative, it will not be because it came later but because it is confused or contains additions from the judgment or the imagination and therefore is not entirely evident. We may imagine that we have some other than a sensuous idea of infinity, though we do not. The search for origins is essentially the one already considered, from the confused to the clear, and only incidentally from the genetically derivative to the original. Or it is the process of skeptically discarding the additions of the imagination and judgment, leaving only the originally given, evident, sense data.

Mental purification and abstractive analysis are closely related. It is characteristic of the philosophy of self-evidence to consider the mind and its objects together; in clarifying the one, we also clarify the other. There is no separation between mind and nature or even between thought and existence. We do not formulate clear ideas as hypotheses and then set out to discover whether they are true; this notion for the most part is a later development. A clouded apprehension will be directed on confused and at least partly false objects, while a clear apprehension will grasp clear and distinct objects, which are also true. While skepticism purifies the mind, abstraction clarifies its objects. The natural light of reason, when it operates freely, grasps evident, primary truths. As we advance from unknown to known, from confused to clear, in experience, we are also moving from conditioned to condition in its objects. Knowing and being, the logical and the ontological, are for the most part inseparable.

They are not entirely so, however. To Bacon, for example, they were partly separate. Skepticism is the destruction of the four

ANALYSIS

kinds of intellectual "idols" which the natural mind worships, and it ends in the uncovering of the understanding. But whether it also results directly in an apprehension of simple natures (which are analogous to clear and distinct ideas) is not clear. So far as he holds that inquiry is the inductive investigation of nature, it appears that the discovery of simple natures will come only at the end of a further investigation. On the other hand, he occasionally says that induction cannot proceed without the previous formation of clear conceptions or notions. He does not tell us how we are to form such conceptions, and the explanation of the omission is perhaps a vague feeling on his part that the destruction of the idols will at the same time be the revelation of clear notions of simple natures. Clear notions—but not the natures themselves. In this distinction lies his desertion of the philosophy of evidence, for the notions are only possibilities, whose reality in nature must be tested by observation and induction. Here is the beginning of another conception of inquiry. To him, the natural reason is weak, even when armed with logical instruments, and needs to turn to observation before it can accomplish anything in the way of understanding the real world. Intellectual purification ends, if not with an empty mind, at least with a mind devoid of any knowledge other than a few verbal definitions and an awareness of its own ignorance.

To Descartes the natural light is strong; to purify the mind is to enable it to think clearly; and, when it thinks clearly, it will see its appropriate objects, the basic principles of reality, such as the true ideas of God, matter, and the mind. The difference between the men is one of emphasis. Bacon emphasizes the importance of particular, factual knowledge. Descartes, while aware of the necessity for observation and experiment, stresses the importance of rules of procedure for the mind and a general method. Rules are for him, however, aids to the mind in wrestling with its own self-delusion, as much as in investigating nature; and he does not separate them from the activity of the mind as Bacon does; an active mind will inevitably be logical—though the logic may be partly implicit, and, so far as it is, the activity will be hindered.

He telescopes the two processes into one and thereby shows his genius. Method is not so much a tool as an attitude. Inquiry and apprehension are to him inseparable, in that success in the one is also success in the other.

We asked a little while ago how the mind can purify itself. A more difficult question, perhaps, is why it needs to do so. If we have the power to understand the reasons of things, must we not actually know them somehow, even though we are unaware of it? We must at least have known them in the past. For the power of reason as here conceived is not a developing, evolving thing; it is complete at every moment. And a power that is not exercised at all seems a contradiction in terms. Nor is it explained how, if man was once rational, he later became credulous. How did he fall from the state in which he affirmed only what he knew? The philosophy of evidence is not interested in this question. It has no myth of Eden and the Fall of man. To be consistent, it must choose between two alternatives: either reason once knew primary truths and then lost them; or else it still has them in some form. The second is the alternative which it tends to adopt.

This is illustrated in the philosophy of Locke. He largely omits the search for primary truths, because he believes that the simple ideas of sense—such as blue, sweet, hard, pleasant, square—which he regards as primary truths, are given to man originally in experience and man still has them. Locke begins his work with a criticism of "innate principles," all of which he denies to be in the mind before experience writes on it. But he does not really consider such criticism an indispensable preliminary to knowledge. The doctrines which he is combating are not, to him, the universal and inevitable superstitions of men; they are merely the views of a school which happens to be contemporary with him and imposes on people who are too lazy to exercise their natural common sense. His real beginning is with the doctrine of simple ideas, and he never doubts that these are present to the mind of everyone. He writes as though we were directly aware of blue, sweet, hard, and the rest at every moment—or, rather, as though

ANALYSIS

we were aware of automobiles and crowds of people, tables, and chairs, as complexes of these qualities. The only mental processes which he discusses seriously are those of building the structure of knowledge from the materials given by experience. His real skepticism is directed not toward the materials employed but toward the unsound construction in what passes for, but is not, real knowledge. One reason for his neglect of criticism is, no doubt, the fact that he is building on the results of Bacon, who had already exposed superstitions in his discussion of the idols; but this is not the whole explanation.

Hume is even more perfunctory than Locke. After a few introductory remarks on the need for a study of human nature, he goes on abruptly to the division of perceptions into impressions and ideas; his real beginning is with sensations and their copies in memory. He does, it is true, feel that the basis of all knowledge up to the present has been shaky, for lack of such a study; but he makes no attempt to explain the errors of his predecessors systematically, and it is hard to see how they went wrong, if the basis of solid knowledge is as obvious as he makes it seem.

If we turn to Spinoza, who bases his philosophy on reason rather than on the senses, we meet with a procedure somewhat similar in nature. He begins his system abruptly, with self-evident definitions and axioms. However, there is a difference, for he had prefaced the system with an earlier, critical work on the improvement of the understanding, ending with an unfinished theory of definition. He may not succeed in bridging the gap between concrete experience and his primary truths; but he tries, and he is keenly aware that the latter are not given. Moreover, he does not regard them exactly as the materials of knowledge.

Philosophical first principles are never given but must be somehow squeezed out of everyday experience: this is the simple moral to be drawn from the theory of methodological skepticism. And it is interesting that the philosophers who relied on reason, in this period, were less dogmatic in this respect than were those who defended the senses. They were more suspicious of the preconceptions of the unreflective mind and therefore more aware of the necessity for some process that would dissolve them. The empirical Locke, on the other hand, thinks that, without effort, we have simple ideas which are direct perceptions of things and provide a solid foundation for knowledge. Either they are not so simple as he claims, we may suspect, or they are not direct revelations of things. And Hume is unfaithful to his own professed method; for in the introduction to his study of human nature he says that he will limit himself to the observation of human life and not make experiments, which would disturb the natural processes of the mind and make a just conclusion impossible—this inability differentiates moral from natural philosophy. But his book is sprinkled with injunctions to the reader to suppose so and so or to imagine such and such—in other words, to perform imaginative experiments. And he falls into an inconsistency in the very first section; for, after saying that simple ideas are always derived from simple impressions, he proceeds to suppose a scale of sensed colors, with only one shade of blue missing, and concludes that an individual who had sensed all the colors but one could fill in the missing item from his imagination. Both men attenuated the preliminary inquiry that is a part of all philosophizing. If they had been more critical, they might have seen that the impressions and simple ideas which they regarded as the self-evident basis of knowledge are no more given than are the innate ideas of their opponents; and if they had seen that, they might have been as critical of the supposed materials of knowledge as they were of the somewhat shaky edifice constructed out of them by the human mind.

To sum up, then, a preliminary inquiry more or less complete or attenuated leads to a direct grasp of basic truths. Their discovery provides the transition to the next process, which is the drawing of inferences from them and the reconstruction of complex objects from simple entities. The basis of this entire process is the self-evident.

ANALYSIS
3. Self-evidence

Philosophy, it used to be said, is not satisfied with a mere description of things but looks beyond for their explanation. What difference may be intended between description and explanation in this statement is not very clear; but, at least in part, it seems to be a matter of completeness. A description of facts is always incomplete, but explanation is complete and final. The statement "The population of Los Angeles is increasing" is susceptible of empirical verification and also of amplification. We can ask how rapidly it is increasing, what evidence there is for the trend, and what its causes are; all these are matters of further description. But the statement "A is A," which says that every entity, no matter what it may be, is identical with itself, cannot be expanded or explained in the same way, although it can be illustrated and commented on. It is as intelligible or as self-explanatory in its stated form as it would be after any further remarks that might be made. Philosophy, the original statement perhaps means to say, looks for the intelligible in this sense. But if this is its meaning, the aim of philosophy is to describe, after all: to describe the intelligible or the self-evident.

This is the view that was taken during the historical period which we are considering. It has sometimes been held that philosophy is concerned with norms or values—with what ought to be, with ideals or imperatives. Some, on the contrary, have maintained that philosophy deals with necessities or what must be, leaving the contingent facts of experience to others. But to the men we are concerned with, philosophy describes what is. It is in the indicative mood and deals with actualities, not with possibilities, imperatives, or necessities. The why of things is a discoverable, describable entity or entities, which are the foundation of everything else. A sound, sweetness, the appearance of a thing, simple mathematical truths, the self as existing, God as existing or being from his own nature—these are instances of such evident and basic entities, rational or sensuous, but in either case real.

This presupposes that there is something to be described; there must be something objective that has the property of being self-evident. The evident is given or presented to consciousness. It forces itself upon the mind and cannot be doubted or denied. Thus the identification of the evident and the true, which was made by all these philosophers, depends on the presupposition that knowledge is apprehension. And the basic claim of the philosophy of evidence might be stated as the proposition, "Reality can be apprehended."

There is in the notion of the evident a mental factor, too. Apprehension carries with it certitude, and certitude is a mental state; it involves absence of doubt in the subject who apprehends. And yet it is not merely absence of doubt, for it is quite possible not to doubt and yet not to be certain. Certitude is a conviction which excludes not only doubt but also the very possibility of doubting. Such a conviction, however, cannot be generated by the mind in itself; it must originate in an object. This is the basis of every philosophy which accepts self-evidence as a valid category. We may persuade ourselves that we are "sure" of something without sufficient evidence, but such a psychological state is not certainty. It is partly subjective in origin, and it is unstable. The concept of certainty excludes both of these. Thus it is a mistake to think of certainty as an independent fact, existing, as it were, in a vacuum. It arises only when an object of the proper sort is presented to the mind—that is to say, is present to a mind capable of grasping it. So the mental factor in self-evidence is not separable from the nonmental. Evidence implies stability in the mind and intelligibility in its object.

To claim that reality can be apprehended is to assert that it is, sometimes at least, directly present in ideas or experiences. This claim was made, in one form or another, by all the classical philosophers. Descartes says in his reply to the first set of *Objections* that "an idea is the thing thought of itself, in so far as it is objectively in the understanding."[1] The doctrine of objective reality

1. *Philosophical Works of Descartes*, trans. Haldane and Ross (Cambridge, 1912), II, 8.

expressed in this statement asserts an identity between idea and object. An idea having objective reality must have an object or thing as its cause; but the cause is present in the effect, so that the idea actually is its object, though incompletely and perhaps imperfectly. Yet this does not mean that the idea should be or professes to be its object in any other sense than "objectively." The idea is the object in ideal or representational form.

It was denied by Spinoza that man has freedom to suspend his judgment, because ideas involve affirmation or negation; as he said, the will, which affirms or denies, and understanding, which perceives and conceives, are the same. The ground of his position is this same contention that ideas, even those of sense, contain reality in the dimension of thought; this is why the understanding in the act of apprehending also asserts or, on some further basis, denies them. There are no mere ideas separate from reality, not even false ones. Again, according to Locke, "our Senses, conversant about particular sensible objects, do convey into the mind several distinct perceptions of things."[2] Our senses are conversant about objects not ideas; and our perceptions are of things. And, while Locke is not unaware of the difficulties implicit in the phrase "perceptions of things" and the ambiguity of the word "of," he is assured that sense knowledge is real; for we cannot create simple ideas of sense, which force themselves upon us and show that nature is present to, and operating upon, us at the time. Therefore he can speak of "the existence of things actually present to our senses."[3] But these are present as idea, and the doctrine is the same in principle as that of objective reality, although Locke, of course, holds other views inconsistent with it—and, for that matter, makes statements elsewhere on the same subject that are inconsistent with this. When he assigns vivacity as a characteristic of impressions and makes it the criterion of experienced reality, Hume follows out the same view that ideas of sense force themselves on us. Belief depends entirely on vividness and varies with it. Why vivid ideas should

2. *Essay concerning Human Understanding,* Book II, chap. i, ¶3.
3. *Ibid.,* Book IV, chap. iii, ¶ 5.

be objects of belief, faint ones not, Hume can give no reason, nor does he feel it necessary to do so. Nature compels us to believe; and, while from the point of view of reason such vivid ideas may be mere experience, from the point of view of feeling and instinct, which have and ought to have the final word, they are true experience. The distinction between reality and imagination stands, for Hume, precisely as long as the claim that reality can be apprehended stands also.

The self-evident has two properties, identity and intelligibility, which, however, tend to coalesce into one. First, the evident has a nature or identity of its own. If an object is evident, it will be clear what its nature is. For example, the number 1 will be seen to be odd, to be unity, and not to contain integers as proper parts. In general, anything evident will be seen to contain a certain property, such as a, and not to contain its contraries, such as b or c. The number 1 is odd, and it is not even. If this were not so, we might be unable to discern whether the object was a or b and whether it was a or not-a; it might even be contradictory, both a and not-a at once. But, if it is evident, its positive nature excludes everything else; what it is, is apprehended and excludes all other qualities and objects. So long as it occurs, it occurs as itself: a is a. It exemplifies the law of identity, of which the law of contradiction is only a negative statement.

The evident is also intelligible, which means that it is in a certain respect self-contained or complete in itself. For this reason, its nature can be understood apart from the relations in which it may stand, or into which it may enter, with other things. We can know what the number 1 is, without knowing its relations to the rest of the integers and the other numbers, because 1 is an entity. The statement of Descartes, "I think, therefore I am," is certainly true for him because the thinking self is an entity, complete as it exists, in spite of the fact that it was created by God.

These two properties, identity and intelligibility, tend to be identified. If we consider a sense-experience of red, for example, we may ask whether the red is self-evident to the perceiver. The

ANALYSIS

answer is that it is if the nature of red is complete and intelligible in itself. The philosophers who denied that such a sense quality is ever evident did so precisely because they denied that it has an intelligible nature. They maintained, on the contrary, that all sense qualities are obscure and confused and are intelligible only through a knowledge of their causes. This implies that they are vague, if not actually self-contradictory in some respect. If we consider the self, the same thing is true. Those philosophers who held it to be evident assigned it a nature complete and intelligible in itself; those who denied its evidence did so because they maintained that its nature is inseparable from that of its cause or causes. Things which have a nature are intelligible, and those which do not have a nature and identity of their own are not intelligible by themselves.

This amounts to saying that the evident is in a certain respect like a substance—both have self-contained natures. Hume actually says in one place that, since our perceptions are each distinct and separable from everything else, they may be considered substances, if that term is defined to mean something which may exist by itself. The most characteristic metaphysical problem of the period was probably the nature of substance—a problem which Hume, of course, in the last analysis rejected as meaningless. Thus we see that a theory of inquiry cannot be separated from metaphysics. We may also see that the concept of self-evidence raises certain problems. For instance, how many evident objects can there be? If the evident is the complete, it would appear that only God, the universe, or all reality can be evident, for only these are complete. Yet it does not seem that these can be directly apprehended. Then is there anything at all that is evident? The integer 1, it would seem, is a poor example, for it is not self-contained; the concept of 1 is part of and inseparable from the whole system of number concepts. On the other hand, if there are many evident objects, each of which is complete, how can they be related, either to each other or to that common-sense world which they are supposed to explain? Let us postpone these questions, however, and consider a further, negative property of the evident.

EXISTENCE AND INQUIRY

The evident is not necessary, although knowledge of it is certain. A good example is again my own existence, which is self-evident and cannot be doubted by me, though it is not necessary, since I am a contingent being. As we said earlier, the philosophy of evidence describes what is; it does not say what must be or what might be. To state the same thing differently, actuality is a more ultimate aspect of the universe than necessity is. There is no necessity higher than this fact, that a thing is what it is. This is an important point and calls for comment.

If a thing must be what it is, the necessity is either (*a*) external or (*b*) internal. In the first case, *a,* the existence of the thing is conditioned by whatever external cause or factor brings it about. In other words, it is contingent things, individual natural objects, that are necessary, because their existence is necessitated by their causes. In that case, either the nature of the thing which is conditioned is not affected by this fact; or, if it is affected by its external conditioning, then it is not evident in itself. To say that every man must die is to assert something about his existence. But either it refers to external causes, nature or God, and leaves his own being perfectly intelligible; or else it refers to the internal corruptibility of his own nature, and then the latter is not self-evident, either because of his own imperfections or because of his dependence on God and nature, or both. So that when it is true to say that A is necessary, either this does not affect its self-evidence; or else A is not evident at all, not because it is not "necessary" but because it is not complete. In the second case, *b,* we say nothing further about the thing when we say that it is necessary. If a thing must be what it is from its own internal nature, then it must be what it is because—it is what it is; the necessity follows from, or is a part of, what it is in fact. God is a necessary being, or the necessary being. But this only means that he is completely intelligible in himself, apart from any conditions, causes, or relations to other things. That is part of the ontological argument, which holds that the existence of God is necessary because he is what he is; the necessity is simply a corollary from the actuality.

ANALYSIS

The evident, then, is neither necessary nor possible but simply actual; this is behind the statement that truth is an intrinsic, not an extrinsic, property of an idea or that clear and distinct ideas are true. When the nature of an object forces itself clearly on the apprehension, it is impossible that the apprehension should be mistaken or the object misleading. Therefore, so far as ideas have reality, they do not need to be examined, tested, or validated. If ideas actually are objects as these enter into experience, their relations to objects need not be investigated to determine whether the ideas are false, for the latter will never be mere experience but always true experience. To say that an object is self-evident is to say that the idea of it is true and the knowledge of it certain.

Not everything experienced is evident. Whatever enters awareness is given somehow; but not everything is given to the understanding. Some things are felt, acted on, believed, or inferred, but they are not clearly apprehended; there are many kinds of experience, of which apprehension is only one. Similarly, there are many kinds of objects, of which the evident is only one; some objects, instead, are imaginary, indeterminate, dubious, pleasant, or baffling. But some ideas and things which at first are not evident may later become so. It will seem strange to some to say that an idea may be had without being completely known for what it is, and may become clear only on examination. One might suppose that an idea is just what it appears to be, and above all for thinkers such as those we are considering, to whom the mind is essentially conscious. But, according to the doctrine of evidence, just as an object is present in its idea, so also the idea takes on something of the independence of its object. It has an enduring identity and may be subjected to analysis. Consequently, inquiry consists not only in replacing inferior ideas by better ones but also in acquiring a more exhaustive knowledge of the ones had from the outset. This is why the statement that the self-evident is the true is not the tautology that it might seem to be. It appears to say only that the evident is the evident. If an idea is evident, it asserts itself, or the object asserts itself in the idea; and if it does not assert itself, it is not evident. If it asserts itself, it is true; if it does not, it is false. To say that an idea is true is simply to repeat that it is evident, so our supposed criterion of truth comes to nothing. But the tautology is specious, for "evident" means intrinsically evident, while "true" means evident to the mind. The intrinsically evident is not always evident to us, though it can become so by changes in our mental attitude and activity. The rights of man and a mathematical theorem are perhaps not understood by children, but that is not the point.

It is not easy to say precisely what kinds of ideas and objects are or can become evident to the mind, and what ones not. To determine this, let us begin by distinguishing three kinds of ideas. The classification is that of the rationalists, but it can be stretched to cover sensuous ideas as well, without doing violence to history. (1) A clear idea is one that appears steadily and strongly to awareness and hence is distinguishable from every other. It is not wavering, unsteady, or weak. (2) A distinct idea is known not only as a unit but by its internal characteristics, all or some of which are clearly perceived. I may have clear ideas of circle and ellipse, so that I never confuse one with the other; but neither idea is distinct unless I can enumerate one or more of its properties. Or I may have clear visual ideas of two men in the distance; but the men are not distinctly perceived unless I distinguish each, not merely as a whole and by the place he occupies in my total visual field but also by intrinsic characteristics of the "idea" I have of him. (3) An adequate idea contains nothing that is not clear and distinct; its entire content or nature is apparent to awareness. The adequate idea of a circle is an exhaustive description of it.

The philosophers of sense did not make much use of this kind of classification because they, and particularly Locke, tended to think that the given idea is simple. Consequently, they were inclined to regard a clear idea as also distinct and adequate, since the simple must be completely given if it is given at all. If the taste in my mouth is definite enough to have a distinct quality and to be called, let us say, sweet, then it is completely presented to my awareness. Their attention was centered primarily on the ways in which simple and evident ideas are combined. But they and the philosophers of reason agreed that there are simple entities and complex ones. Their difference was over the classification of specific ideas. From the sense point of view, ideas such as blue, solid, and warm are simple and evident; from the rational, they are complex, obscure, and confused. From the first point of view, the idea of substance is complex and perhaps hopelessly confused; from the second, it is an evident and, in the sense of being irreducible, simple idea. The two seemed to agree on the simplicity of some ideas, such as unity, motion, and spatial figure; but the agreement was only verbal, for they understood different things by the same word.

The question is, How many kinds of ideas are evident? Clearly, an adequate idea must be, for it is completely before the mind, so there is no possibility of mistaking its identity. It is understandable why philosophers have looked for simple ideas and simple entities of all sorts, for the simple or unanalyzable must be apparent to the mind in its completeness, if it is present at all. It cannot be partly apparent and partly not, since it is without parts; nor can it be mistaken for anything else, since there is no basis for similarity, if it is completely simple. In short, simple ideas must be adequate if they are clear; the clear and simple is indubitable and altogether intelligible. And any other ideas which are present to the understanding in all parts and respects will also be adequate and therefore evident. At the other extreme, a complex idea that is merely clear will not be evident, for its nature will not be present to the mind, except in a confused way. The problem lies in the intermediate class.

A distinct idea is clear and something more, for it is known not only as a unit but also in its parts, or some of them. It comes closer to being evident than does a merely clear one, for its nature is better known. But is it really evident unless it is also adequate? It seems not; I cannot know it in the full sense, it would appear, unless I know everything it contains. Suppose I have the idea of a right triangle and think of it as having three sides and three interior angles, one of which equals 90°. This idea is not altogether indeterminate; I have distinguished some of its parts. Yet my idea is not evident, for I have not stated that the remaining angles must total 90°; I may be under the impression that one of them could be obtuse. It might be objected that in that case I do not really have the idea of a right triangle, or even of a triangle at all. That may be; but, if so, the consequence seems to be that to have an idea is to grasp it either in its entirety—adequately—or else simply as a unit, without distinct parts—in other words, that there are only clear ideas and adequate ideas, while the distinct merge with the latter. Perhaps even clear ideas drop out, leaving only the adequate. For instance, if I have a clear sensuous idea of a man in the distance, as I look down the street, it might be said that it is an adequate idea of a man, though not of a tall or short, intelligent or stupid man, and not an adequate idea of Smith or Jones. To have an idea is to *have* it, adequately. What such an objection forgets is that we are talking of ideas of things or objects—which ideas, therefore, can, in their intrinsic characters, be better or worse representations of those objects. And the three kinds of ideas form a valid classification because they constitute three different ways in which ideas can represent objects.

To return to the problem of whether a clear and distinct idea is self-evident, let us take two test cases characteristic of the period: the ideas of space and of God. Now ideas and things have both intrinsic natures and relations to other ideas and things. We may say that an idea will be evident, although not adequate, if enough of its intrinsic nature is apparent to convey to us the uniqueness of its object, even though we do not know everything which the latter contains. In that case we can never confuse it with other ideas, or the object with other objects. Such seems to be the case with the two ideas in question. Is the idea of space simple? Yes and no. Space has parts, and in our idea of it we do not apprehend them all; or if it be objected that space does not intrinsically have distinct parts, at least it has various aspects and qualities. On the other hand, there is an extensiveness, or quality of being spread out, which is simple, unique, and directly apprehended; and if this is what we mean by "space," then the idea is simple. Grant that our idea of space includes extensiveness. Then it is distinct and evident, for extensiveness is enough to differentiate space from all other things, in spite of the fact that space has many other characteristics. (We may ignore in our illustration the fact that there is a more general extensiveness which comprehends both space and time.) Here an intrinsic character guarantees relational distinctness; the idea conveys the essential nature of space to us, without communicating its complete nature. Similarly, our idea of God is clear, distinct, and evident if we know that God is absolutely infinite, even though we do not comprehend his nature in its completeness; for, although our idea of infinity is itself inadequate and perhaps largely negative, it enables us to distinguish God from everything else and the idea of him from all others, through our grasp of an essential property.

Thus the difference between "distinct" and "adequate" is one in degree of analysis. Something like the ancient distinction between essence and accident is suggested; but there is a difference, for it is not implied here that the unknown characteristics are only accidents. Distinctness involves the translation of essential attributes of the idea into simple or primitive notions; adequacy requires the translation of all attributes into these terms. Leibniz, doubting whether the process could be completed by man, at least in most cases, added a fourth class of ideas, or perhaps rather a fourth way of knowing: an intuitive idea is one whose full nature is apparent to the understanding at a single glance, without the use of symbols representing to the mind parts of its nature.

Here, then, is a test: an idea is humanly self-evident and true if it presents enough of the nature of its object so that we know in it an essential property of that object. Truth, clearness and distinctness, self-evidence, and the full analysis of some essential attributes belong together. Adequacy involves something more. An adequate idea is not more true than one which is only distinct, nor is it more evident, for a clear and distinct idea is evident and true in itself; but it is more completely known. Truth and evidence, however, do not require that idea and object be completely known. Thus truth and certainty are attainable by man, even though his knowledge is limited, for they are definable in terms commensurate with his finite mind.

We are now in a position to classify the ideas and objects which may become self-evident. No formal definition can be given, beyond what has just been said: we can only say that they are those entitities which can be immediately apprehended by the mind. Also the ones with which we are now concerned are attained without the necessity for any but a critical process of reasoning. However, we can broadly distinguish three groups of entities which, according to the tradition, can be so apprehended.

First of all are the simple entities; why they are evident has already been indicated. There are various possible ways of classifying simples, almost as many as there are philosophies which admit them. But there are two main types which we need to note here: the simple natures of reason and the simple ideas of sense. Descartes is a good representative of those who accepted the first, Locke of those who primarily, though by no means exclusively, built on the second. For the one, God, the self, and motion are instances of simples; for the other, such qualities as white, hard, and sweet. As we have noted, some ideas, such as motion, unity, and even the mind, appear to be accepted by both. But I think examination would reveal subtle differences in these cases, implied if not always explicitly stated. To anticipate, these simple entities are the ultimate constituents of the objects of knowledge; at present, it need only be said that they are the ultimate products of a process of analysis or the ultimate materials or data which an examination of experience discloses. For most, and probably all, of the philosophers they include relations as well as terms, though it was the latter which were most stressed, particularly by the advocates of sense. They are unanalyzable by the mind. Locke is more extreme on this point than is Descartes, who admits that there are relatively simple entities which deserve the name. To the latter, for example, a universal, which is, from one point of view, simpler than a particular, is yet complex, since it is related to the various particulars from which it was abstracted by a comparison of them.

Second, there are complexes which are immediately grasped rather than seen after a process of construction. They consist of simple elements in relation; and, in order to be grasped both as units and in their details, the relations as well as the elements involved must be seen. For instance, "red to the left of green" might be directly grasped as we look at objects; or "3 greater than 2" as we think of numbers. To Locke, some relations between simple ideas are immediately self-evident; yet it is doubtful whether he would say that they are as directly given as are simple ideas. However, it seems that the complex impressions of Hume clearly belong here, although they are probably clear and distinct rather than adequate. As I receive impressions through my eyes or ears, I do not at first acquire merely separate and simple sensations, which I then combine. I actually perceive patterns of sounds and of colored shapes, as well. That is, parts are discerned in a complex impression; yet it seems doubtful whether Hume believed that all the parts and their relations to one another are necessarily seen in any such case. Historically speaking, this is the least important of the three classes; yet it must be admitted, at least as a possibility, that skepticism and analysis might never reach the simple and that the evidently given and primary materials of knowledge might be complex—as Hume saw.

Third, there are axioms or common notions. These are principles or laws that are universally valid and can be abstracted from crude experience and common-sense objects. They are simple in that they cannot be broken up into other and constituent propositions; they are laws which cannot be derived from other laws. Their importance lies in the fact that they provide a means of uniting simple, and perhaps complex, natures and so forming a system of knowledge. Representative items are the laws of identity and of contradiction, the principle that things equal to the same thing are equal to each other, the principle that substance is prior to its attributes, and the principle that every event has a cause. And it is here, more than in the other two groups of simple entities, that we find clear common ground beween the various thinkers involved. If they disagreed over simple ideas, they agreed on axioms. Everyone accepted the laws of logic, and perhaps certain elementary, quasi-mathematical principles as well. But when others were introduced, protests arose. There has always been disagreement concerning the items that belong on any such list. Hume turned the criterion of self-evidence against the principle that every event must have a cause, by arguing that its contradictory satisfies the criterion. We can clearly and distinctly perceive an event in isolation, and therefore it is false to say that every event has a necessary relation to some preceding event, its cause.

However, although there was disagreement as to detail, it was generally agreed that there are both formal and material axioms, in the sense of self-evident principles. This is important, for it means that the classical philosophers, partly under the influence of the older metaphysics and partly under that of the newer science, universally regarded philosophy as systematic knowledge about existence or matter of fact and not merely about possibilities. If the elements of things as they are for knowledge are evident and if the principles by which these are united are also evident, then systematic knowledge of things is possible.

It might be questioned whether a skeptic like Hume believed in any self-evident principles concerning fact. When reading his attacks on a priori reasoning, one might reasonably suppose that all propositions having to do with matters of fact are for him, at best, probable inductions and, at worst, irrational beliefs. But this is not the case. He believed that by observation of men and manners it is possible to abstract from the human scene principles of human nature which have complete certainty. Although observation leads at first to skepticism as to the validity of customs, it eventually results in knowledge of unvarying principles. He says: "It is universally acknowledged, that there is a great uniformity among the actions of men, in all nations and ages, and that human nature remains still the same, in its principles and operations."[4] Observation reveals the unvarying passions and even, to some extent, sentiments of man and the principles that govern his thinking and hence enables the student of human nature to establish politics, morals, taste, logic, and other branches of the study of man on a sure and scientific basis. Thus Hume can speak of "universal axioms" and "eternal political truths" in the science of politics;[5] and he regards it as "a priori" impossible for man to be totally indifferent to the well- or ill-being of his fellow-creatures.[6] In short, he believes no less than anyone else that it is possible to abstract evident truths from particulars; and, while he points out the limitations of sense knowledge and the problem of induction latent in it, he agrees with Descartes and Spinoza that the light of reason can discern principles in existence that are universally valid for human knowledge. These views are not so well known as is his analysis of causality. Perhaps they are not so characteristic. But their existence cannot be denied, and they link him definitely to doctrines which he rejects in other connections. It is interesting to note that he does not regard axioms as given, as he does the "materials" of knowledge.

There are two sides to the philosophy of Descartes, too. The more familiar account runs as follows: Everything in experience can be doubted except the idea of God. All other ideas are worthless, taken by themselves; they are mere subjective, mental phenomena, completely separate from their causes. Thus, except for this one idea, man is cut off from all reality beyond his own immediate consciousness; he can neither know his own body or nature nor trust his reason. But the idea of God is so clear and distinct that it cannot be doubted. For this reason (as well as for others) we know that God exists, and thereby we have a link with the world. So we can believe in our own existence and that of

---

4. *Enquiry Concerning Human Understanding,* Sec. VIII, Part I.
5. *That Politics May Be Reduced to a Science.*
6. *Enquiry Concerning the Principles of Morals,* Sec. V, Part II.

nature and in the truth of mathematics and in whatever else may be trustworthy, for God would not deceive us. Alternatively, the indubitable idea is that of the self, and the rest depend on that. But there is another side to the Cartesian philosophy, and it is the one we have been considering: All clear and distinct ideas are true, because they contain within themselves direct evidence of the reality of their objects. Knowledge is not a deduction from any one idea. We have an ontological proof for the existence or reality of everything which is clearly and distinctly perceived. The idea of God carries existence with it; God must "exist" because he is perfect. But all other clear and distinct ideas carry existence with them, too, in proportion to the objective reality which they contain.

If this second doctrine were carried out to its logical conclusion, it would lead to a theory of degrees of truth, proportional to the degree of reality in the idea that is true. Descartes did not carry it out; instead, he distinguishes sharply two classes of ideas, the true and the false. Nevertheless, he holds that there are many clear and distinct ideas, and therefore many which carry their truth with them. The two sides of his philosophy are incompatible. But which are we to accept? The first is the side which most influenced subsequent thought; but it is the second which is philosophically sounder.

It is now clear in what sense of the term "true" ideas can be said to be true. They are true when evident because they are real or embody reality. Truth is not correspondence with reality but is reality itself. Or, rather, the correspondence between ideas and facts is a consequence of their partial identity: if an idea agrees with its object, that is because it is a manifestation of its object. This is why, as Spinoza says, "He who has a true idea knows at the same time that he has a true idea, nor can he doubt the truth of the thing."[7] Now truth and evidence depend on the reality contained in the idea, but this reality has degrees. Then do truth and evidence vary by degrees? They do not. There are quantitative gradations of reality in ideas; but, according to the phi-

---

7. *Ethics,* Part II, Prop. 43.

losophy of evidence, truth and evidence depend on distinctions of kind, not of degree. Much of the power of this philosophy lies in its insistence on sharp distinctions, and its refusal to soften them into differences of degree. One might almost say that it declined as it lost this tough-mindedness. There is a sharp distinction between the evident and the nonevident. Whether, as now appears to be the case, it always coincides with the distinction between true and false or whether, instead, it sometimes marks the difference between knowledge and true opinion remains to be seen.

It should also be clear why ideas as well as propositions have the predicate "true" attached to them. The reason is that the truth of propositions is simply a consequence of the truth of the ideas which they contain. It is usually said that only propositions can be true or false, because only a proposition can be asserted. But, according to the theory under discussion, ideas are capable of truth and falsity because they assert themselves or make a claim to truth. Propositions refer to things as they are for knowledge, that is, under the form of ideas. A proposition either analyzes a complex idea—for instance, "Green is a color"—or else it unites or separates ideas—for example, "The clock is on the wall." But in either case, on the present theory, if the proposition is true, the ideas must be evident; and that means that the elements of the totality referred to and the relations between them must be evident, too.

If truth and self-evidence are equivalent and there is only one kind of truth, the significant distinction is not between idea and proposition, since propositions are either ideas themselves or combinations of them. This is one reason why the classical philosophers talked so little about propositions—the other being their tendency to unite possibility and actuality. The significant distinction is, rather, between idea and judgment, for judgment goes beyond direct perception and introduces the possibility that the mind may distort what is presented, by addition, subtraction, or alteration. If I could directly see the complex, "clock on wall," my knowledge would be certain; it is because I interpret what I see that I may be mistaken. Direct apprehension of what is given to the understanding is never mistaken; but judgment introduces the possibility of error; for if the mind alters what is given, by the intrusion of such activities as imagination, will, or habit, error is the result.

We can now answer the questons raised earlier in the discussion. It is not possible to say in advance how many things are intrinsically evident. This is a matter to be ascertained by empirical investigation; the procedure of methodological skepticism, if carried out rigorously, will enable us to classify each thing examined in turn, as either evident or nonevident. But some things, at any rate, are evident, for we find them to be so. Nor are they restricted to one; there is a number of things, in each of which we can grasp the essential nature or enough of it to see the thing. And we can also see that they are, or may be, related. There is no reason why identity and intelligibility in a thing should exclude relations, unless we ourselves exclude them arbitrarily, by definition; a thing can both be and be related. The number 2 is an intelligible entity, and it is related in many ways to other numbers. But it is the number 2, not some concept of it, that is evident. A self-evident object is not to be identified with our "concept" of it, in the modern sense of that term; for, as the term is often used, one concept is unintelligible apart from the system of which it forms a part and is nothing by itself—concepts are essentially contextual. But the number 2 is evident in itself, in spite of the fact that it is essentially related to other numbers. And the idea of 2 is evident because it embodies the nature of its object.

This brings us to an important objection which may be raised against the whole doctrine of self-evidence; and with an answer to it we may close the discussion. It may be said that there is an ambiguity in the notion that a real entity, A, can be so directly apprehended that we can say, in consequence, "A is." And therefore the whole argument is fallacious, for it is not clear in what sense A "is." It may be as a possibility or as an existent; and it may be in the act of apprehension only, or it may be independent of and going beyond that apprehension. The notion of self-evidence, if it is admissible at all, applies only to possibilities (universals, concepts, essences), or at most to these plus the immediate data of sense. I may be able to see that it is impossible for 2 to be not 2 but, for instance, 3; or for this red to be not this red but, for example, that green. But I cannot see that it is impossible for these objects, seemingly two, to be actually three; or for this thing, apparently red, to be in reality green. The only immediate and indubitable apprehension is of universals and of sense data. Things and events can be known only probably, for they are inseparable from causes and effects that go beyond them; if they can be said to be given at all, at any rate what is given is inseparable from what is inferred.

Now this objection presupposes the separability and even independence of things which to the philosophy of evidence are absolutely inseparable. The most important of these are, first, possibility and existence and, second, subjective certainty and objective fact. In the basic claim of the philosophy of evidence that reality can be apprehended, the term "reality" includes both possibility and actual existence, while the term "apprehended" unites mental certainty and an object independent of that psychological state. In such apprehension, the real asserts itself rather than being asserted by the subject who is aware of it; and it is assented to just because it does assert itself. There is no question of inference here. Such propositions as "Some dogs are vicious" are not evident. In thinking about them, we ask whether possibilities are exemplified in existence. Dogs may be vicious—but are they actually so? It is the contention of self-evidence that such propositions are not the ultimate units of knowledge but are ideally reducible to a dimension where the separations which they involve disappear. The entire objection is based on a distinction between necessary and contingent truths, the first dealing with possibilities, the second with existents. It is necessarily true that 2 and 3 are 5; but if some dogs are vicious, as they may be, that fact is merely contingent. But this distinction and the consequences which it entails (some of which will be considered later) are foreign to the concept of self-evidence that we have been considering. We shall soon see how the distinction arose. But it is not a part of the present concept, which, as we have seen, is concerned with what is, and not with what may or must be.

4. Reconstruction of Familiar Facts

The difficulty of philosophy does not lie primarily in its abstractness. It is comparatively easy to formulate a set of abstractions which have the appearance of profundity. The difficulty lies in the interpretation of familiar facts in the light of the abstractions. The reason why the construction of a system is often considered the duty of the philosopher is that it is supposed to supply such an interpretation; and this is, indeed, its only point and the only measure of its success. Our present task, accordingly, is to return from thin to thick experience, to reconstruct the world from those clear and distinct elements which constitute, as it were, the alphabet of the universe—to form syllables, words, and sentences from the letters. Primary facts and truths must be related to the unreflective world. Clearly, the two are not the same, for, if they were, the second would not call for explanation. Yet they cannot be simply different, for then the first, no matter how evident intrinsically, would not explain the second. There is a gap between the two worlds. But it can be narrowed or eradicated if crude fact can be reconstructed out of simples; for if a fact of common sense can be deduced or synthesized from primary facts without remainder, its explanation is an evident truth, and the fact is fully real.

The term "reconstruction" refers to a mental activity; but the aim of the activity is not to impose an interpretation on the facts. It is essentially deductive in character. The mind deduces the complex fact from the terms and relations which are its simple constituents. These latter are given data which result from analysis; and the goal of the deduction, like that of the first analysis, is the intuition of something presented to the mind. The intuition of an objective complex is an ideal which, admittedly, is rarely, if ever, attained. Its pattern is mathematics, and no existent has the simplicity and clarity of a mathematical structure. But it is the contention of self-evidence that it can be approximated and that it is the only possible ideal for the sciences and philosophy. Politics and morals, no less than physics, must be guided by it. And the human mind, no less than a moving body, has an intelligible constitution, if only we can discover it.

Reconstruction presupposes two things: first, that objects actually have a structure. There is order and relation in them; the only question is whether we can discover it. Second, that the process of synthesis, which is to result in apprehension of the whole, follows that of analysis. The object is the point of reference throughout; we begin and end with it. We do not begin with simples, nor is it implied that they have an independent reality. They may or may not be independent; but it is certainly not a part of the inquiry to assert that they are. For the starting-point of inquiry is crude fact, not simples, and the function of the latter in inquiry is to make the former intelligible.

The crucial problem which this notion raises is whether we actually do see the elements as they are combined in the object or whether we combine them according to some principle of our own. The concept of reconstruction implies the first, for the goal of our deduction or combination is an apprehension of the total fact. To understand the magnet is to see its total complex structure at a single glance. But inquiry may not always reach the point where this goal is attained. Consequently, the nature of combination is sometimes difficult to determine.

It is in empiricism that the concept of an interpretive activity of the mind, adding something to the given facts, first developed. Empiricism compensated for its comparative neglect of analysis by stressing heavily the activity of synthesis. The reason is that it was largely concerned with those sense qualities whose objective relations to each other appear largely accidental. Why should fluidity, wetness, transparency, and a sweet taste be combined in water? It is we who assert that these qualities, as Locke said, "coexist" in water. They are related in our experience; but we do not know what their relation is to the internal constitution of that substance. Locke believed as firmly as anyone that things have an intelligible structure; but he did not believe that the human mind is able to grasp it. Therefore, we must classify and order data from the point of view of our experience and, as he says, be satisfied with the nominal essences of things instead of the real ones.

It is in this way that the doctrine of mechanism grew out of the very different theories of self-evidence and analysis. So far as we are unable to discover a structure in things, the given element in knowledge will be limited to simples. Objects will be for us "collections" of simple ideas. The mind will be able to combine and separate such elements in knowledge without departing from given facts, for the relations between the simples are not given. Terms and relations, which originally had been co-ordinate materials for knowledge and both discoverable by analysis, gradually become separated, with respect to both their origin and their function in inquiry. The assertion that the whole is the sum of its parts comes to mean that the parts have no intrinsic relations in the natural complexes from which they are abstracted; the relations are contributed by the mind, and the parts are prior to the whole and, indeed, are the whole. The source of this theory, however, was not a "mechanistic" theory of nature, in the popular sense, but a split in philosophy between knowledge and existence.

Returning to the process of synthesis, we observed that the ideal of reconstruction cannot be completely attained. The gap between primary truths and crude facts cannot be entirely closed. If we adhere strictly to the identification of the true and the real with the evident, it follows that the residue of crude fact which cannot be made intelligible is unreal and that any statement about it is false.

Anyone who is unwilling to accept this consequence—and it does follow strictly from the premises—must hold that there is a second kind of reality. He may call this new reality "nonevident," or he may make a distinction and say that it is practically or morally, though not intellectually, evident. Then he will have to say that, in addition to intellectual truth, there is practical truth or true opinion or something else that is their equivalent. If he has come as far as this, accepting two kinds of reality and two kinds of self-evidence, he has, in effect, arrived at the distinction between necessary and contingent truths. The first is the truth of reason, the second the truth of given fact, rationally unexplained and inexplicable. The second is what falls outside the sphere of the evident, as we have understood this term. Thus statements of causal relations are contingent truths to Hume, and "Socrates was snub-nosed" is a contingent truth to Leibniz, because they are not evident or reducible to the evident. They are not intelligible but just happen to be so; and when we explain them we can only relate them to other facts that also just happen to be so.

We must now follow the development by which the nonevident changed from being the false to being the contingently true, from being unreal to being real. And the first point to consider is the notion of contingent truth. This notion may, or may not, be of merely human import. If there are any familiar facts that are intrinsically irreducible to the self-evident, then there are intrinsically contingent truths; but if all facts are intrinsically constituted of evident, primary elements without remainder, then contingent truths exist only in relation to our defective understandings, while truths which adequately stated the real nature of familiar facts would all be necessary. Perhaps, if we knew enough, Socrates' snub nose would appear as intelligible as geometry; and perhaps it would not.

All this raises questions. What does it mean to speak of "contingent truths" in relation to our understandings only? This is as much as to say that they are not really truths at all but only opinions or beliefs which do not correspond to fact. They may be the natural starting-point for reflection, but they should not be called "truth"—or else we shall be giving truth a new meaning, as something relative to human knowledge and experience. And how can we know that there is anything intrinsically incapable of becoming evident, unless we know everything? How can we know that the most confusing events of history, for instance, do not have the clarity of logic and mathematics, if only we could understand them? We never can know this, so it appears that the distinction between two kinds of truth is invalid. Yet it is a very natural one. These are not problems of the relation of knowledge to its objects, so much as of the relations between those experiences which are knowledge and those which are not. But, before considering the new concept of reality to which they gave rise, we must see how far crude fact is translatable into evident fact.

To simplify the problem of the relation between the evident and the nonevident, let us ask what an ordinary object of perception, such as a stone or a plant, is, in philosophical terms. There are two possibilities. When such a thing is understood, either it is seen to be altogether intelligible, or else there are some aspects of it which are still confused, opaque, obscure. Either it is a complex of evident elements in relation, or it is such a complex plus certain associated manifestations of a different sort. The problem is implied in a statement by Bacon about forms, which in his philosophy are closely related to simple natures, being, in fact, their laws or causes: "... the Form of a thing is the very thing itself, and the thing differs from the form no otherwise than as the apparent differs from the real, or the external from the internal, or the thing in reference to man from the thing in reference to the universe."[8] It is the relation between the "apparent" and the "real" that is in question; and the point at issue is whether the real excludes or includes the apparent.

Consider a blade of grass, for instance, in terms of the theory of atomism. The atom, let us suppose, is rationally self-evident; certainly, some philosophers have come very close to considering it so. What, then, is the blade of grass? Either it is a complex of atoms, moving in relation to one another, according to the laws of matter, laws which, ideally, might be considered self-evident; and in this case the sensuous appearances of the grass are not a part of it. Or else the grass is a complex of atoms plus certain sensuous manifestations which are associated with, and dependent upon, them. To take another example, and one which interested Bacon and Descartes, the magnet might be considered to be a complex of

---

8. *Novum Organum*, Book II, Aphorism 13.

simple natures, such as attraction, and this complex would then constitute the real nature of the magnet; it would actually be the magnet. The interesting sensible phenomena of magnetism would then be explained by the nature of the magnet, but they would not be a part of it. Or else, on the other hand, the phenomena might be considered a part of it, over and above the simple natures, so that the magnet would be a set of constituent natures plus a set of sensible manifestations.

This problem arises, no matter whether it is the rational or the sensible which is identified with the evident. One may begin with the rationally intelligible and raise a queston concerning the status of the sensible; this is the procedure of Bacon and Descartes, who mistrust the senses and hold that simple natures, rationally apprehended, constitute the intrinsic nature of things. If heat is "really" a certain kind of material motion, what are we to say of the heat we feel, which is not a motion at all but a sensation of pain? But it is also possible to begin at the other end, with the sensible, and raise questions about the nonsensible; this is the procedure of Locke and his successors. Given the sense qualities, they ask, what is to be said of such notions as substance, force, and matter? Is a thing simply a complex of qualities, or is substance an additional, nonsensible aspect of it? Are force and causality sensible; and, if not, what is their relation to sense qualities? Whether a philosopher begins with the rational or with the sensible, the problem is the same. It is that of reconciling the evident elements of objects with the crude, confused elements; or of deriving the full, concrete object from certain partial aspects of it.

The problem seems to admit of two possible solutions: the apparent aspects are either real or unreal, in the sense that they either are or are not part of the object that is evident. Bacon clearly chose the first alternative. He searched for the simple nature or form of heat, the nature of heat in itself or "in reference to the universe," and he found it in motion. But he did not conclude that sensible heat is unreal; instead, he called it "heat in reference to man." And for him the total fact of heat was motion plus sensible heat, the real plus the apparent. And so, in the last analysis, he did not reject the senses; he simply regarded them as inadequate and, when unaided, often misleading. To Leibniz, similarly, sense knowledge is phenomenal but well founded; although confused, it is not illusory. And the complete account of an object for him would have to be given not only in metaphysical and rational, but also in physical and sensible, terms. Again, Locke begins with simple ideas and admits that he does not find the idea of substance among them, strictly speaking; yet he maintains that a thing is substance having qualities or attributes—a composition of evident, simple ideas and a not-so-evident idea of a substratum. Substance in the sense of substratum is nonsensuous and is not reducible to terms of the sensuous; yet it is real for him. To these men the true object is the inclusive object; it is the thing in both its evident and its merely apparent aspects.

If we accept this first alternative, a further question suggests itself, which, however, will not be considered here: What is the relation between the evident and the apparent in the object? The theory of Bacon will serve to illustrate the point. He seems to hold that the apparent is the realization of what is, in the object existing by itself, only potential. When the hot object—the object in appropriate motion—interacts with the mind, the result is the actualization of sensible heat.

The other alternative is that the apparent is unreal. This is the solution Descartes chooses when he says in the twelfth *Rule* that "the whole of human knowledge consists in a distinct perception of the way in which those simple natures combine in order to build up other objects." Objects consist of simple natures and complexes of these; everything else is excluded. All knowledge is of the same kind; so sensations, which cannot be derived deductively from simple natures, must be consigned to mere experience and are unreal, since they do not form parts of objects. Similarly, for Hobbes only the material motions are real; and thought, which he reduces to motions in the organs of the body, is nothing over and above these. Again, the idea of substance is unreal or fictitious for

ANALYSIS

Hume, because it cannot be stated in terms of primary impressions. The rule is the same: whatever cannot be reduced to, or accounted for, in terms of primary data is unreal or imaginary. Here we have the exclusive object, consisting solely of the evident, and distinct from those misleading ideas of things which men find themselves believing. To Descartes the exclusive object is a complex of intelligible natures; to Hume it is a complex of impressions and the ideas derived from them.

If the exclusive conception of the object is accepted, it is not enough, I think, to say that the excluded features of experience are "subjective," while the rest are "objective." This suggests that they have a reality, but that it happens to be of a different kind from the reality which objects possess, or in a different place, namely, the mind. But when Descartes is maintaining the views indicated just now—and he is not always doing so—he goes further and asserts that sense qualities are strictly unreal; they do not exist, they are nothing. And when Hume is defending the exclusive conception of things, he does not maintain that substance is in the mind rather than in the object; what he really does is hold that substance in the old sense is nothing, simply a word without logical or empirical meaning. He substitutes for it something entirely different, namely, a collection of impressions and ideas, to which he gives the same name. Similarly, he holds that causality in the old sense is merely a word, and he substitutes for it the expectation of a certain sort of event upon the occurrence of a certain other sort of event; to this expectation he gives the old name, but he holds that the name formerly referred to nothing at all.

Now, if these nonevident aspects of experience are not real, the result will be a new skepticism. Methodological skepticism preceded the apprehension of primary truths. A systematic and dogmatic skepticism will follow the reconstruction of the common-sense world in terms of them, beginning where the reconstruction, of necessity, leaves off. Hume was a systematic, not a methodological, skeptic. Beginning with impressions, which he regards as given in the most direct sense, he proceeds at once to the task of describing the familiar world of the plain man in terms of them; methodological skepticism is for him practically unnecessary. But he is unable to finish the job; there are elements of that world which cannot be traced back to impressions, and these he rejects. They are all those metaphysical concepts for the repudiation of which he is famous. If the question is asked, "How do men come to think there are such entities as, for instance, substances, when, in reality, there are only impressions?" his answer is: "By the inventive power of the imagination"; it is in this way that true experience gets perverted into mere experience.

Descartes, too, was a systematic skeptic, as well as a methodological one. He finds men not only apprehending sense objects and using them as guides to life—attitudes which are perfectly legitimate and not deceptive—but also attributing reality to them, regarding them as valid accounts of what the world is like. Here he is forced to stop and be skeptical, and he explains the errors of men at this point by their failure to restrict themselves to affirmations of what is clear and distinct, through the tendency of will and judgment to make assertions beyond what is really known. But sometimes his skepticism goes further, and he denies, or seems to deny, the very reality of sensations. To the question, "How do men come to think there are sensations, when in fact there are only simple natures in combination?" he then replies in effect: "That is not my problem; I begin with men as I find them, with all their beliefs and illusions." But at other times he holds that sense experience is not false or unreal, so long as no judgments about the constitution of things are based on it.

Here we might formulate a law of inquiry: The more you insist on one perfect and complete type of knowledge, the more necessary does a radical skepticism become, to reject everything which does not measure up to the criterion. If knowledge is limited to the self-evident, and only primary truths and whatever can be directly constructed for them are known, then everything else must be rejected as false, irrational, and illusory. Here Hume betrays his affinity to the philosophy of reason. He still regards logical demonstration as the ideal of knowledge, and when he fails to find it he becomes a skeptic. In spite of his discussion of reasoning concerning matter of fact, he is really unwilling to call causal reasoning knowledge at all, because it is not demonstration; instead of regarding it as knowledge of an inferior order or of a different kind, he calls it instinct, sensation, and feeling. Reason has not yet become association of ideas, although by this time the eventual identification is almost inevitable. But since the world now appears to be an irrational succession of isolated, unrelated facts, reason can no longer be trusted. It would, in fact, be irrational to trust reason in an illogical world, and skepticism is the only reasonable attitude. Reason refutes itself, and we can believe only the imagination. If Descartes really means that all knowledge is of one kind, he, too, must be completely skeptical of everything which is not of that kind.

If you do not insist that all knowledge is of the same kind, however, it is possible to admit the reality of objects which are not clear and distinct, and systematic skepticism will become proportionately less important. The result will be the differentiation of degrees or kinds of knowledge. Spinoza made such a distinction, between imagination, reason, and intuitive understanding. It is not a coincidence that he also denied the possibility of suspending judgment; for, if some experiences, such as ideas of the imagination, are totally lacking in reality, it is quite understandable that they may be apprehended without being affirmed, since there is no reason to affirm them; but if, as Spinoza asserted, even imagination is a kind of knowledge and its objects possess some reality, then affirmation of them is inevitable, because they force themselves upon us. Locke also enumerates, in addition to intuitive and demonstrative knowledge, a third type, namely, sensitive. And Leibniz, in disagreement with Descartes, claims that confused perceptions, as well as clear and distinct ideas, provide genuine knowledge, though only of contingent truth.

Whether, corresponding to the various degrees of knowledge,

there are objects possessing various degrees of reality depends on the doctrine of the philosopher in question. Certainly, Spinoza would have maintained this, if by "reality" we mean "being"; for substance, known by reason, has more being than an object perceived by the senses. On the other hand, the notion of degrees of reality is entirely foreign to Locke, who would have said that, although the objects of sensitive and intuitive knowledge are different, they are equally real.

As for the main problem, however—the nature of familiar objects and the status of their apparent aspects—the result seems to be a dilemma. If the nonevident aspects of things are real, the criterion of self-evidence is abandoned, and philosophy has to start over again and find a new conception of truth and reality; but if they are unreal, then much of the familiar world has to be abandoned, and philosophy, instead of explaining the world, has explained it away.

Before attempting to find an escape from this dilemma, it will be advantageous to consider in a general way the relation between knowledge and reality, as it appears in the philosophy of evidence. In the basic proposition that reality can be apprehended, the subject is reality as it is for knowledge, and this cannot be identified with reality as it is in itself. That the two are not necessarily the same was widely recognized. For instance, Locke admitted that substances, and Berkeley that spiritual substances, although real, are not, strictly speaking, objects of knowledge, since the medium of knowledge is ideas and we do not have ideas of them, literally. And Descartes regarded the simple natures as primary elements for human knowledge; he was not sure that they are absolutely simple, only that they are unanalyzable by the understanding; and he did not assert positively that, apart from knowledge, all objects are constituted of them. Therefore, we cannot say that the evident consists of things as they are in themselves, while the nonevident is merely things as they are for us; but both refer to things as they are for us, both terms have reference to human knowledge and experience. Therefore, the only reality in question is reality as it can be known.

Since this is so, one might ask whether knowledge is true or real after all. And that the latter term is not misapplied in this connection is indicated by the fact that Locke devotes a chapter to precisely this subject: "Of the Reality of Our Knowledge."[9] The question arises as to whether ideas truly or really represent things. Now the doctrine of self-evidence assumes an affirmative answer to this question because of the partial identity, which is all the nature of the case requires, between ideas and objects. And it accounts for ideas in terms of things, not vice versa, by holding that the evident has a cause beyond itself; and if, as in the case of mathematical and logical ideas, the idea is not directly of and caused by a thing, it still was abstracted from things indirectly. But the discovery that there are nonevident ideas or aspects of experience which are, if the doctrine of evidence is to be maintained consistently and to the bitter end, illusory and unreal brought out the possibility that there are ideas without objective reality.

Here is the beginning of a split between objects and ideas. Such ideas cannot be explained, since that which is nothing does not require or admit of an explanation; and experience, so far as it consists of them, will not be knowledge, since it does not represent things as they are. But there is another possibility: perhaps they are something, after all. All that has actually been shown is a discrepancy between ideas and things. The existence of ideas which are false in the sense of not corresponding to fact, therefore, suggests the thought that perhaps ideas may be related to things in some other way. Perhaps they are clues to, or signs of, something in the future. In that case there would be no reason why they should correspond to the things toward which they point. Or, approaching the problem from another side, perhaps things are embodiments of ideal forms. In that case the relation may be one of correspondence, but it will have the opposite sense: things will

9. *Essay*, Book IV, chap. iv.

correspond to ideas more or less perfectly, depending on how perfect embodiments they are.

Some such alternative must be developed, for the theory that entities are unreal is never acceptable for long, because it is obvious that they are not annihilated by the epithet. The thinning of experience and nature to the evident, therefore, results in an unstable situation. The nonevident has become separated from things and has turned out to be mere experience; the rejected entities or aspects seem to be left without a locus, the rejected experiences or ideas without a function. But if philosophy is to make good its claim to account for all kinds of things, the rejected entities must get back in some way, since they still exist outside reality. As a matter of fact, the process of re-establishing them began as soon as their existence was seriously recognized. The prevalence of the view that the rejected entities and ideas of secondary qualities were "subjective" has, I believe, been exaggerated; for the classical philosophers instinctively regarded the process of experiencing as having objects, and the notion of a subjective object must always have had to them the flavor of the paradoxical. In other words, the concept of what we have called the "exclusive object" was not widely or very consistently accepted. Although there was the view that some objects, or perhaps all objects in a certain sense, are ideas, this did not mean that they were subjective or merely "in the mind"; it would be more accurate to say that they were presented to the mind. It is admitted on all sides that the illusory, unreal, and false present great problems. But the notion that some common, dependable, and familiar objects of experience, or important and conspicuous phases of them, are merely subjective or merely apparent must always have left the reflective, as well as the unreflective, man with an uncomfortable feeling.

It has been pointed out that these problems and dilemmas can be avoided without abandoning the criterion of self-evidence if the latter is broadened to include degrees. There is an alternative, however, which may also provide an escape: the nonevident is neither real nor unreal, but useful.

ANALYSIS

This view developed simultaneously with the recognition of such rejected entities, and that means actually from the beginning of the doctrine of self-evidence. It is maintained by Descartes in the sixth *Meditation* when he says that certain sensations, although they do not reflect the nature of the object, indicate what is beneficial or hurtful to us. It is suggested by Locke when, stepping outside the limits of human knowledge for the moment, he says that our senses, although they do not give us an adequate knowledge of things, enable us to secure the conveniences of living and to know our duty; if our senses were more acute, they would be less advantageous to us in our dealings with our environment—we could not see the forest for the trees, the object for its minute parts. Here Locke reverses the position that he usually holds and considers sense knowledge, although it be self-evident, as useful rather than as true, because it does not represent faithfully the real, intrinsic essence of things; but how he knows this, he, of course, does not explain. Hume asserts, at least by implication, that the non-evident aspects of experience are useful when he admits that the exigencies of action bring forth such fictions as that of the enduring external world and the belief that causality resides in empirical objects rather than in the mind—notions which have no basis in our impressions and, therefore, no rational justification.

And yet the notion of the useful is an anomaly. Either the useful is not true because it is not clear and distinct; or it is not real because it does not faithfully represent the intrinsic character of things. The first is the view of Descartes, the second that of Locke. At the same time, it is not false, for it enables us to make correct predictions; and it is not unreal, for it represents things as they exist in our experience. The first is the view of those who hold with Bacon that knowledge is power—and on occasion both Descartes and Locke defend this thesis—while the second is the position of all those who hold that things can be represented by their effects even if these are not in any respect identical in nature with their causes. In short, the notion of the useful does not fit into the scheme of concepts of which self-evidence is the nucleus; and, as the former advances in importance, the latter will recede. Finally, the notion promises to provide a new criterion of truth and perhaps a new definition of reality as well.

5. Decline

In its attempts to solve the problem of the contingent, philosophy split and entered three divergent paths, each of which leads away from the traditional body of ideas and criterion of truth. The beginnings of these movements were clearly distinguishable at the time when the philosophy of evidence was at its height.

One path opens up with the recognition of degrees of knowledge. If this notion is carried out consistently, it means the abandonment, sooner or later, of the criterion of clearness and distinctness as an effective category in philosophy; for, if degrees of knowledge are admitted in a philosophy which accepts that criterion of truth, degrees of clearness and distinctness must also be admitted. And from here it is a short step to the position that all ideas possess some degree of distinctness or evidence and so are true in some degree. Then the distinction between true and false, real and illusory, disappears except as a distinction of degree; everything has some measure of truth and reality. Everything has some degree of falsity and unreality also, and complete self-evidence becomes an ideal to be approximated but never reached. This is why evidence ceases to be an effective category; since it is never found, it cannot provide a means of distinguishing between true and false and thus further the search for truth. The task of philosophy now will consist in clearing up confused ideas rather than in separating the true from the false. This conception of philosophy is to be found in both Leibniz and Spinoza; but it is more prominent in Spinoza, although it is Leibniz who states it more explicitly. Everyone, including himself, feels the difficulty in what Spinoza has to say about intuitive science. The reason is that he regards it more as a goal than as an actual achievement of human knowledge. There are abstract ideas and propositions, of course, which he knows intuitively from the beginning of his system; but he does not start with an adequate apprehension of the real, and it is doubtful whether he believed that such an apprehension is possible for men.

This path leads to Hegel, who abandoned the category of self-evidence for that of inclusiveness. He recognizes evidence, which he calls "immediacy," as an aspect of every idea and object. But, whereas the older philosophers had regarded the evident, rational, and true as possessing positive reality and had tended to exclude the nonevident, irrational, and false as unreal and merely negative in character, Hegel holds that both must be included. True and false, rational and irrational, evident and confused, real and unreal, must be combined into an inclusive whole if philosophy is to account for the world. And since there are degrees of inclusiveness, there are also degrees of truth and reality—in his sense of these terms, fixed by the standard he uses. Therefore, the immediate face value of an idea or object must be transcended, as thought passes on to its work of synthesis. Every philosophic idea is a means by which experience is organized and made intelligible, and its validity is measured by its effectiveness in performing this function. Understanding is a never completed process of organization, instead of an insight or a series of insights, each complete at a moment.

One of the virtues of self-evidence is that it makes intelligible our instinctive feeling that it is possible to know one thing without, at the same time, having to know everything else. If the dialecticians are correct, that feeling must be mistaken. However, dialectic does preserve one distinction of kind, that between analytic understanding and speculative or synthetic reason. The first is clear and distinct because it works with sharp and rigid distinctions; but for that very reason it is not the kind of knowledge that is capable of the truth. One is tempted to say that speculative reason, on the other hand, is more true because it is less clear; and, taken in one sense, the remark would be just. But it would be more accurate to say that the mind is unsatisfied with the clarity of abstractions, and in its attempt to understand the concrete is forced to give up that clarity for something confused and obscure, in the hope of arriving at eventual understanding. Whether that hope is misplaced, when based on the conception of reason in question here, is another question.

A second path explores the concept of usefulness. So long as the true is identified with the evident, the useful can have no legitimate cognitive significance; for the useful has a reference to action, but the evident, being complete in itself, does not point to anything further for its truth. A certain discrepancy between truth and utility, knowledge and action, is half-admitted by two philosophers who, though in different ways, both adhered to the criterion of evidence: Descartes and Hume. For Descartes says that his method of doubt is not dangerous, since his object is not action but knowledge; and Hume admits that his theories cannot be believed in practice. The extent of the separation in the rationalists must not be exaggerated, for they identified the good as well as the true with the evident; to them reason was the proper guide to life and therefore eminently useful. And yet, even for them there is a contrast between the arbitrary customs, laws, and institutions of everyday life, on the one hand, and the rational good, on the other, analogous to the contrast between mere experience and true experience. So that for them, too, there is sometimes a tendency for knowledge to lead away from action, so far as action is concerned with concrete, obscure fact, even though they recognized that the existence of man must always remain subject to natural forces that are largely beyond his control and, perhaps in part, even beyond his understanding.

The concept of the useful practically amounts to the admission of a second sort of reality, existing side by side with the evident but out of touch with it. This, however, was not realized by the philosophers who belonged to the tradition and had no suspicion that they were introducing a new idea which one day would largely displace their own central doctrine in popular thought, science, and philosophy.

The notion of the useful took two main forms. First, it was a supplement to, or substitute for, other contact with reality, in those cases where human knowledge is defective. Locke and Descartes held that, in knowing, man is in direct touch with independently existing things. But they also held that things in some cases cause ideas which are not like them; and these latter, taken in themselves, do not tell us anything about the nature of their causes, only that they have causes. Such ideas are useful because they indicate what will probably happen and enable us to deal more effectively with events as they affect us. True ideas are preferable for knowledge, but useful ones are practically indispensable and at least tell us what the future effects of things will probably be, even if they do not communicate the intrinsic natures of their causes. And, while this is not knowledge, at least it is closely allied to it.

In its other form, the useful becomes identified with reality as it is for human belief. This theory is the contribution of Hume, who also accepted usefulness in the first sense. In his theory the forthright realism of "ideas of things" and the more dubious realism of the view that things cause ideas have finally given way to the claim that things are constructions out of sensuous materials. This sensationalism demands the rejection of an independently existing real world, as a part of, or even as a legitimate inference from, human experience. But realism is deeply rooted in human nature and cannot be eradicated by any amount of reasoning. And so Hume finds that the sensationalism of the intellect is opposed by the realism of the imagination. The consequence is that he regards man as incurably and pervasively anthropomorphic in his thinking. We project our experiences onto the universe. Concern for the happenings of human life leads man to imagine anthropomorphic gods, whom he makes responsible for his fate. A desire, perhaps, for security induces him to project the necessary connections of events, which exist only in his own mind, onto nature; and similarly with such concepts as law, substance, and matter. Our intellects tell us to explain the universe in terms of ideas; but our instincts tell us to explain ideas in terms of the universe.

Here are two concepts of reality for Hume, and the second is stronger than the first. These metaphysical conceptions, or rather fantasies, which seem to lend independence and solidity to the known world, are indispensable to the natural man, however ridiculous they may appear to the philosopher. As fictions necessary to living, they constitute the basis for an invented reality and a substitute for the reality which, if it exists, we can know nothing about—so speaks the philosopher. If we are to act at all, we must act as if bodies existed, causes produced effects, and so on; and belief in the fictions of the imagination is produced by the communication to them of the forcefulness of our impressions. Here is a different kind of usefulness; it is not the predictive utility of sensations which are correlated with certain other sensations in recurring patterns, as pain is with heat, but the usefulness of what satisfies a human need so basic that its satisfaction is requisite to the very continuance of life. The first utility provides means to specific ends; the second provides the means to life itself.

The concept of usefulness begins with Descartes and Locke and finds a developed expression in Hume. It is echoed in Kant, who develops something like the first form of usefulness in his doctrine of possible experience and something analogous to the second in his postulates of practical reason. However, the analogy cannot be pressed, for his ethical notion of the practical differs in fundamental ways from the concept of the useful. This latter concept continues down to the present, in some versions of pragmatism and positivism. The philosophers who employ it seem to retain the criterion of clearness and distinctness more faithfully than do those who distinguish degrees of knowledge; for they usually distinguish between formal and material truth; and, while they make usefulness the criterion of the latter, they keep self-evidence as the test of the former, perhaps giving it some other name, such as "consistency." So Hume, with his relations of ideas and his matters of fact. But, in reality, this distinction is a surrender of the whole doctrine of evidence; for the heart of that doctrine was the claim that reality can be given, even if imperfectly; but these philosophers deny its applicability to objectively existing things and restrict

ANALYSIS

apprehension to what is possible, or to that plus sense data. In the face of reality, they say, we need other weapons; reality is not to be apprehended but dealt with.

The third path lies in the direction of history. The concept of the evident is nontemporal in its implications. A temporal process is necessary, to get to the place where the intrinsically evident idea can be grasped by the mind; but apprehension itself is not a process. And so the elements of human nature which contribute chiefly to understanding—namely, reason and sense—are, in the tradition that we have been considering, without any important reference to time. Neither, as they were understood, has any essential connection with past or future; each operates in the present and is, from a certain point of view, hardly in time at all. Memory and imagination also have some cognitive value, but they are auxiliary and always suspect because they are temporal, and the second because it is subjective as well—we arbitrarily rearrange the traces of what we once perceived.

The philosophers of evidence were not uninterested in history, but it had no philosophic significance for them. Spinoza, for instance, developed a critical historical method, as well as his better-known, analytic one. But, in studying the Bible historically, his only object is to arrive at nonhistorical truth. His purpose is to disengage the universally valid elements of religion and ethics, which can be known by the light of reason anywhere and at any time, from the merely historical elements, which have no universal significance and are only contingent. To him the historical is only something to get away from as fast as possible; there are truths in history, but none about history. And so his penetrating observations on the evaluation of historical evidence have no effect on his philosophical method. The same thing is true of Hume. As a philosopher, he uses history primarily for the purpose of supplying examples of principles that are eternal in human nature, which has not changed through all the past, so far as he can see. There are, of course, individual differences between men, and the influence of geography and custom is by no means negligible; but they do no more than supply a superstructure. The main determinant in history is the unvarying passions of man. Since human nature remains the same, the working-out of its principles has been episodic and has produced little, if any, cumulative effect; changes are only local and fluctuating. For both men, a fair sample of history is accessible to any careful observer, and the task of the philosopher is to abstract from it nonhistorical, evident elements; although truths are to be found imbedded in history, there are no principles, laws, or categories of history.

And yet both hoped that man, or at least some men, might become more rational in the future than they had been in the past. Spinoza perhaps had the greater right to such a hope, since he believed in the power of reason; but it was stronger in the skeptic Hume, for whom it amounted almost to a faith. This may seem surprising, for the age of reason to which he belonged was, of course, in its implications an age of unreason and disillusionment; and Hume clearly and candidly turned many of those latent implications into explicit inferences. The explanation of his attitude lies in the concept of habit or custom—and the two were practically synonymous for a time, because "custom" or "collective habit" was only a name for an aggregate of individual habits. Although he was skeptical of the constructive power of reason, he believed strongly in its ability to disintegrate and destroy the prejudices and superstitions imbedded in custom. This is why he was able to view the future with hope, although study of the past afforded small ground for optimism. Gradually the theory that reason disintegrates custom gave place to the theory that reason is itself a kind of custom or habit. But custom develops through time. It follows that man and his knowing are parts of history.

We have seen that the movement of experience was conceived as a progress from obscure and confused to clear and distinct and that the accompanying analysis had other dimensions as well. The temporal quality of the movement was of little interest at first, attention being focused on the levels of analysis rather than on their historical succession in the course of inquiry. Nevertheless,

ANALYSIS

the presence of the temporal dimension of experience was recognized, particularly by the philosophers of experience, who asked what the origin of knowledge was and found the answer in the gradual filling of the white paper of the mind. Gradually a shift of emphasis occurred, from the contrast of simple and complex or of logically original and derivative to the contrast of temporally earlier and later.

There is another source for the concept of custom. As men reflected on material and scientific progress and as their knowledge of other peoples increased with the improvement of communications, they began to compare themselves with those others and to ask whether the superiority which they seemed to see in themselves had any explanation in human nature. And one explanation of the difference seemed to lie in the subjection of earlier ages to the bonds of custom and their own emancipation from these. Past history and the present lives of savages show us a strange and endless variety of customs, forming the structure of backward and often oppressive social institutions. The variety is due to their irrationality; and, as knowledge progresses, reason will gradually supplant custom as a guide to life, with an accompanying spread of uniform rational institutions and an increase of happiness for all concerned. Man's growing awareness (and frequent misunderstanding) of history as the spread of enlightenment and the conquest of customs by scientific understanding contributed to the formation of a historical conception of reason itself—though reason had originally been conceived as changeless and though the gradual accumulation of knowledge was at first explained by the uniform and ceaseless application of a constant rational force to the problems of life.

The result of the shift in emphasis was that experience is no longer conceived as the building of complexes from simples but as the formation of habits by association through repetition. Habits are the impression of natural order on the individual mind and thus enable man to apply past experience to the prediction of future events; the stability of habit mirrors the stability of the laws of nature, from which it was derived. Apart from habit, man would be helpless; in fact, he would hardly be man at all, for his memories, expectations, aims, thoughts—even desires, in part—all depend on habitual associations. And the present strength of habit depends directly on the number of past repetitions and is unintelligible without them—a view which contrasts sharply with the theory of clear and distinct ideas, which bear on their faces no trace of their origin in the process of doubt and analysis. This is an important difference.

The new conception of experience carries with it the novel idea that reason is predictive rather than contemplative in nature. Hume signalized the change by calling reason an "instinct." It still deserves the name of reason in one respect, for habit, like a logical structure, contains regularity and order. But the order now is causal rather than deductive, and it must be passively experienced rather than actively discovered and contemplated; when A occurs, B is expected. There is order and stability in man, so far as experienced nature is stable, but no longer for man. Whereas formerly his reason had grasped the order of nature in its various parts, he has now himself become a part of nature, though a peculiar one. At first, this concept of reason existed alongside the other one, but gradually it began to overshadow the older. When the older had been supplanted, the status of man became such that the power of his reason was, in his own eyes, limited to the performance of the practical function of providing more effective means to the ends of security, comfort, and power. From this to Darwinism is only a step. Truth is more and more equated with usefulness or else subordinated to it.

Dialectical synthesis, pragmatic usefulness, and changing custom have much in common. To begin with, all three concepts agree in their rejection of an important doctrine. Second, they are united in the contention that the validity of ideas must be determined not by what they are but by the functions that they perform in experience. And, finally, all presuppose that time and process are of the essence of the human mind, as they are of reality. But they differ in their interpretations of becoming, and the relation of ideas to it. In the idealist dialectic, the relation of ideas to process is that of real to apparent and of eternity to time. Being the essence of historical process, ideas shape it; this is why they enable man to understand it, as they unfold subjectively in the human mind. To pragmatism, present action is the central category if we go beyond method; and the validity of an idea lies in its contribution to the interpretation of the situation in which action occurs or to the construction or furtherance of the concrete act, in one way or another. The study of custom, on the other hand, gradually developed into an investigation of origins.

Since all these concepts are concerned with change, the distinction of three separate lines of development might be challenged. What really took place, it might be said, was the emergence of a single historical or evolutionary concept of reality; and these three concepts are simply different ways in which the new view was recognized. They are different ways of saying that the object of inquiry is change, and they are all variations on one basic theme. The connection between usefulness and custom is obvious; with both, knowledge is predictive and pragmatic. A custom is justified by its usefulness and dies out when it ceases to serve its purpose, just as an idea is discarded when it ceases to predict the future. And dialectic, too, soon became materialist and scientific; like the others, it is concerned with the empirical investigation of change as soon as that occurs.

But the matter is not so simple. It is true that reality came to be understood more and more in terms of change; but not everyone in recent times has understood the same thing by "change." Moreover—and this concerns us more immediately—there has not been agreement about the character of inquiry into change. To understand a thing, it might be said, is to know its causes, and science seeks the causes or laws of change. Here is one theory of inquiry. The concept of the useful led to a philosophical interpretation of science as prediction of the future. But the study of custom led to the development of the genetic method; and, as we shall see later, the experimental and the genetic methods, while allied, are by no means the same. Moreover, while the study of custom pointed in the direction of history, it became at times notoriously unhistorical. The past was concrete, but laws and causes are abstract. Can we then understand the first in terms of the second? Must not a study of origins inevitably result in a statement of uniformities, and will not causal uniformities always miss what is unique and characteristic in history? This is, at any rate, a problem. Of the three methods, only dialectic seriously attempts to grasp things in their uniqueness; its ideal inclusiveness leads it to look for all sides of existence. And only dialectic attempts to understand the past—or the present, for that mater—in its own terms. Thus, while all three lines of development are concerned with change, they are nevertheless distinct.

In the philosophy of self-evidence, knowing involved a nice balance of activity and passivity or, rather, receptivity in the mind. Rational contemplation suggests passivity to modern ears; but apprehension is an act, and the reason why the intrinsically evident is not evident to everyone is that most people are not prepared to perform that act. If the mind were passive, the truth would impress itself on everyone alike, whether willing, unwilling, indifferent, or ignorant. In sensation, it is true, the mind had always been considered "for the most part" passive. But the organization of sense materials into knowledge by such processes as comparison, relation, combination, separation, and abstraction was an active process. And knowledge itself was an act of perception of the relationships between ideas. As the tradition declined, this balance was lost.

With the development of empiricism into sensationalism, mental processes came to be thought of more and more as taking place in conformity with rigid psychological laws. The laws of the mind were of the same sort as the laws of motion in their inevitable operation; and, as the mind became assimilated to nature, mental events took on the mechanical character of physical ones. A material particle persists in its state of motion or rest until acted upon by a force from without; although it is self-moving to this extent, one would hardly consider it spontaneously active. Similarly, the mind is acted upon by the external forces of experience and reacts appropriately; but its reaction is not an action. Locke classed judgment as an act of the mind, the results of which were difficult to distinguish from passive perception. But judgment later came to be classified as a form of belief, and belief to be explained by association, which operates almost automatically. Thus, by the assimilation of mind to a mechanical physical world, empiricism lost the element of activity which had originally formed an essential part of it. And yet, as we have seen, paradoxically, along with this conception of mind there developed the view that knowledge is interpretation, for the order among phenomena is due to lawful psychological operations on the data of sense.

With the gradual discovery that time enters into knowledge, reason, on the other hand, became more active. It had first been conceived as an apprehension that would occur spontaneously when prejudices and confused opinions had been cleared out of the way. But, with the breakdown of the sharp antithesis of reason and sense, it came to be regarded increasingly as an active synthesis of experiences. Moreover, the relations by which the synthesis was effected came to be attributed increasingly to the mind itself, while the experiences lost form and order to a corresponding extent. The end-result was, as with sensationalism, that all order comes from the mind, while the data of experience are reduced to a formless swarm of impressions. But this account does not correspond to fact; for, if anything is evident to an unbiased mind, it is the presence of order and relationship in experienced nature—not a wholesale uniformity but a great and unending variety of relationships, together with some regularity. Belief in reason once implied the presence of order in nature, discoverable by man. Now it came to mean the opposite, and it is fair to say that it thereby became unempirical.

The development of the new modes of thought proceeded as the idea of self-evidence declined, and its decline consisted largely in an increasing restriction of the sphere of the evident. In the beginning, that sphere had included the whole of reality: God, nature, and man. It would be difficult to determine whether it was God or nature which first lost the characters of clearness and distinctness in the eyes of thinkers; if either preceded, the interval was a short one in any case. But after both had definitely passed into the area of probability and belief, the principles of human nature still seemed to have the highest degree of certainty and clarity. The proper study of mankind is man, and he can know himself though he knows nothing else. This belief would have seemed very strange to a Greek, for whom man is a part of nature and to be understood as one instance of universal principles; or to a Christian, for whom man, like every other creature, is unintelligible apart from God. The explanation lies in the individualistic attitude of the modern world, which here finds expression in a belief about the extent of knowledge.

The doctrine that reality can be directly apprehended rested on the view that reality, the cause, is directly present in idea, the effect. But as has been indicated, another concept of causality was also operative from the start, according to which cause and effect are distinct and effect does not participate in or necessarily resemble cause in any respect. It followed from this that an idea and its object need have nothing in common. It was assumed that the difference was complete in such cases as the sensible idea of heat and its physical cause, the motion of material particles. Criticism gradually extended the sphere of ideas which do not resemble their causes, until it threatened to become coextensive with the entire range of ideas. But this is secondary for our purpose. The point is that, as soon as it was asserted that cause and effect need have nothing in common and that an idea is an effect, the notion of clear and distinct ideas was doomed; for if that is true, it is impossible to tell from inspection of the idea anything about the nature of the object which caused it. It may still be "true," but it is not self-evidently true. Reason no longer apprehends the structure of existence. Instead, it becomes a process of organizing the experiences which are always pouring in upon us. It becomes more active, less contemplative; but it also becomes increasingly cut off from objective fact. Men talk less of truth and more of knowledge; and the change of terminology reflects the change of attitude.

There was, however, a tendency to believe that cause and effect must both belong in the same sphere of existence. This principle was first invoked against supernaturalism; all physical events must have a physical or natural explanation. Nature is a closed system. The principle was then applied explicitly to man, and it was asserted that a bodily effect must have a bodily cause. Finally, the rule of the homogeneity of cause and effect was applied to the sphere of ideas, and it was said that only an idea can be the cause of another idea. But in the case of the mind, it was easier to believe that idea and cause are one. The self seems to be present in the idea that the subject has of it; the idea seems to be of the mind, "mental." And so the concept of self-evidence persisted longer here than elsewhere. A direct apprehension or intuitive knowledge of the self was the last to go. The principles of human nature still appeared self-evident after others had lost this character, because the new concept of causality did not, at first, seem applicable here. Mind seemed directly present in the ideas of it, although neither nature nor God seemed present in the ideas of them.

But at last self-evidence was crowded out from the actual entirely and limited to the possible. It is self-evident that the number 3 is greater than 2 and that red is not green; but nothing as to the character of existence can be inferred from this. Then new theories of concepts removed self-evidence even from the sphere of the possible, and the chapter is finished; for an operational concept is in one respect incomplete through its implicit reference to endless relationships; and, if it is an empirical concept, it also contains an element of denotational vagueness; and in neither case is the concept self-evident.

For the old doctrine, to know what you mean was also to know whether your ideas are true. Every clear and distinct idea was true, every obscure and confused one false, or at any rate rationally inacceptable. But now, "What do you mean?" and "Is it true?" have become two independent questions. When this point is reached, the old doctrine has been abandoned, for it held that the questions are, in the last analysis, the same.

6. Clarity and Existence

So far as they accepted the notion of clarity, the empiricists and rationalists agreed on the nature of knowledge and its objects. They disagreed only concerning its source and the means of acquiring it. It is because of this fundamental agreement that we find such a vigorous defense of reason in the philosophers of sense; the corresponding, though limited, acceptance of the senses on the part of the rationalists, however, was more a concession to their common sense than it was the result of agreement with empiricism. To both, reality as known to man is simple natures related in definite ways. All knowledge is of one kind, and all is on one level, except so far as some doctrine of degrees of knowledge complicates the theory.

With the growth of the new modes of thought which we have indicated, it is the function of ideas that comes to be stressed rather than their intrinsic nature. The question asked is no longer "What kind of idea is this?" but "What will this idea do?" And a moderately probable theory, or even a rough generalization, may serve well enough in many cases. Even if it is not clear and distinct, it may provide a degree of knowledge, possess a modicum of explanatory power; it may be useful either for purposes of prediction or as a means of reorganizing experience in some other way or as a necessary fiction. The clear and distinct idea did not so much have the function of explaining the real or dealing with it as of manifesting it; for, strictly speaking, it was the real in human terms. It did have a function, for it had a place and relations to other ideas within the conceptual system. But it was not formed for the purpose of aiding man to grasp conceptually and deal practically with a pervasively temporal and changing world, which is perhaps different from himself in fundamental ways. This is a change of tremendous importance.

It is interesting to observe that the hierarchical classification of the sciences, with which we are so familiar, did not appear until after the doctrine of degrees of knowledge had developed. The distinction between simple and complex was not merely familiar to the philosophers of evidence; it was in many respects basic to their entire point of view. Yet they did not use it to classify the branches of inquiry according to the relative simplicity or complexity of their subject matter. This suggests that, as I have said, they did not hold that the simple is prior to the complex except from the human point of view; we know the simple first, but it does not necessarily exist first. Reality is all clear and distinct, all intelligible; and it is so unified and systematic that the distinction between simple and complex is chiefly of human or epistemic, rather than of ontological, significance. Some things are more complex than others; but it does not follow that they depend on those others causally or follow them in an order of temporal development. All knowledge is on one level, whether it is mathematics, physics, politics, or theology. The classifications made at this time are based, rather, on such contrasts as those between philosophy and history or between theoretical and descriptive knowledge; and these suggest at once the distinction between evident and nonevident. Or they have some such basis as the contrast of nature and man, as when we find natural and moral philosophy distinguished, or the natural sciences and the arts.

It is only later that the hierarchical arrangement of the sciences appears. It seems likely that, aside from such factors as atomistic modes of thought, the theory of degrees of knowledge may have had something to do with this development. The arrangement of phenomena and sciences in terms of such subjects as physics, chemistry, biology, psychology, and sociology gives a series which proceeds from simple to complex. Add the doctrine of evolution, and it becomes also an order of temporal development, from earlier to later. Apply evolution to society, and it is the order of development of the sciences themselves; for man and his institutions grow from simplicity and relative homogeneity toward differentiation, complexity, and heterogeneity, and he understands the simple when he himself is relatively simple. But it is also, in the sciences, a series which moves from the better understood to the less well understood, from more probable and exact knowledge to the less probable and less exact, and from clear and distinct concepts and precise laws to less well-defined concepts and rough generalizations.

It is the altered conception of the world that is ultimately responsible for the new conception of knowledge. To ask what an idea does is meaningless if knowledge is apprehension of an unchanging object; but if the world is pervasively changing, the relation of man to nature is a dynamic one, for the individual must deal with, manipulate, and operate upon it practically. The intellect must approach a world of change obliquely, for the relation of concepts to change is not simple. A philosophy attempting to interpret such a world must make a place for action; and, once action is admitted as a category, it is the individual rather than reason or sense, or even mind, that takes the center of the stage. Also, if the human environment is in many important ways a social one, the living organism develops into a reflective human individual only within society. If this is true, the old theory was too individualistic, failing to see that the power of the mind is limited or released, but in any case shaped, by the culture in which it matures. And the theory was too optimistic in its advocacy of universal skepticism, overlooking the difficulties implicit in the fact that our presuppositions, power of thought, and even the skeptical attitude itself are all saturated with cultural content.

In the philosophy of self-evidence there is no point in demanding the verification of an idea, for in apprehending it we already possess truth. And so, in place of verification, there is preparation. The problem is not how to test an idea but how to find it; and when the apprehension comes, it is final. It is the inquirer who needs to be tested. This is as true of the empiricists as it is of the rationalists. Hume, for all his emphasis on the useful, has no concept of verification. Knowledge of the relations between ideas does not need verification, being intuitive in the last analysis; while knowledge of matters of fact is not susceptible of it. In place of verification—a rational, deliberate process—he has formation of habit—a non-rational, involuntary process and a work of nature. To him nature is the last word, and nature is to be trusted, not tested; the natural is the useful, but this does not imply any skepticism as to what is natural.

As the tradition declines, the situation is gradually reversed. Indeed, Hume (or Kant, who here provides a parallel illustration) is the turning-point. He finds it hard to decide whether philosophy should be on the side of reason or of imagination. But the very fact that he uses the term "imagination" shows that he still casts his lot, as a philosopher, with reason and evidence. As philosophy progressively takes the side of imagination, instinct, and utility, nature comes to be tested rather than trusted, until finally the testing—the verification—comes to be the criterion of what nature is. When that happens, new definitions of truth and reality have emerged. Instead of being the end of inquiry, ideas now constitute its starting-point. If an idea is accepted because it satisfactorily performs a certain function, it must be tested in order to discover whether it actually does perform that function and, if so, how well. In the tradition, it was the thinker who had to be purified, corrected, altered; now it is the idea, never entirely free from a certain hypothetical character, that requires such treatment.

The first object of the classical philosophers was to free the mind from preconceptions by a purification which should enable it to grasp the truth unhindered. The skepticism which they employed for this purpose expressed a normative approach to experience, which strove to discard the false in order to leave the true behind as a separate and definite object of knowledge. The contemporary preoccupation with skepticism is very different, both in content and in purpose. We are still fascinated by Descartes' method of doubt, but for reasons that he would not have understood or, if he had, would have rejected. The difference lies in the fact that to the classical philosophers skepticism either preceded or followed the body of philosophic doctrine but did not form a part of it, for the body of doctrine consisted of ideas and propositions that could not be doubted. Today, on the contrary, skepticism is considered an intrinsic part of philosophy, so far as thinking is regarded as experimental in nature; for to think is to justify ideas logically and test them empirically, but to justify and test is to doubt. Testing, doubting, validating—these are attitudes which the classical philosophers never took toward evident ideas. It would have seemed nonsense to an adherent of the principle of self-evidence to assert that the best approach to experience is not freedom from preconceptions but, rather, a wealth of preconceptions, together with a readiness to examine, develop, test, and apply them. Yet this is what his successors have been saying. This does not necessarily reduce philosophy to methodology; for, if the use and validity of each single idea are limited, it may be possible to combine ideas systematically to attain reasonably dependable knowledge; but it does seem to imply a great deal of unfinished business and the impossibility of an old-fashioned system.

Since modern skepticism doubts even ideas, it goes beyond the classical in its subject matter; and, since it is concerned with their function in experience rather than their intrinsic character, its purpose is different. It need hardly be added that the meaning of "idea" has also changed. One might almost say that recent philosophy has not been primarily concerned with ideas at all but with hypotheses, propositions, and judgments; for, strictly speaking, it is the latter three rather than ideas that have implications and consequences and so call for examination and testing.

The character of contemporary skepticism arises from the separation between two notions which were united in the classical doctrine of self-evidence. The first is determinateness of character and structural definiteness. The second is efficacy, force, vividness, or urgency. The first is essence, the second existence; the first is the "what," the second the "that," in things. Some might call this second component "reality," but that would be an error, for it

ANALYSIS

would imply that reality does not necessarily include form. On the contrary, anything real contains the two components together, and the experience of reality includes both. Historically, the rationalists stressed the first, the empiricists the second; but until the decline set in, both branches implicitly recognized the existence of both elements, without clearly distinguishing them. The theory that there are clear and distinct ideas which therefore are true by their intrinsic nature implies that we have ideas in which both logical clarity and existential immediacy are sufficient for purposes of human knowledge, although they need not be at a maximum and the idea need not be "adequate." With the rejection of self-evidence, possibility and existence, meaning and truth, concepts and data, universals and particulars, form and content, fall apart. Then the relation of every idea to existence becomes problematic and a matter for doubt.

In contrast to this point of view, the basic contention of the philosophy that we have been examining is that we have a direct cognitive experience of the world. Reality is directly given in experience; it is not simply inferred from experience, although we do also make such inferences, and for certain purposes always make them. Our experiences are iconic, with respect to both their characters and their stuff: they are likenesses of reality, for they are reality as it is experienced from our own particular perspective. The second contention of this philosophy is that the basic structure and content of reality can be discovered by us. This is in accord with that persistent conception which holds that philosophy is an attempt to understand the nature of things. It presupposes that the world has a "nature," that there are first principles or categories which can be uncovered and apprehended by an effort of thought.

These two propositions—that reality is given and that its nature can be apprehended—together with the concept of analysis constitute, I think, the permanent truth in the philosophy of self-evidence. The two propositions are related by the concept of analysis, for it is through analysis of the given that we discover the categories. The method of analysis and the ideal of self-evidence are not necessarily connected, but they naturally go together; for we analyze and abstract in order to explain, and the self-evident is the self-explanatory. For practical purposes, explanation is relative. The accounts of social phenomena such as wars, depressions, or religious movements which will satisfy a businessman, a politician, or a military man are all different in important respects; yet each may be adequate for the purpose of the individual in question. The accounts offered by psychologists and economists differ from all of these; they are scientific. A philosophical account is still different; it, too, might be called "relative," and the purpose to which it is relative is philosophic insight. Its aim is the formulation of first principles, which are not derived from other and prior principles. Such first principles, if we can reach them, have the quality of self-evidence.

Analysis is often identified with atomism. This, as we have seen, is a mistake. Analysis is a method, while atomism is a theory about the ultimate constituents of reality and their relations. Atomism is a philosophy which one might conceivably reach as the result of analysis; whether one would actually do so could be determined only empirically, by making the analysis. But, while one is analyzing, he is not yet an atomist; and when one becomes an atomist, he is no longer an analyst in the basic sense. If one assumes the truth of atomism, it is, of course, still possible to practice analysis, but not as the fundamental kind of inquiry which we have been describing. Analysis will then be, instead, an established technique for translating crude facts into refined data. The method which is really identified with atomism is not analysis but synthesis or construction. Atomism begins with abstract and relatively simple elements and attempts to construct out of them the concrete and complex things and facts of unreflective experience. Analysis, on the other hand, begins with the concrete, the nature of which it attempts to understand by abstraction; ideally, it also returns to the concrete by a synthesis.

In addition to its permanent significance, however, the philosophy of evidence contains elements which can no longer be accepted today. Of these, the most important is its theory of ideas. The sensory "ideas of things" which Locke described have become for us sense data; and in place of the "simple natures" of Descartes we have logical concepts. No one would wish to return to the earlier theory of ideas—if such a suggestion has any meaning—any more than to the world view of which it formed a part. Yet reality is not given in sense data and logical concepts. We need a fresh analysis of experience, in order to describe the nature of that experience of reality which everyone has at every moment. And any such analysis must give a more adequate account of its relational nature than the older philosophy did; it cannot be described as an "idea" or a set of ideas. This is a task on which some contemporary philosophy is engaged.

Again, while classical philosophy tended to assign objective reality only to clear and distinct ideas, we recognize that it is found also, and originally, in confused and obscure ones. Reality is first given in the primitive and unreflective experiences of men; and in such experiences reason is not the only, and—at least in the usual senses of the term—not a dominant, factor. They are conspicuously experiences of practical urgency and emotional vividness rather than of logical clarity. A skeptic would say that a law of inverse ratios is operative here: the more direct our contact with brute existence, the more vague, confused, and obscure our ideas; and the clearer our meanings, the more abstract, hypothetical, and detached from fact and reality they become. But philosophy is the belief that we can clarify our ideas without getting out of touch with reality; it is the search for truth by clarification of ideas, and these without the other are not philosophy at all.

If we consider the nature and problems of philosophy in relation to the ideas and intellectual framework provided by early modern thought, two alternative conceptions present themselves. One is epistemological. It begins with the two notions of logical clarity and empirical verification. These it regards as distinct and complementary components in the knowledge of existence. It would not be accurate to say that they are independent and separate, for the second implies the first. However, the first is independent of the second, except for psychological connections; and the basis of the second, namely, sense data, is independent of the first. As has been suggested, these components may be regarded as derivative from rationalism and empiricism, respectively. The task of philosophy, on this view, is primarily criticism of ideas and beliefs. The criticism consists of a reformulation of ideas in logically clear and consistent concepts and a translation of beliefs into terms of rationally credible propositions which are directly or indirectly verifiable in terms of sense particulars. Whatever ideas and beliefs do not survive this procedure are to be rejected as meaningless.

The aim of this program is the validation of knowledge, that is, the substitution of logical beliefs whose content and strength are proportionate to the evidence for beliefs which were vague, inconsistent, unempirical, or unfounded. This process involves the substitution of constructed for inferred entities, since the logical structure of the former and their empirical basis in sense particulars are believed to provide a higher degree of probability in knowledge and to involve less risk of unempirical, meaningless expressions than is the case with many inferred entities. The actual validation of empirical knowledge, however, is left to science, for all empirical knowledge is scientific. Philosophy is concerned, rather, with the meaning of basic concepts, such as knowledge, inference, probability, meaning itself, and perhaps others, such as matter, space, time, causality, good and bad, real and unreal, and so on.

This program is a familiar one in philosophy today and is widely accepted, though it differs in details from one writer or group to another. There is difference, for instance, over the question of which concepts and how many are the proper concern of philosophical analysis. The implication, or rather presupposition, of the program is that cognitive contact with reality (or, as its adherents would say, with the objective, public, and common world) is indirect. This statement taken by itself would be consistent with the view that we know reality by means of perceptual experiences which represent things that lie beyond them. But the traditional theory of representative perception has been pretty generally discredited by this movement as well as by others. So the statement implies, in effect, that objects of empirical knowledge are definable in terms of sensory acquaintance under specified conditions or are constructed in terms of sense data and their relations.

The other conception of philosophy suggested by early modern thought is the one which has been developed in these pages. It is ontological rather than epistemological; its starting-point is existence rather than knowledge; and its theory of knowledge will be based on a theory of existence. On this view, too, philosophy involves the examination of beliefs, but its concern is with their clarification rather than with their validation. We are not concerned primarily with sorting out the empirical beliefs from the non-empirical and meaningless ones and the valid from the invalid, because every important belief has some objective meaning and is founded on some experience of real existence. It is the task of philosophy to define that meaning as clearly as possible. Which are the important beliefs is obviously a further question; but they will not in any case coincide with those which, from the other point of view, would be called "empirical," for the meaning of empirical will be different where reality is held to be directly given in experience.

We begin with experience and go on to abstract its traits. Philosophy does not ask "Do I exist?" but "What am I?" It does not ask "Does the external world exist; or what reasons are there for believing in its existence?" It seeks, rather, the characteristics of the outer world or environment and of those situations in which we experience a polarity between ourselves and other existence. It attempts to define the concept of the external world. It looks for the characteristics of God, freedom, good, and evil and for the proper definitions of these terms, instead of asking whether the words have meaning or describe any entities. Such questions as those about my own existence are not asked by the critical school with practical intent. It is assumed that such terms as the first person singular pronoun are acceptable and practically indispensable in common usage. The questions concern their theoretical meaning, which is to be investigated quite independently of their practical utility. But, from the ontological point of view, philosophy is descriptive, and no account would be complete which left out the practical or translated it into other terms.

Modern philosophy has gradually turned from the second to the first conception. As it did so, it became more and more closely identified with scientific method, and with the processes and conceptual forms by which we know, to the neglect of the objects of knowledge. As ontological concepts have declined in importance, one of two things has happened: either philosophy has become preoccupied with problems of secondary importance, or it has become progressively assimilated to science, which has provided the subject matter which philosophy itself no longer could supply. We, on the other hand, have noted some of the ontological notions involved in inquiry during an important period of Western thought. The conclusion I wish to suggest is that the survival of philosophy is bound up with its firsthand analysis of existence.

PART II

Dialectic

THE distinction of pairs of opposites is very old; it must go back almost to the beginning of human thought. Men seem always to have noticed the alternation and contrast of life and death, light and darkness, day and night, good and evil, permanence and change, and to have wondered about their relations. These aspects of the world are striking and dramatic in their opposition. They pervade all experience and are constant in their bearing on human life. Their discovery requires no special training and no particular vantage point of observation in nature and history. Yet systematic thinking, which builds its understanding of man and the world on opposites, occurs only at intervals, or at least reaches a high development only at certain times. Why is this? The persistent recurrence of the idea indicates basic truth, while its intermittent appearance suggests that the truth is only partial.

To understand is to relate, so far as the facts of experience permit; and this activity cannot get very far without a small number of inclusive concepts, which can bring many diverse facts together. Here is the importance of opposites in human thinking; they enable us to make sense of the world, by seeing in it the same principles at work everywhere. Everything is permanent or changing, one or many, good or evil, positive or negative, real or illusory; and the more we reflect, the more we see that not just one, but both, opposites of any pair are involved in a thing, for they are inseparable.

The doctrine of opposites also implies that the world is unified. If the aim of inquiry were simply to describe things as they come, as accurately as possible, the unit of study would be the single thing, event, or property, and no one could say to how many others it might be related and in what ways. To claim that everything is a manifestation of the same universal opposites would be senseless dogmatism. Again, if, as is sometimes said, all knowledge is scientific and the ideal of science is measurement, they are equally useless; for measurement has to do largely with quantities that are continuous. Its formulas contain variables that take many values, not merely two. It is concerned, not with rest and motion, permanence and change, but with the quantity of motion, the degree of permanence, the rate of change. It deals in curves, not polar opposites. Or if the aim of inquiry is only prediction, opposites will give us no help in forecasting the weather, population trends, or the top speed of a new airplane. But if the aim of inquiry is to gain some conception of the world as a whole, the doctrine of opposites will be very relevant indeed; for it is an attempt to state the most general aspects of the world, so that we may see how the most ordinary and familiar, as well as the extraordinary, happenings all illustrate the same principles.

A philosophy of opposites is a theory of what the world is; dialectic, in the most common sense of the term, is a theory of inquiry. But successful inquiry must conform to facts. Dialectic presupposes a theory of reality; and, if it enables us to understand reality, that will be because the structure and process of the world themselves have the nature of opposites. Our concern is primarily with inquiry. But it cannot be exclusively so—above all, in this philosophy, where knowing and being are so closely related. We must deal with both. And so, in what follows, the term "dialectic" will be applied both to the method of inquiry and to the theory of reality on which it rests. This broad meaning is not uncommon: people speak of "dialectical" idealism or materialism, as well as of the "dialectical" method. Where there is danger of ambiguity, it will be stated whether the term refers to human thinking or to its object.

"Dialectical inquiry" is here understood to mean thinking in terms of opposites and their relations, and it has two sides. On the one hand, it is a criticism of abstractions, the purpose of which is to show that concepts and truths which, at first glance, appear to be final and complete and hence "absolute" are limited, partial, and relative when seen in perspective. For instance, there are individuals, and the individual is an irreducible datum. But there is also society; and, unless this is seen, the individual does indeed become an "abstraction." But the "also" shows that we have simply opposed a second abstraction to the first. Similarly, there is quality, but also quantity; there are things with properties, but also interactions. And so, moving on from these abstractions, dialectic is the construction of a truth less one-sided and incomplete, by the organization of the various opposites which show themselves in the course of inquiry into a totality, a unity that may be called "concrete" because it is the concretion—the growing-together—of the various concepts that have been criticized. We must think of the social individual and the individualized society; of the quantified quality; of the interacting (and intra-acting) things.

Later we shall have occasion to consider dialectical materialism, but for the present we are concerned only with idealism. This philosophy, which culminated in Hegel, is distinguished from other theories of opposites by the intermediate position in reality which it ascribes to these. There is in the world a double process of the generation of opposites and their absorption, their differentiation and their integration. But there is also the unity out of which they are differentiated and the unity into which they are absorbed. For example, before the emergence in experience of the oppositions of self and not-self, thought and existence, there must have been an immediacy in which these were not yet distinguished; and there is also a time, or a phase of experience, in which they are, or are being, overcome. There never was a time before which opposites did not exist or one at which they began to be; neither will there ever be a time after which they have ceased. But, with respect to any specific, historical opposition, there is a stage before it arose and another after which it has been overcome. At the same time, there are great elementary opposites presupposed in every historical process. In any process there are one and many, being and not-being, and even, perhaps, good and evil. These are not generated but are the presuppositions of generation. Yet they, too, occupy an intermediate position; for they are aspects of a unity that includes them, which they split but which, nevertheless, holds them together. Thus the dialectical view of reality involves a greater degree of unity in the nature of things than is accepted by those who regard the world as a balance, mutual limitation, struggle, or other relation between opposed principles that are irreducibly plural and perhaps even mutually independent.

This basic unity is that of the absolute, or spirit; the process is its development or manifestation. But, say the absolutists, in manifesting itself it ceases to be absolute and becomes relative and hence other than itself. Now the absolute can be known only in its appearances; in fact, if the statement is properly understood, it may be said that the absolute is its appearances. Philosophy, then, is the study of this process of differentiation or manifestation. The process contains two basic elements, opposites and negation. These two are the essence of dialectic. Only if we can describe them can we give any real meaning to such expressions as the "absolute," and the "generation" and "absorption" of opposites. But, if we can understand them and their relation, we shall understand dialectic.

1. Opposites

Consider any of the familiar pairs of opposites, such as form and content, good and evil, one and many, or positive and negative. The key to their nature lies essentially in the mutual relations of the two terms. On this point a number of theories have been put forward. Some have maintained that they are simply correlatives, such as we find in the familiar dualities of light and darkness, male and female, or up and down. Others have regarded them as mutually limiting one another. Such seems to have been the view of some of the pre-Socratics with respect to hot and cold, moist and dry, especially when these were made concrete elements of the cosmos, for instance, in the form of fire and water. Still others have described the relation as a conflict, the clearest instance of which is the struggle between good and evil. On the other hand, it has also been maintained that opposites are complementary to each other and so do not conflict but are in harmony; and this harmony may be interpreted either as a static relationship of complementary elements or as the balance of opposed forces in equilibrium. The dialectical theory of the relation, however, is different from all these. To make a start, we may describe it in terms of three properties: opposites are correlative, mutually exclusive, and in conflict.

First, they are correlative; they have a positive relation of interdependence. There is no affirmation which does not contain a latent negation, and there is no negation that does not imply an assertion; "is" and "is not" are inseparable when we understand the implications of any assertion or the nature of any fact. And similarly in other cases. Without necessity, freedom would have no meaning, though, of course, freedom must have some intrinsic meaning of its own in order to be a correlative at all. And, conversely, without freedom, in the sense of alternatives that might have been chosen but were not because of factors that excluded them, necessity would be no more than a simple actuality; it would no longer be itself. But opposites are more than correlatives; for parent and child, in and out, lock and key, center and periphery, are correlatives, yet they would hardly be called opposites.

Second, opposites are mutually exclusive. What is good is not bad, and vice versa. Necessity excludes freedom; and freedom excludes necessity, though not order, law, and discipline. The same thing is not both one and many: a house is one, and, although it is made of many bricks, it is the bricks, not the house, that are many. Or if the house is many, it is no longer one, as when it is cut up into a number of apartments and, becoming an apartment building, ceases to be a house in the former sense. But opposites are more than mutually exclusive, for this morning and this afternoon are temporally exclusive of each other, and my desk and typewriter are spatially exclusive; yet they are not opposites. For that matter, everything is identical with itself and so excludes everything else through the fact of differing from it; but not all exclusions are oppositions.

Finally, opposites conflict or, as dialectic says, contradict each other. This is their most characteristic and most important property in dialectic; and it is the one that most stands in need of explanation. Unless a clear account of it can be given, the whole theory is nonsense. Without attempting to justify the use of "conflict" and "contradiction" as synonyms, we may note in passing that the assumption behind the usage is an agreement of thinking and reality. For thinking, contradiction is the ultimate conflict. Therefore, if it is granted (as, of course, it may not be) that opposites conflict and that thought and reality agree, opposites may also be said to contradict. But the important thing is what the words refer to, not the words themselves. Let us approach this problem negatively.

If opposites were simple contraries, they would not conflict. Contraries may be defined as extreme differences within a kind or genus. Hot and cold are contraries within the scale of temperatures, assuming that the scale has extreme points; black and white were once considered contraries within the genus color. But, while hot and cold are incompatible, they do not contradict each other. If a thing is hot, it is not cold; if it is cold, it is not hot; when one quality is present, the other is absent. This is interesting; and the fact that some qualities, such as cold and smooth, are compatible while others, such as cold and hot, are not deserves investigation. The relation of contrariety is important. But to say that a pair of qualities which exhibit it contradict each other is simply false.

Opposites, however, are not contraries, for there are intermediates between contraries, but there are none between opposites. Between hot and cold are all the various degrees of warmth and coolness. Between good and evil, on the other hand, or between permanence and change there is no middle ground. Where these are relevant, one and only one holds, as is the case with contradictories. Yet opposites differ from contradictories, too, in that both terms of the pair are positive: red and its negate, not-red, are contradictories;

but the opposites, permanence and change, are both positive notions. In this respect, opposites are like contraries. They are contraries that are contradictory. To the statement that both terms of a pair of opposites are positive, such instances as being and not-being, affirmation and negation, appear to be exceptions, for one term of each seems purely negative. And there are other similar instances: evil is sometimes considered the absence of good, matter the absence of form, and so on. However, the exceptions are only apparent, as we shall see, and there is positive content even in negation. This is a point that may be postponed for the moment.

But, even though opposites were contradictories, they still would not conflict. Of contradictory statements one is true, the other false; and of contradictory properties one is present, the other absent. Either "This is red" or "This is not red," and not both, must be true; and a sweater itself is either red or not-red. The two possibilities are incompatible, just as was the case with contraries. But there is no conflict. Strange as it may sound, contradictories do not contradict, because they do not meet. The entities of which contradictory terms are predicates hold them apart, and this saves them from conflict; one thing is red, another is not-red. And in thought the mind holds contradictory terms and propositions apart; it cannot unite them. Whatever contradiction, in the sense of conflict, may be, it is not a relation between logical entities such as these. If permanence and change were like ordinary logical entities, there would be no difficulty—and no dialectical opposites; for we could be sure that of the two statements, "This thing is permanent" and "This thing is changing," one would be true and the other false; and the thing itself would be one or the other but not both. Nothing could be both permanent and changing at the same time and in the same respect. But the problem is more complicated than this because, in making the distinctions in order to be consistent, we may lose the unity of the object with which we began.

Contradictions arise because we attribute both opposites to the same thing, and we cannot avoid doing so. We say that this person is both changing and permanent: changing in his actions, surroundings, experiences, but permanent in that he has the same personal identity and biological endowment. We say that this salt is one and many; one substance but with many predicates, such as white, hard, crystalline, salty. Again, the same experience is both immediate and mediated: immediate because everything, even abstract thought, is directly felt, and mediated because anything that was pure feeling and nothing else would fall outside consciousness and we could not be aware that we had experienced it. The logician immediately feels the economy of his mediated, abstract proof; on the other hand, a man in the grip of strong love or hate still is conscious of the object of his emotion, and so his feeling is partly mediated.

Unless we can understand how the two sides are related in such cases or can suspend judgment until we do understand, we fall into contradictions. But on some things we inevitably reflect and find ourselves unable to suspend judgment—whether everything changes, whether good and evil are the same in the end, whether man is free, whether the physical world is reality or appearance. So the question is how we can best understand these things. We cannot do it simply by making distinctions, though distinctions are necessary; for we do not understand until we relate, but distinctions separate. We cannot say salt is one, but to our five senses it is five; for we want to know the relation between the one salt and our five impressions of it. And it does not help to say that Smith's personality is one, but it expresses itself in various ways; for the question is: Are these ways consistent with one another and with what Smith thinks he is, and how far do they reveal his deeper traits of character?

People differ widely in their reactions when confronted with such problems. Some say they are only semantical confusions, to be removed by a proper definition of words and by making the necessary distinctions. Others dismiss them as paradoxes, harmless though undeniable; they think that time and familiarity will

DIALECTIC

harden us, until the air of paradox disappears. But to the dialectician they are central philosophical problems.

The question is whether or not the contradictions can be removed without losing the unity. It cannot be done, at any rate, unless we abandon the old concept of substance with its predicates; for, if we say that a person is permanent and changing, good and evil, we must explain this, in accordance with that concept, by saying that he is permanent and good in his own eyes, changing and evil in the eyes of his fellows, or something of the sort. We make good the quality of one person and locate evil in the judgment of his fellows; but we still want to know how he can be both good and evil; that has not been explained. The fact is that, if there are dialectical opposites, things cannot be understood in terms of substance, predicate, and relation; for opposites are none of these, and neither are they relations between them. When we say that this thing is permanent and changing, good and evil, one and many, and so on, these expressions must be understood as crude, though sometimes useful, ways of stating the facts. It would be more accurate to say that here good and evil are struggling and somehow related; permanence and change are factors in this situation; this unresolved process is unified and yet diverse.

A second question also arises: How, if at all, are the various pairs of opposites themselves related to one another? Are they a haphazard collection, or are they ordered? Is there a definite number of them, or are they indefinitely many? Or are they reducible to some one basic pair? The answer to these questions, which will also furnish a clue to the problem of the contradictions, can best be found by a reference to the historical development of the ideas involved.

The historical origin of dialectic lay in the problem of subject and object in knowledge. For a time no one was able to give any satisfactory account of their relations. It seemed necessary to derive one from the other; and yet there were equally good reasons for assigning each an independent status in the process of knowing. This dilemma led to their being considered conflicting opposites;

and their conflict became the pattern and point of reference for all other pairs of opposites.

The opposition between subject and object in modern philosophy had its roots in Cartesian dualism. The two notions are very different, of course. The dualism was based on a distinction between mind and matter, thinking and extended substance; the opposition was a contrast between subject and object in experience and involved the problem of how the subject can know an object other than itself. The first had to do with being, the second with knowing. To Descartes, the opposition did not exist; for him there was no gap between subject and object known. If the opposition is accepted, on the other hand, substance must eventually be given up, for it is not an object of knowledge or of any other experience. Nevertheless, the first position gradually led to the second, as the implications of dualism became apparent. With Kant, the transition is almost complete; substance has become merely one of a number of categories by which objects are known. The question to be asked is no longer What is reality? but What is the object of sense experience? Or, at any rate, the first question can be answered for knowledge only in terms of the second.

The new point of view, however, led to a difficulty. Subject and object are different, though they are related in knowledge, and their meanings are even correlative; subject is one thing, object another. But the self or subject can become its own object. In fact, it is a subject only so far as it does so, for it is precisely self-consciousness and freedom (which are inseparable) that distinguish the self from a determined, passive, unconscious, natural object. In other words, subject is object. On the other hand, all the structure of the object, including spatial and temporal order as well as conceptual, is attributed to the subject. Only the given, sensuous material has another source, and it is not objective; for sensation is private and chaotic, while the objective is public and orderly. The object, or what makes it objective, comes from the subject. Subject is also object, or not-subject; and object is mostly subject, or not-object. This was the discovery of Fichte, who began his system of philosophy with the proposition "I am I." Having thus postulated an unlimited self, he set over against it, antithetically, the not-I or not-self. He then went on to say that the not-I can be opposed to the I only within consciousness, which means that the not-I, or nature, is a part of experience. He now has on his hands not only subject and object but two subjects. There is the first, absolute I, independent and complete in itself; and there is the thinking I, which is relative to its object. There is the unlimited self and the limited self, the free and the determined. These two selves or subjects are themselves opposed, and Fichte attempts at some length, with great ingenuity but no success, to reconcile them. He cannot generate the relative I of knowledge from the absolute I; nor, starting from the other end, with the mutually limited subject and object of consciousness, can he find the "ground of experience" which will unite them.

There is a practical, as well as a theoretical, conflict in the self. The I is primarily activity, effort, striving, rather than thinking; and the goal of its striving is to overcome the sense world, nature, the not-I, to make itself infinite. But it is limited by the latter, which acts as a counterforce or barrier. Fichte thinks of the not-I as inert and dead, accepting the mechanical theory of nature completely; so the opposition is between active and passive elements. It falls within experience, as before. But why the I should be opposed by a not-I is, in the last analysis, inexplicable; it is simply a fact. It makes sense morally, since moral and reflective action would be impossible without something to act upon; but why there should be such action at all cannot be explained, although in this philosophy, which first postulates an unlimited self, an explanation is called for.

These contradictions were implicit in Kant, just as the philosophy of Kant was implicit in Descartes; but Kant was not too troubled by them, being concerned for the most part either with the object of scientific experience or with the subject of moral and religious experience, rarely with the two at once. When he did think of them, he quieted his philosophic conscience, though without solving the problem, by making a distinction between the theoretical or scientific, and the practical or moral, spheres of experience. But the important point, for our purpose, is that to him contradictions lie in thinking, not in existence; they are always logical, never ontological. He never says that mind in its actual existence, things in themselves, or nature is contradictory.

Fichte, however, takes a different point of view: there is a contradiction in the nature of the self, as well as in our thinking about it. Man is somehow both infinite and finite: finite as an intelligent, conscious being, infinite in his striving. And there is a contradiction in nature, too, for it is both dependent on and independent of the self. Thus the notion that opposites conflict is first clearly developed in his philosophy of the self. To him, conflict and contradiction are closely related, since he derives the laws of logic from the nature of the self. The law of identity, "A is A," is derived from the basic proposition about the self, "I am I"; the law of contradiction, "A is not not-A," is derived from "The I is not, but is opposed to, the not-I." Logic is based on existence, the study of logic on an analysis of the self. Therefore, logical contradiction is an abstraction from the real, concrete conflict between freedom and necessity, act and limitation, subject and object. Practical conflict and theoretical contradiction are inseparable, though the second depends on the first.

Opposites, we said, are correlative, mutually exclusive, and conflicting. But a philosophy built on this notion alone would have to admit that the world is irrational and that no coherent account can be given of it; it could present only a mass of contradictions. Fichte was really forced to this conclusion. Not only does he find subject and object in conflict because each "limits" the other, but he is unable to unite the relative standpoint of knowledge with the absolute standpoint of the original, unlimited ego. Hegel solved the problem and thereby formulated a completely dialectical philosophy, by definitely adopting the ontological point of view and consistently adhering to it. He always talks primarily of reality, and knowledge is either a form of reality, a kind of being or existing—or else, as reason, it is the essence of reality. He never begins with knowing and asks whether we can know reality. His point of departure is always, in one way or another, implicitly or explicitly, reality, being, the absolute.

The basic opposites shift to fit this approach, and in place of self and not-self they become reality and its manifestations. This duality could be stated in many ways. I think the most adequate, on the whole, is essence and appearance. The absolute must manifest itself; essence must appear. Both terms are essential to reality. The inner nature of anything—for instance, a man—which does not achieve outer expression is itself only an "outer," that is to say, superficial and unimportant; and, conversely, overt actions which are not the expression of an inner purpose are not really actions but blind discharges of energy. This basic notion of inner essence and outer appearance repeats itself again and again under many different forms. It is universal reason and its manifestation in nature and history. It is the contrast between the universal and the particulars in which it is embodied. It is the contrast between quality and the quantitative expressions which quality assumes. It is form and content, substance and attributes, one and many, identity and differences. At its sharpest, it is being and nothing, for appearance, taken apart from essence, is nothing.

If we view the historical development as a whole, it is fair to say that the problem which had gradually emerged was primarily a problem of knowledge: How can the subject know objects other than itself? And, if the question is answered, How can it know itself as a subject? The problem was set by certain theories about nature and the relation of man to it and by the whole individualistic, subjectivistic tone of modern thought, which more and more had isolated the individual from the cosmos. It is the same problem that we find in the psychology of sensations, the epistemology of primary and secondary qualities, certain characteristic beliefs about substance, the ethics of hedonism, the economics of private profit, the religion of Protestantism, the politics of the social contract. Hegel solved it by going back beyond the whole period to earlier sources in Greek and Christian thought. From the Greeks, and especially Aristotle, he took the concepts of form and matter and of the process by which form or essence, as a potentiality, actualizes itself concretely. Form and matter, however, become essence and appearance in his philosophy—a very un-Greek transformation. From Christianity he took the concept of an infinite, eternal God, manifesting himself through creative activity in the natural world. The rational essence is the divine logos; the appearance is the whole of nature and the process of history. But, again, absolute spirit is not the God of Christianity. And from the science and philosophy of his own time he took the theory of a mechanical nature, which is interpreted as the "other," the negation of active mind or spirit. In this way he overcomes the dualism of mind and matter and abolishes the isolation of subject from object and from everything else, which had been the outcome of the previous development. The strength of the position lies in the fact that it incorporates and welds together so much that had been central in Western thought.

It resolves the conflict of opposites, for, while the absolute contains opposites, it reconciles them. Its self-expression is a single, continuous, indivisible process. There is no contradiction in the fact that God or universal reason manifests itself in nature and history. On the contrary, since it is the nature of this absolute subject to be conscious, it must have an object; and, since it is infinite and free, it makes and is its own object. But conflict is also real, for everything finite is in conflict with and contradicts itself.

What does this mean? To be finite is to be a particular, different from other particulars, which exist in other times or places. This stone is not that tree; this person is not that one; this nation is not that nation. But particulars, though different, are also related to and limit one another. The stone cramps the roots of the tree; the territory and power of one nation set limits to the expansive ambitions of another, or even to its continued existence; and individual persons are dependent on and limited by one another. As a manifestation of the absolute, the nature of a thing is to be self-

DIALECTIC

realizing; but, as one particular among others, it falls short of the ideal. Because of this incompleteness and failure to realize itself, the opposites within the particular fall apart. That is, the thing does not contain the explanation of how they can be together in it; no analysis of it will give the answer. If it could hold them together, it would be complete in itself, the absolute; but it cannot. It is not unified, and that is why we are unable to unify it. The single tree, man, nation, stone, are each both one and many, identical and full of differences, permanent and changing. Each is one, identical, and permanent in essence but many, different, and changing in appearances. The nation is one; but the classes, institutions, and individuals within it are many and oppose its unity. Everything finite is striving to be one, to bind together its many aspects and properties. But the many aspects oppose the effort, and eventually the thing flies apart, dissolves, comes to an end, dies. "The nature of the finite lies in this, that it dissolves itself."[1] Such conflict is simply contradiction in concrete form—for to Hegel, too, the logical is an abstraction from the real, although his dialectical logic is not the logic of Fichte. Opposites, then, are the ways in which the absolute manifests itself in finite things and to finite minds; opposites appear in knowledge because they are already in things.

The absolute is not in conflict with itself, but its manifestations are. How is this possible? Opposites contradict, but the absolute does not, though the opposites are in it. Here is a problem which the dialectic does not solve. It need not deal with the paradoxes of the self and the not-self in knowing, since its standpoint is existence rather than knowledge; but the problem of existence is no less crucial. Reason gives rise to nature—its other—and these two are mutually exclusive and in conflict. It is true that they are not completely different, for nature could not be at all unless it embodied law and reason and order; nature is, therefore, the manifestation rather than the sheer other of reason. Nevertheless, it is also opposite. Spirit—and reason is implicit spirit—at the same time both generates and unites opposites everywhere, just as in

---

1. *Enzyklopädie*, ¶ 81.

this instance. And so far as they are generated, they are real and contradictory, although so far as they are reconciled, they are not. Perhaps we may say that, so far as spirit is a being, entity, finished reality, it has overcome and united the opposites which it contains; but, so far as it is becoming, activity, process, it is continually generating and overcoming them, and so they are real. But which is the case? "So far as" is not an answer, for it says they are real, yet united; opposite, yet reconciled. This only repeats the same paradoxes.

There are three ways in which one might attempt to answer this objection. First, we might say flatly that the concept of opposites does really apply to the absolute, just as it does to everything else. But then it would be difficult to see how the absolute really differed from particulars, in spite of statements that it "unites" its opposites. Second, we might say that "opposites" has two meanings, one that applies to finite things, the other to the infinite. But this would simply restate the problem, for we should then have two sets of meanings to reconcile and two kinds of truth. The most satisfactory interpretation of dialectic, I think, is different from both of these answers. We must say that the term "opposites" has a single meaning; but, while they give as adequate an account of the nature of particulars as can be found, opposites are inadequate descriptions of the absolute because they do not portray adequately the single process of its activity. They give the complexity but not the unity. However, some are more adequate than others. For example, quality and quantity are more adequate than being and nothing; essence and appearance (or existence) than quality and quantity; subject and object than essence and appearance. Inquiry must try to find those which approximate as closely as possible the nature of reality. The difficulty is that, while the approximations form a series and derive their positions in it from its limit, the limit does not have the character of the series, that is, of opposites. In what respect, then, do they approximate it? The series of fractions which approach the integer 1 as a limit have in common with it their arithmetical character; the integer 1 itself

DIALECTIC

may be regarded as a fraction. But no character can be found which applies identically to the absolute and its appearances. This means that the application of opposites to the absolute is analogical, not literal; they are philosophical metaphors. For that matter, the picture of the categories as a linear series is also a metaphor, for the later members of the series include the earlier—this is precisely what makes them later. They are a system, not a series. But let us defer this topic for the time being.

It is now clear why opposites are not the greatest differences within a genus. If they were, they would be co-ordinate species, as hot and cold are with respect to temperature. But essence and appearance are not co-ordinate species at all. They are not two kinds of reality, like two kinds of triangle or two species of vertebrates; but everywhere there is essence that is appearing, and similarly with all the other pairs of opposites.

It might be supposed that the relation between opposites is that of form to privation; and this interpretation would be especially plausible if we should choose such examples as being and nothing, good and evil, actuality and potentiality, freedom and necessity, where the second term in each case seems to signify a lack or absence. Necessity, it might be said, is the lack of freedom, evil the absence of good, and so on. But this interpretation would be mistaken. Let it be granted, for the sake of argument, that evil, taken in abstraction from good, is nothing, unreal, illusory; and, in general, that the second term of each pair is privative in character when taken in isolation from its correlate. But the point is that it cannot be taken in isolation, for that is not the way it exists. And when it is seen in relation to the first, it must be recognized as having positive force. Good cannot exist or have meaning without the struggle against evil; if a way of life could be imagined without evil, it could no longer be called morally good, it would have no moral quality. Without necessity, law, and order, freedom is only anarchy; real freedom implies its opposite, necessity.

The opposites are not co-ordinate, and neither is one simply the lack of the other. Rather, the second is always the manifestation of the first; and this makes it both positive, because it goes beyond the first, and, at the same time, subordinate because derivative. Fichte calls such judgments as "I am" and "Man is free" "thetic judgments";[2] they lay down a thesis, without reference to any antithetic notion. The existence of the self here contains no reference to nonexistence or to the existence of anything else; the freedom of man does not imply necessity, which characterizes nature, or its absence. Man as a free being has nothing in common with nature, so there is no similarity to form the basis of a comparison. But he would never call thetic such a judgment as "Nature is"; its essence is to be antithetic to spirit, it is the not-I. Yet the I must manifest itself in the world of sense, and it realizes its moral nature there. This is exactly the relationship defined by Hegel, although he rejects the Fichtean notion that there is a conflict between nature and spirit, so that nature is a mark of our imperfection and a completely free being would have nothing of it. But in his dialectic there remains and is developed the idea that the first of two opposites is thetic, basic, primordial, and the second antithetic, dependent, derived. The relation between them is asymmetrical, and the second is the development and actualization of the first, though this is not immediately apparent in some sharp oppositions, where the second term seems purely antithetical. The first always requires the second; essence must appear.

The contention that opposites cannot be synthesized because they are incompatible is as important as it is old. The explanation of their synthesis can now be stated. They can achieve synthesis because the second is simply the development of the first. But in finite existents or, rather, in existence as finite, conflict arises because the antithesis sets itself up as independent and equally real with the thesis; this is only a way of saying that the finite does not contain in itself the absolute, which is the active principle in all existence. So evil claims to be as real as good; the individual claims to be a substantial person, independent of the community; appearance takes on the character of essence, as when we judge

---

2. *Grundlage der gesamten Wissenschaftslehre* (1794), Teil I, ¶ 3.

things or people by "appearances." The antithetic tries to make itself purely positive, thetic, by severing itself from its base; but the result is conflict, evil, and falsity, since it is not really independent. This is the source of contradiction.

The discussion of the nature of opposites has led to an indication of how they come to be, as well as how they are united; for they are not primary data or facts but are the product of a process of opposition, of opposing. This process dialectic calls "negation," and we must now examine it more closely.

2. Negation

The first and simplest form of negation is otherness. It is first because any other or more specific kind of exclusion, absence, or denial entails it. Today is not yesterday: yesterday is excluded from, and therefore other than, the day now passing. He is not here: he is absent, in a place different from the one in question. The political parties do not really differ in their principles: there are certain possible principles which either party might hold, but, in fact, these are other than the set held in common by both. The same is true of the qualities intrinsic to things and events. The metal bar is not heavy but is a light alloy, other than heavy; the conversation was not long, but of a different kind, namely, brief. Otherness or difference is also the form of negation closest to common sense, which accepts plurality as given. But negation goes beyond the concept of a plurality of different entities, each itself; for it sets up a relationship between them, which may be regarded either as a factor intrinsic to existence or as our interpretation of it. In other words, negation may be interpreted in terms of either thought or existence or both.

If each existent thing and fact is entirely positive, and just itself, and if the aim of inquiry is to describe the facts and correlate them, negation will not be an important concept. The word "not" will indicate that we are approaching the facts by a roundabout way, for one reason or another, instead of going straight to them. Negation will be a concept relevant to knowledge rather than to existence, and its role in knowledge, moreover, will be secondary—to correct an error, to deny the reality of the nonexistent, or to express our ignorance. We correct a mistaken impression about the length of the conversation by pointing out that it was not long; we do not know where the man is, but he certainly is not present. If this is all that negation is, we should be justified in giving it a subordinate place in our thinking, for it would form no part of the final account of existence. But if, as is implied by every philosophy of opposites, facts include both "is" and "is not," are in some way both positive and negative, then the concept of negation is essential for understanding them. For dialectic, negation is primarily existential and derivatively an aspect of thinking; we must use it in thinking about existence because it is a factor in existence.

Three aspects of the concept may be distinguished. It may refer to (1) a process or operation, (2) its resultant or product, or (3) a relation. In logic one may take a class term, such as "round," or a proposition, such as "Texas is larger than New York," and perform upon it the operation of negation. The result of the operation will be the negate of the original: the term "not-round" or the proposition "Texas is not larger than New York" ("It is not the case that Texas is larger than New York"). Also, a relation holds between the original and its negate. Between the term and its negate there is the relation of mutual exclusion, as well as joint exhaustion of the possibilities in the universe of discourse, expressed in the statement that nothing can be both round and not-round and everything must be one or the other. Between the two propositions there is the relation of contradiction. The concept has all three senses in common speech. We speak of an act of negation: "He negated their proposal," or "He refused to accept the conditions." But we also say, "His absence was conspicuous," using absence, itself the result of the act of staying away, as a noun. Finally, negation is a relation, as when we say, "Dictatorship is the negation of freedom," not only because it destroys freedom, but because the two are mutually incompatible.

DIALECTIC

Which of the three aspects is basic? This is an important question, and it has been partly begged by our formulation of the concept; for to call the negate a product implies that it does not exist until it has been created by an act, and this assumes that the operation is prior to both entity and relation. But this is only one possibility. Most thinkers who have been concerned with the subject have considered the relationship primary. They have regarded the universe as a system of limited and complementary entities, each separated and joined to the rest by negative relations. The tree is not the stone, the green leaf is not yellow, courage is not justice. Tree and stone, each of the colors and virtues, is positive and limited; and they form disjunctive systems of complementary elements. Things are either birds, houses, trees, hills, stones, or something else; anything colored must be either red, yellow, green, brown, or one of the other colors; and similarly with the virtues. On this theory, negation may be regarded merely as a relation between things, or it may also be considered an ingredient in them—"not to be a bird" may be part of the being of the tree—but in any case it is not a separate entity and not a process. A few philosophers, however, have held that it is an entity, almost a thing: not-being. Thus some of the Greeks maintained that there must be a void if there is motion, for things can move only where there is nothing. And the English language has the substantive "nothing," which in some sense may be the subject of discussion and thought. Now if negation is primarily a relation or an entity, it may be said that otherness is an ultimate fact, an absolute datum. But if negation is an operation or an act, analogous to a verb, then otherness has an explanation, though it is possible that the act itself has none.

Dialectic takes the act as basic, and the entity and the relation as derivative from it. This is characteristic of absolute idealism, which places becoming before being—or, rather, holds that the being of spirit is an endless becoming. The category of substance which was typical of the period preceding idealism may have put static existence before change, though the truth of this familiar generalization becomes increasingly doubtful as one turns from Descartes and Locke to Spinoza's *natura naturans* and the Leibnizian centers of force. The category of subject, at any rate, cannot do so; for to be a subject is to experience, and experience, whatever form it takes, is a process. The idealist conception of the absolute was formed under the influence of historical circumstances already noted. The difference between nature and spirit was formulated as the contrast between a dead, material substance, on the one hand, and a free, creative subject, on the other. In fact, the idealists often identify spirit with freedom, which they interpret as a spontaneous act of creation. This notion is best illustrated by art, because in art the self is most clearly creative. The artist objectifies his ideas in a medium. He puts himself into his works so completely that they could not have been made by anyone else. They are different from their author, and yet they are himself in another form, for in them he expresses or, better, actualizes himself. Their full nature is lost if they are taken in abstraction from him; in fact, to suggest this possibility is to imply their imperfection, by an external relationship between artist and work. Ideally he, as artist, can be adequately seen in them. The difference is that the work is finished, a created thing, while the artist is creating; it is the difference between being and becoming.

Let us consider the three aspects of negation in turn.

1. Dialectic calls the process of objectification "negation." It is variously described: creation, objectification, actualization, self-expression. But these are all ways of stating the same idea. It is the activity by which spirit objectifies itself, not an operation performed on a pre-existent substance. To continue our analogy, we must suppose that the artist creates his own medium. Also, the act is double, for it both results in an object which is other than spirit and relates this to spirit. The artist paints a picture, which is outside himself; he may sell it or give it to a friend and forget about it. This is the "first negation." Yet at the same time the work is himself; it does not really have an independent being, although it may be elsewhere in space and time. This is the second negation, the

"negation of the negation." The two phases are not separate, nor do they succeed each other in time. To become other is to become more completely one's self. Thus objectification is a process of differentiation and, at the same time, of integration; it is both exclusion and inclusion, antithesis and synthesis; the first cannot occur without bringing the second along with it.

The same process is repeated in all the opposites. Just as subject develops its own objects, so essence negates and affirms itself in appearance, the universal takes on the form of particulars, quality expresses itself quantitatively. Particulars are not the universal, quantity is not quality. Yet the universal is potentially the particulars and achieves actuality in them; and quality, in order to exist, must take on quantitative expressions. There are men as well as man; and redness exists in the form of coats, banners, fire, and flowers, with spatial and temporal extension. Also, the relation between the opposites is positive. Essence and appearance, or rather essence appearing, is actuality, in which the negative character of mere appearance is itself negated. Quality with quantitative expression is measure; the universal existing in the particulars is individual. So, while objectification is creative activity, it is not formless and chaotic but has a definite structure. Every negation is specific; it is the negation of one category, and no other. Particulars are the negation of the universal, and not of quality, essence, or subject; and the universal is objectified in the particulars, not in quantity, appearance, or objects.

We have a paradox on our hands: negation is positive. It is really affirmation, for which the negative is only a means. Here the religious and ethical principle, that we must lose ourselves to find ourselves, is generalized into a metaphysic. This is why there is no such thing as "mere negation" in dialectical logic. It is subordinate to affirmation in thought, just as it is in existence. "He is not here" is a denial and expresses a distinction and physical separation between person and place. But there is also an affirmative element implied, though unexpressed: "He is at home, or in his office, or attending a conference." Since we view existence from our own limited perspective, we sometimes fail to notice the affirmation underlying the negation, the identity underlying the differences, but it is always there.

This is not common usage, for which to negate is to deny or exclude. And it might reasonably be objected that to call "negative" something essentially positive is confusing and that the term should be restricted to its accepted meaning. It might indeed have been better to call the process under consideration by another name, such as "actualization," and to distinguish two elements in it, the negative and the positive. But, regardless of what it is to be called, there are two reasons why the common notion of negation is inadequate for dialectic and must give place to another concept.

The first is that dialectic is an attempt to explain the source of plurality, and this concept is the explanation. We usually assume plurality and use negation to express a relation between two or more elements which are taken for granted. We assume the identity of everything with itself and its difference from everything else; affirmation expresses the first, negation the second. So the real question underlying the difference about the meaning of negation is this: Can plurality be explained? To some people a negative answer is so obvious that the question itself is without meaning. They can never make any sense out of dialectic, for precisely this reason.

We took art as a concrete illustration of the doctrine of objectification. As a matter of fact, it is almost the only one we could have found. And, even so, the account of artistic activity required the supposition that the artist creates, instead of finds, his medium. But the various forms of practical activity, as well as knowledge, morality, and religion, all presuppose something simply "given." Knowledge presupposes the existence of independent objects. For this reason, Fichte and Schelling regard it as an inferior form of experience; in it the self is relative to something else. It follows, as they see quite clearly, that the absolute can never be "conscious" of itself. The act by which it grasps itself, in which intuiting and intuited are identical, is utterly different from the events which we find in consciousness. Again, morality involves recognition of and respect for an independent individual. It is conceivable, perhaps, that an infinite artist might create his own material; but it is inconceivable that an infinite moral being could create the objects of his own moral respect—his relation to his creatures would have to be different from this. That is why absolute idealism in its developed form has a theology but no ethics; a deep conception of the identity of the individual with his community but no real conception of the individual himself, or of respect for his individuality. Finally, religion—or rather Christianity, which alone is in question here—involves faith in a God who, though certainly immanent in the believer, is also transcendent. Instead of being explained, he is the explanation of everything else, the ultimate given.

Now Hegel saw that any philosophy not incurably romantic must recognize necessity, the givenness of reality, first of all—in some sense, as a first principle. But he also saw that a philosophy which gives to that principle the name "absolute spirit" must include the relative and differences within it; an absolute which excludes these is misnamed. The doctrine of negation is his solution of the problem. However, this solution involves a revision of the statement that experience is a process. To hold that the ultimate given is not objects for a subject but the subject itself means that spirit is its own object; and this implies that spirit knows itself intuitively. Here is the classical doctrine of intuition, which, instead of opposing intuition and thought, identifies them. The difference is that the classical doctrine separated such pure thought or contemplation from change, whereas here they are not separate. The negation of the negation is the intuitive phase of experience. In its highest form it is intuitive knowledge; but every experience has something of the character of intuitive knowledge in it.

In addition to the fact that it is an attempt to explain plurality, the dialectical theory of negation differs from common usage in another way. We are accustomed to connect negation with some theory of the limited character of existence and to hold that there is a factor of nonbeing in reality. Something which might be, is not, so that the world is other, and perhaps also less, than it might have been. Thinkers have occasionally maintained that the world is a plenum, where every possibility is realized, where everything that could be, is. But this speculative theory goes against our instinctive logic and direct experience. To common sense, reality is limited.

We inherit this point of view from the Greeks. For them, change was from not-being into being and from being into not-being. There is coming into existence and passing out of existence, generation and decay. Underlying this theory is the doctrine of contraries. The characters of the existent always represent a selection from a range of possibilities between contrary extremes. Coffee must be hot or cold, or something in between, and it can have only one temperature at a time. To become cold, it must cease to be hot. An action with moral quality may be moderate, excessive, or deficient—brave, rash, or cowardly—but it cannot be all of them. What exists at any given time is limited; and when something comes into existence, something else is lost. Change can never be just the taking-on of form by matter, but because of the contraries it must always involve some loss, though this may be only in the sphere of accidental qualities. It is true that the idea of a plenitude of being is to be found in the Greeks. But there is also another concept, even more deeply rooted in their thought and incompatible with the first: the teleological view of nature. To say that nature is striving to realize certain ends is to maintain a selective doctrine of process. The actualization of essence is a selection from possibilities. It may be that all essences are realized in nature. But, even if this is asserted, existence will be limited, for only some of the possibilities in matter will be actualized in the realization of essence. A fully developed man may be tall or short, and a cat is black or white. Also, teleology implies a distinction between success and failure, normal and abnormal, health and disease. If a process is not interrupted, it will reach its normal termination; and a thing may be either normal or abnormal. Nature may either hit or miss the mark.

But, for dialectic, change is sheer creativity. There is only creation and generation, with no decay or passing out of existence, except for what is accidental (in a derogatory sense which the word did not have for the Greeks) and unreal. The present includes the past, which has not really gone; and even the future is real, though it does not yet exist, for spirit is eternal. To say that spirit is both in process and eternal betrays a fundamental difficulty in the whole point of view. Nevertheless, both notions are there, and the result is a doctrine of negation which excludes limitation. From one point of view the doctrine results from the fact that dialectic has no theory of contraries; for, according to the philosophy of opposites, the contrary is also the contradictory; and, since every term demands its opposite, there is really no selection. Take such a statement as "This tree is not a maple." From some points of view one might interpret it to mean that some one of the various possibilities is realized here, while the rest are not. The tree is an oak—or a chestnut, hickory, or magnolia. The kinds of tree are not exactly contraries, but the illustration will serve. This account obviously corresponds to the observable facts and would be accepted by dialectic. But dialectic goes on to interpret the facts by saying that the essence "tree" is appearing in many forms, of which oak is only one. The universal is particularizing itself, the identity is differentiating itself completely. The idea of plenitude has won out over the ideas of purpose and selection.

2. Negation is also an entity, the result of the process, and it appears in many forms. First of all, it is the opposite of being: the category nothing, which is pure negation. It is also appearance, the opposite of essence; negation, the opposite of reality; death, the opposite of life. Each of these specific, determinate forms of negation participates in the indeterminate character of sheer negativity or nothingness. But each, as a determinate form of negation, has its determinate character set by the first term of the pair of opposites to which it belongs. The term "negation," for example,

has the generic meaning which it has carried in this discussion. It also has a specific meaning, as the unique correlative of the category "reality." But whatever form it takes, the negate is always a correlative, being derivative from a process. Therefore, it has no reality independent of its correlate. That is why the puzzles arise about how we can think nothing, when we try to take nothing by itself.

Since negation is not a substantive from the dialectical point of view, we need not be troubled by the old questions, "How can what is not, be?" and "How can we think what is not?"—if they are asked with reference to the substantive meaning. In the first place, since, for dialectic, reality is a process, it is unnatural to phrase the problem in these static terms. In the second place, if we think of spirit in terms of being—and it has being, though this is not its essence—it would be erroneous to think of a second being, "not-being," set over against it. The problem for dialectic is better formulated by reversing the questions: "How can what is, not be?" The answer is, as we have seen, that what is can be only by objectifying itself, by creating its own "other"—that is, by not being. Again, "How can we think what is?" We think it, paradoxically, by thinking what it is not. Spirit is known through its other, nature; force is known in its manifestations; the man is known by his actions; and God can be understood only through his creatures—and his creating. So it is true that what is not, also is, and what is, somehow is not.

Nor should we speak of "negative" facts and "positive" facts; for a fact is a state of affairs, such as is expressed when we say that it is raining. Such a state of affairs taken as a whole is like a term. So, to speak of negative facts is like saying that negation is a term, a substantive. And to speak of positive facts, similarly, is to suggest that being is found separate from not-being. But to accept opposites is to hold that every fact is both positive and negative at once, since being and not-being are correlative, as are all the determinate forms which they take. However, unless it is said metaphorically, to call facts a mixture of being and not-being is mechanical, as if they were two ingredients dumped into a bowl.

The question may be asked, Is a negate a second reality; or is it unreal; or is it an inferior, lesser reality? The answer is None of these three. If it were another reality, the result would be two realities, side by side; and the unity would be gone. Simple unreality, on the other hand, is unthinkable, a contradiction in terms, a nothing that is something. And to call the negate an inferior reality, a kind of shadow or imitation of the first, is only a compromise between the other two alternatives. When the "other" is taken by itself and in abstraction, it is a self-contradictory concept. But when it is taken as other, then the question can no longer be asked, for instance, whether nothing is as real as being, or appearance as real as essence; for to ask this is to imply a separateness which is not there. Being and nothing, essence and appearance, are two sides of the same reality, two aspects of a single process.

3. As a relation, negation both unites and separates its terms. At first glance, this may seem a strange way of describing the situation. Negation, one might think, does not unite. When I point out that a certain large building is not the post office, I do not unite the two terms in question but deny that they can be truthfully combined. Nor do I separate them, for the post office and the building before me were separate in the first place, and so were the terms that refer to them. I unite the terms in my statement, but its form recognizes or formulates their separation. This is awkward, and it might seem better simply to say that negation relates. The reason why the point needs to be raised is that the claim is sometimes made that terms are independent of relations, and not only of specific relations but, it seems, of any at all. Dialectic denies the priority of things and terms over relations in this or any other sense. It holds that process is prior to both of them and that they are co-ordinate elements in it. Now, since terms and relations are components of the process, they are not fully intelligible apart from it; their status is not accidental but essential to what they are. For this reason, the dialectical relation of negation is not symmetrical. If it

is abstracted from the process, it may appear symmetrical. We shall then have two related terms, which can be taken in either order: A is not B, and B is not A. But, if the relationship is examined further, it will be seen that the order of the terms is not indifferent.

Here, again, the dialectical theory of negation differs from others, and for the same reasons as before—it is primarily a theory of process, while most views are concerned only with structure and being. In logic, for instance, there are complementary classes, A and not-A. That they are symmetrically related is shown by the fact that either one may be considered the negate of the other. Let the class concepts be "red" and "not-red." It is a matter of indifference which one we label A, and which not-A; and the reason is that they are mutually other in the peculiar manner of contradictories. Red is the contradictory other of not-red, just as truly as not-red is the other of red. The same holds of contradictory propositions, p and not-p. This fact is the basis of double negation. Since it is a matter of convention whether a term is considered original or negate, we may treat the negate itself as our original term, and negate it. "Not-(not-p)" is a perfectly good proposition, and "not-(not-A)" a respectable class term. Negation here is not a property of class or proposition but a relation between two classes or propositions.

In the same way, negation may be considered a relation between two or more existents, as when we deny that a certain building is the post office or say, "William did not do this deed." We can equally well say, "This deed was not done by Willam" and "The post office is not this building." The latter statement seems a bit unnatural because of the word "this," which raises problems not relevant to the present discussion. We can correct it to read, "The post office is not the large, red building at the intersection of Market and Main streets." We regard the world as a set of mutually exclusive things and events and qualities, and we consider the events themselves to be a kind of things. We may consider these entities to be simply different; or, if we have a speculative turn of mind, we may think of them as complementary, together mak-

DIALECTIC

ing up some sort of totality or system, which we call "reality." In either case, negation expresses the relation between any two items in the set.

But it may be that we can attain a stage of knowledge where things are seen to have a closer unity than this. Dialectic claims to have reached such a stage, and it expresses the unity in terms of asymmetrical negation. "Man is not free," "Death is not real," and "William did not do this deed" will serve as examples of such negations. Natural necessity is a denial of freedom; yet, in coming to terms with it, we achieve a higher freedom than we should do if we insisted on considering all the natural necessities of life as limiting and frustrating, instead of making them opportunities for development, so far as we are able. But we cannot say that freedom is the negation of necessity, for necessity is only one element in a dialectical process that is creative and free when seen in its unity. Death is the negate of life, but it is itself negated in the process in which the life and death of individuals are component parts. We cannot say that life is the negate of death, for it is death that is a phase of the life-process, not the converse. William did not do the deed, but it was done by someone; so, while it is a negation of William, it is an affirmation of human nature, of which he is only one instance or manifestation. We can say of it, "This deed is human." But we cannot say, without modifying the meaning by implication, "Human nature is exemplified in this deed"; for the deed is only one partial expression of human nature. In all these cases the direction or sense of the relation is determined by the nature of the process in which it occurs.

The most famous remark on negation is that of Spinoza, *determinatio negatio est*, "determination is negation."[3] Let us consider two cases—"The tree is not the stone" and "The tree is not God." These are instances of symmetrical and asymmetrical negation, respectively. The determination or nature of a tree is not that of a stone, and it is not that of God; but the reasons are different. The tree and the stone are two mutually exclusive particulars, of which

3. Letter 50.

God or reality contains an infinite number. We can just as well express their relation by saying that the stone is not the tree. The tree and God, on the other hand, are not mutually exclusive. The tree is a manifestation of the infinite and eternal activity of God; as a finite, determinate thing it is limited, but God is unlimited. It depends on God for its being, as the part depends on the whole or, more accurately, as the finite mode depends on the infinite substance. Therefore, we cannot convert the statement and say that God is not the tree without changing its meaning. Spinoza, however, did not see that there is a difference between the two kinds of negation, although he uses both in his philosophy.

Dialectic is often mistakenly identified with the theory of "internal relations," which is supposed to be one solution of the "problem of relations." This theory may be defined as the claim that relations are rooted in the terms which they relate, that they make a difference to their terms. Many objections have been raised against it. We shall consider only those which bear directly on the subject of relations and shall pass over others which are really concerned with different issues. An example of the latter is the objection that, according to the theory of internal relations, every relation is necessary; if terms are related, they must be related; for, since, according to the theory, relations make a difference to their terms, the latter would not be the same out of relation as they are in relation. A term that is related is, by definition, different from any that is not related. Therefore, it would be false and even meaningless to say that a related term might have been unrelated. If a man is father of a child, he is changed by this relation, a different person from what he would have been had he not been a father. Therefore, it is a contradiction to say that he might not have been a father; for, if he were not, he would no longer be himself. This is an argument against determinism and in favor of real potentiality and a plurality of individual substances rather than an argument against internal relations, which theory is merely incidental to the other issues.

The objections arising directly out of the nature of relations reduce to two. The first is that dialectic cannot account for relations at all; the second, that it has the wrong theory of relations—which, if examined carefully, will be seen to imply their unreality. Let us consider them in this order.

There are, it is said, two types of facts and propositions. One type is concerned with objects or things and their intrinsic properties; the other is concerned with relations between objects. An example of the first is "This book is blue," and of the second, "This book is on the table." Since dialectic holds that there is only one thing in the world, namely, the absolute, it cannot account for the second type of fact and proposition but must say that all are of the first or attributive sort, in which the subject of the proposition is reality or the absolute and the predicate is some attribute of it. It follows from this that, since there is only one thing, which is indivisible, and since every aspect of it is internally related to every other, there is only one truth. But the objection is not valid, for it rests on the mistaken supposition that dialectic accepts "thing" or object as an adequate category. On the contrary, to accept the philosophy of opposites is to reject the concept of "thing" and the subject-predicate logic which goes with it. The absolute cannot be the "subject" of a proposition, which has a "predicate." Reality can be understood only as a process of the generation and unity of correlative opposites. Things and their properties are aspects of the process, but they cannot be adequately understood until we take the latter into account. Therefore, it is subject-predicate propositions, if any, which dialectic rejects, not relational ones.

It is only philosophers in the so-called "empiricist tradition," which holds that the world is a collection of particulars, who have said that dialectic accepts subject-predicate logic. According to them, "Reality" is the implied subject of every dialectical statement that we can make. If this were the case, we should have to alter the above illustrations to read, "Reality is such that the book is blue" and "Reality is such that the book is on the table," the word "such" referring to those unexpressed internal relations which make it necessary for us to qualify every possible statement. But the truth is that for dialectic the term "reality" is only one of a pair of opposites, not a subject which has properties; and if we are to use it, we must also use its correlative. And if we could reach final truth, the statement of it would have to be impersonal in form, like "It is raining." We should have to say something like "There is a process of the actualizing of essence" or "It is differentiating and integrating."

I think it is fair to say that for dialectic all facts and propositions are relational and that the subject-predicate sort is simply one species of these. Thus the relation between book and blue is simply one type of relation. What, after all, is the reason for classifying propositions and facts as relational and attributive? Why would it not be equally justifiable to designate those containing triadic relations as one type and lump all the rest together in a second class? The real answer is that the authors of the classification hold a philosophy which rests on the concepts of substance and attribute. They believe that the world is made up of particulars with properties, bearing or able to bear certain relations to one another. The merits and limitations of the concept of particulars, however, is another subject, which need not be considered here. Of course, if dialectic is unable to account for particulars and their properties, that is an important and perhaps fatal objection to it; but it is not the one with which we began.

If the first objection to the theory of internal relations held, it would follow that, since dialectic had no theory of relations, it could not account for asymmetrical relations, which are one subclass of these. But this objection, which has been raised by Russell, is mistaken, since, as has been pointed out above, the basic negative relations of dialectic are always asymmetrical. The real difficulty is the other one—namely, to account for symmetrical relations, such as that of otherness between tree and stone.

The second objection is that the theory of internal relations involves difficulties which make it untenable and which do not arise if we suppose that relations are external (what this means will appear presently). In the first place, it is said, the theory of internal relations leads to the conclusion that nothing can exist or be understood except in relation to the whole of reality, for all the relations of a term contribute to its nature. So there is only one thing and one truth in the world. The meaning and validity of such a statement as "The book is on the table" involves a knowledge of the relation of the book to the printer, to its author, to society, history, evolution, and, in short, the entire universe; and the same is true of the table. But this implies that we cannot know the truth of any statement, including statements to the effect that dialectic is the true philosophy. If an exception is to be claimed for this latter, there are as good and better reasons for maintaining that we can also know the truth of ordinary propositions referring to perceptual objects. Further, the theory implies that there are no terms and relations at all, that these concepts are self-contradictory; for a thing or quality must be and must also be related. The book must have intrinsic qualities, as well as being related to other objects. So the necessity arises of explaining and stating not only the relation of the book to the table but also the relation of one part or aspect of the book to the other, the relation of book-as-blue to book-on-table. If we succeed in stating this relation, we shall only find ourselves confronted by the problem of understanding book-as-blue, which will prove to be the same problem all over again and will lead to the same kind of internal split. Any term, upon examination, proves to be infinitely complex internally, just as its relations to the rest of reality are endlessly extensive. So the theory is untenable on two counts. It leads to the unverifiable assertion that nothing is or can be known except the absolute, an assertion which implies its own falsity. And it leads to the denial that there are any terms and relations at all.

These difficulties, it is said, are avoided by the theory of external relations. The latter may be stated in two ways. First, as indicated above, it is the doctrine that there are two irreducible types of facts and propositions, relational and attributive. But this doctrine really rests on the assumption that there are terms (whether particular or universal) and relations in the world and that they do not affect one another with respect to their intrinsic properties. So the theory may be stated, second, as the contention that relations do not make a difference to their terms or are not grounded in them. This means that an object in relation does not have any intrinsic property which that object out of relation does not have. The book on the table does not have any intrinsic property which it would lack if it were not on the table. In order words, it is the same book off the table as on. The first formulation implies the second, unless we suppose that no term ever enters or leaves a relation—a supposition which none of the advocates of the doctrine would admit, since it implies that change is unreal.

It is true that the theory of internal relations leads to the difficulties stated. The alternative, however, leads to difficulties equally as great and is equally unsatisfactory. One might ask, What does it mean to be related, if not to be modified or affected by the relation? If Smith is not changed by becoming a father, is he really a father? If "father" is a purely physiological term, we ought to say that begetting a child is a relation but becoming a father is not. And is not "being half of four" part of the nature of the number two? The defect of the theory of external relations is that, while it properly distinguishes between intrinsic and relational properties of terms, it has nothing to say about their connection. In its anxiety to show that the book on and off the table is the same book, it fails to explain what being blue and being on the table have to do with each other; it does not relate being a father to being a male. These are rather serious omissions, and the position is fully as weak as that of the theory of internal relations. The only difference is that, while the latter has two books on its hands which it cannot get together, the theory of external relations has two types of property. Neither theory can explain relations.

The problem of relations arises when terms and relations are taken to have different origins. Its most common, as well as historically most important, form is the theory that terms are sense data, while relations are the conceptual patterns in which we arrange them. The sensory terms are supposed to come from "outside" the mind, while the relational patterns come from "inside." Experience, or at any rate knowledge, is made up of patterns of sense data, actual or anticipated. For instance, "onion" is a concept which states how yellowish-white color, flatly oval shape, a smell that makes the eyes water, and other data are related, simultaneously and successively. Natural laws are conceptual patterns which state that under certain conditions a sensation of one sort will be followed or accompanied by, or will vary functionally with, sensations of another sort. The question is How do the sense data and the patterns get together? It is an important question because knowledge conforms to fact or reality; but on this theory knowledge is relational, while the only available data to which it can conform are nonrelational. In certain respects sensory data of the sort in question may properly be called "relational" in character, especially with respect to temporal and spatial characteristics. For instance, areas within a colored patch may be distinguished, having such relations as inclusion or exclusion. So far as this is the case, the problem of relations does not arise because the relations as well as the data are given and knowledge has something to conform to. But the exceptions, such as this one, which are consistent with the sense-data theory will not take us far.

The problem of relations arose because of the prevalence of certain mechanistic theories, which ignored or failed to explain important unities and kinds of change. The theory of internal relations arose as a protest against these theories. But, as always happens, it was infected by the position that it was designed to refute and is itself mechanical. Its adherents regard nature as material, the material as spatiotemporal, and space and time as quantitative. They consider quantitative relations to be external, based on atomic-unit terms, which can only be added or subtracted to form aggregates. And, finally, they maintain that the material and the quantitative are unreal. Their claim that a term is related not only to another term but to itself, and each of its aspects to itself and so on endlessly, was suggested by the infinite divisibility of space and time. Just as an area or segment of one of the latter can be endlessly divided internally, so can any term within itself. The externality of supposedly quantitative terms and relations was extended to all terms and relations, which were then seen to involve an infinite regress. Finally, as in the ancient paradoxes of space, time, and motion, the conclusion is drawn that relations are contradictory and unreal. The problem of relations might, of course, just as well be called the "problem of terms," since the difficulty, if any exists, lies in the mutual relation of terms and relations. But so to state it is to make clear the mistake involved. To ask for the relation of terms and relations is to begin an infinite regress, to assume that, first of all, we have terms and relations, which we then try to put together. But to believe in relations is to hold that relatedness is an original and irreducible aspect of reality. The fact is that the problem of relations is simply the focus that other problems assume when the opposites, form and content, are applied to experience and become conceptual structure, on the one hand, and sensory content, on the other.

For dialectic the problem does not exist, and dialectic does not subscribe to the theory of internal relations. The problem does not exist because the process of development generates terms and relations together. One does not exist without the other; terms are united and separated primarily by the relation of negation. Moreover, the relations are as objective as are the terms; and relatedness, or rather the double process of relating, is an original datum. The problem of dialectic is that of permanence and change, of identity and difference. How can things become different, yet remain the same? It is the problem of process.

In summary, then, negation is primarily a double process that separates and unites elements. It is also a resultant and a relation; but these, while they can be considered in terms of their own characteristics, do not have a status independent of the process. The so-called "problem" of relations and the solutions offered for it are the consequence of mistakenly taking relations and their terms to be independent of the process of existence and of each other.

We must now turn to the consideration of dialectical inquiry itself. To this subject our analysis of negation has provided a useful introduction, for the pattern of inquiry is set by the pattern of existence, which it exemplifies. Inquiry has two phases. First, it is the separation and analysis of the various ideas which are factors in belief; this phase is critical, in that it shows the limited character and validity of the separate elements. Second, it is the construction of a system of ideas that is more valid than any of the beliefs criticized, because more inclusive. The basis of these two phases lies in the double character of negation.

3. The Course of Inquiry

Philosophical thinking is both critical and constructive. And the criticism is not merely preliminary to a later construction; the two occur together; for to criticize philosophically is not so much to test a theory about specific facts as it is to assess the relative validity of an attitude, such as trust in the senses. The result is that we see better than before the place which this attitude should have in our experience, how large a part it should play, how far we can rely upon it, and for what purposes. In criticizing beliefs and attitudes, then, we are also relating them. But, while these two activities occur together, they must be partly separated for purposes of exposition, and we shall begin with the first.

Philosophy is an examination of beliefs, a criticism of opinions, an analysis of attitudes, a clarification of ideas—this is as old as Socrates, and it will be new as long as men think philosophically. The accent here is on an attitude of mind; the reflective attitude is implicitly contrasted with the unreflective or the dogmatic. The reflective attitude implies a continual readiness to examine one's opinions; so, while the goal of reflection is knowledge, no one ever attains it completely. The emphasis, then, is on the activity of philosophizing rather than on its result.

Criticism emerged as the primary concern of philosophy in the modern world when the skeptical reaction set in, after the first great burst of speculative activity in the seventeenth century. With the rise of skepticism, men began to ask whether it is possible for us to know such realities as God, material substance, and the soul; but they did not ask directly whether these existed. When doubt had been cast on the possibility of knowledge, they gradually changed the form of the question and began to ask whether it is possible to experience them in any way, or even to think them at all. The first is a question of knowledge; the second, of meaning. When it had been decided that such presumed realities could be neither known nor thought and that the very words used in speaking of them are meaningless, the question of their existence no longer had a point. The stress throughout was on experiencing rather than on things experienced. The outcome was complete skepticism.

The reason is that at the basis of the criticism lay such questions as: Is the mind capable of attaining truth? How much can we know? What are the limits of knowledge? The critical method of the period insisted on the necessity of making a preliminary study of man and his capacities before undertaking any survey of existence. All knowledge is human knowledge; and, before using the tool of reason, we must first find out what it can do. With a little practice it proved easy to doubt the capacity of human faculties for knowledge and almost impossible to set any limit to the doubt. It was the distinction of Kant to have seen the implications of doubting and yet to have set clear limits both to it and to human knowledge. He adopted a moderate position on the entire matter. But this is his weakness, as well as his strength. If there are limits to human knowledge, how can we be sure that we really do have knowledge of them? How can reason limit itself without begging the question of its own capacities? Perhaps to set such limits transcends our limited powers.

The method of criticism, like every skeptical movement, tended to get out of hand and become an end in itself. Kant attempted to keep it in its proper place and to use it as a means to something constructive. Having found a critical weapon in the age of reason, he turned it against the times, in order to develop a positive philosophy of man. But he could not complete the positive philosophy, because he never overcame the early oppositions which he had set up between theory and practice, phenomena and noumena, thought and reality—or, we may say, inquiry and existence. A philosophy of man must include a theory of human practice; but such a theory will carry us beyond man. The peculiarity of human nature lies, for Kant, in the fact that it combines necessity and freedom, what is and what might be. But if this is true, we cannot understand man without examining such ideas as necessity, possibility, being, and not-being. How, then, can we discuss human freedom without considering nature and its necessity and the relation of man to these? And, if human freedom is a striving for unrealizable ideals, must we not also consider their place in reality? In short, we cannot know man without going beyond him; and we are carried beyond him as soon as we begin to reflect on our own existence. But, while Kant thoroughly investigated the possible limits of our knowledge of objects, he did not really consider what might be involved in the attempt to know our own knowing and ourselves as free, reflective beings.

Hegel did consider it and came to the conclusion that it is impossible to set limits to knowledge because, in the language of dialectic, knowledge of a limit is at least the beginning of knowing what lies beyond it. A stone conforms to the necessity of natural law but does not know it. Man knows that he is limited by nature, but, in knowing it, he is already partly free. Kant used this principle in his argument for freedom: I ought, therefore I can. The fact that I feel my choices limited by the selfishness of natural impulse, while at the same time I am aware of moral obligation, shows that I can progressively overcome the influence of impulse on my will. The feeling of obligation proves that we are not determined in our choices by natural causes; if we were, we should, like the stone, be without a sense of either duty or constraint. But Kant was unwilling to apply the principle to the problems of knowledge. Dialectic does so and thereby changes the meaning of criticism.

EXISTENCE AND INQUIRY

It assumes the existence of truth, its accessibility to man, and a standard of criticism for inquiry.

The standard is the agreement of belief with itself. It is applied by subjecting the belief to analysis. The standard is logical, for agreement is just another name for internal self-consistency. It is also allied to historical criticism. The historian, it is often said, should take the age he studies on its own terms. He should try to understand its aims, interests, beliefs, and institutions and ask how far it succeeds in doing what it set out to do, instead of imposing his own attitudes on it; this is historical objectivity. The needs and character of the people provide the immanent standard of criticism for its historical achievements; if the beliefs and institutions meet the needs of the age, they are valid for it. Similarly, the critic of ideas should not impose on them his arbitrary notion of what they should be. The principle of internal criticism holds that examination of beliefs will reveal their limitations, by making evident any lack of internal consistency that they may contain. Thus dialectic combines the analytic and the historical in its criterion of truth. It denies that there is any external "test" that can be applied to ideas, to determine whether they have the mark of truth. When such a test, for example self-evidence, has been formulated in the past, it has turned out in practice (and that was really the meaning of its authors) to be a procedure, such as analysis, not a mechanical rule. But consistency, which is the core of self-evidence, is too formal a word; we must add "with itself," to indicate that it is with a concrete, human belief that we are dealing, not an abstraction.

The principle of internal criticism is used to argue that (*a*) no idea is simple and therefore unanalyzable and (*b*) no idea is completely intelligible and certainly true in itself. These properties—simplicity and certainty—were the characteristic traits of clear and distinct ideas, the "simple natures" in which analysis was supposed to end. Dialectic examines beliefs and shows (*a*) that they are all internally complex and inconsistent because they contain latent opposites and (*b*) that each implies other beliefs in-

DIALECTIC

compatible with it—that is to say, that each is its own negation. These two defects belong together; it is because every idea is incomplete that it proves to be inconsistent when considered by itself as though it were complete.

But objects are inseparable from our ideas and beliefs about them; the notion of a pure object which contains no categories of human interpretation is naïve. Conversely, every belief, even the falsest, has an object of some sort; it is about something, though that something may not be what the believer takes it to be. Subject and object are correlative; this is a cardinal tenet of the whole dialectical tradition. Therefore, the defects of ideas also belong to objects. An examination of attitudes, such as sense perception, faith, aesthetic appreciation, conformity to custom, or reason, will lead to an analysis of the corresponding objects; an examination of objects, on the other hand, will lead back to the attitudes and categories which are implicit in them. So the examination of beliefs involves us in the whole problem of knowledge and truth. Consequently, dialectic may be regarded as a criticism of everything limited, incomplete, or finite. It is to be contrasted with the undialectical attitude, which assumes that individual ideas and facts can be or be known apart from other ideas and facts. This is what Hegel means when he says: "Dialectic, on the other hand, is that immanent process of passing beyond, in which the onesidedness and limitation of the concepts of the understanding shows itself for what it is, namely, their negation."[4]

The moving force of inquiry is contradiction. It is because of contradictions in our opinions that we are forced to examine them and look for a new idea that will resolve the conflict. Contradiction is also the moving force in existence. What this concept means for dialectic can be stated in terms of the fundamental concepts already analyzed—opposites and negation. To say that things are contradictory is to say that they contain opposites; and, conversely, to describe the world in terms of opposites is to say that it is full of contradictions, for the members of a pair of opposites are mutu-

---

4. *Op. cit.*, ¶ 81.

ally contradictory. Moreover, it is because things and concepts are contradictory that they negate themselves. However, what is true of opposites and negation also holds of contradiction: it is not a symmetrical relation, and this differentiates it from the meaning which the term has in formal logic. To say that a thing is contradictory means that its existence does not measure up to its essence; its real existence is not the complete fulfilment of its potentialities. For example, "Nature in itself, in idea, is divine, but as it is in fact its existence does not correspond to its idea; rather, it is an unresolved contradiction."[5] Again, man is essentially free; but his existence does not measure up to the ideal, for he is subject to many kinds of natural necessity beyond his control. His existence contradicts his essence. But we cannot say his essence contradicts his existence, for that would be to take the material and temporal as the measure of the ideal and eternal. Contradiction is the effort, conatus, or drive by which things strive to realize themselves. It is the presence of the infinite in the finite and the attempt of the first to overcome the second. It is not simply a relation but a force.

Contradiction is, for dialectic, internal to the nature of whatever it characterizes. It holds between opposites that are inherent in an idea, a thing, or (in the last analysis always) a process; and it becomes manifest when the latent opposites are developed. So conflict between elements is reducible in the last analysis to contradiction within an element. Contradiction between things reduces to contradiction within a system of interaction, or implies it. It is often said that thought begins with a problem and that an intellectual problem arises from a conflict between our ideas and facts or objects. We say there is disagreement, failure of verification of the ideas, or, perhaps in the beginning, simple mental confusion. But, since dialectic does not accept the independence of objects, it regards such conflicts between ideas and objects as contradictions within experience; and, since it does not accept the independence of reality from experience, it considers them also as contradictions within reality. Here logic seems to substantiate dialectic, in one

5. *Ibid.*, ¶ 248.

respect. We say that two propositions, p and not-p, are contradictories. But there is no actual contradiction unless the two are brought together—unless they are asserted together by the same individual, or unless one seems to imply the other, or both to be implied by a third. In itself, surely, no proposition is contradictory. Contradiction, according to dialectic, always implies some kind of unity between the elements involved.

Readiness to examine one's beliefs is one of the marks of empiricism. Criticism is empirical, and dialectic is therefore an empirical theory of inquiry. It asserts the truth of no proposition a priori and makes no assumptions but examines every belief and concept as it comes, on its own merits. It will accept nothing merely because it is given. However, we must distinguish between application and implication. Although it can be applied to any belief, dialectic itself presupposes certain doctrines, as we have just seen; if it did not, it would have no character of its own. They might be called "assumptions"; but they cannot become explicit without changing their character. The difference between implicit and explicit assumptions is the distinction, present in all reasoning, between the premises of an argument and the principles in accordance with which reasoning takes place. The laws of identity and contradiction, for example, are always among the principles by which we reason. If we wish, we can make them explicit premises, too, and give notice that we are assuming their validity. But if we do so, their logical role as premises is different from what it is when they operate as principles; and by making them explicit we do not get rid of their implicit function. We can even prove them, if we like, by starting from suitable postulates; but if we do, we employ them throughout the proof. So it is with dialectic. Since it can be applied to any concepts, it can be used to examine opposites. And it is so applied in the analysis of such concepts as universal and particular, subject and object, form and content. But the notion of opposites is part of the method by which the concepts are analyzed, so its validity is presupposed all along. We touch here on the relation between method and result. To adopt a method is to determine, up to a point, the kind of result which will be reached by its use. To understand the relation, however, we must examine further the course of dialectical inquiry.

Dogma has both an intellectual and a moral sense. The moral dogmatist is a person who obstinately holds to his position and refuses to be shaken by any considerations that may be offered. He deliberately refuses to "listen to reason," and his refusal is an act of will. But intellectually any idea may be called a dogma which is present in the mind to the exclusion of everything else. When a single idea occupies the mind, it is inevitably believed. It asserts itself without restriction and unconsciously claims to be absolute, simply because it is given and there is nothing else present to cast doubt on it. The difference between such dogmatism and intelligent belief is that the latter involves comparison of the accepted idea with others. It is reasoned or mediated, while dogma is immediate and unreasoned. Criticism is nothing but the examination of dogma; and, according to dialectic, every belief stands in need of criticism, so far as it is unreasoned, unsupported, unmediated. If it should prove that no idea can be completely mediated and that none is self-evident, then we must all be intellectual dogmatists in the end. It would follow that there can be no end to inquiry.

If all beliefs contain a rational element, there could be no beginning either, since this would mean that every belief had already been partially mediated in a prior inquiry. Actually, this is the case. There is no such thing as sheer dogmatic belief, except in the moral sense of an act of faith, and this does not exclude reason. Every belief contains an intellectual component. In other words, sheer immediacy or givenness is not a separate kind of experience. It is only one pole in the process of experience, the other being mediation, which means analysis and synthesis of constituent terms and relations. To speak of "immediate experience" as an entity or state is undialectical. Immediacy is the form which the latent, potential, implicit, or inner assumes in experience. There is an analogous phase in all the processes of existence. The seed might be called the immediacy of the plant, potential energy the immediacy of its overt discharge, human character the immediacy of the acts in which it expresses itself. Anything is immediate so far as it is undeveloped, and its development is its mediation. But immediacy exists only in relation to the process of mediating. A seed which was purely potentiality could never grow, but would have to be acted upon entirely from without, and then react mechanically. But even mechanism involves something like a notion of self-development; for, although it suggests what is merely inert and passive, it also includes the concept of force, which implies an inherent tendency to act under appropriate conditions. Similarly, a purely immediate experience would be cut off from all possibility of rational analysis.

It is true that Hegel speaks of immediacy as the starting-point of inquiry, and he distinguishes two forms of it—sensuous and conceptual. In sensuous immediacy, experience is such an undivided flow that not even the distinction between subject and object has emerged, let alone any criticism of the object. Conceptual immediacy, on the other hand, is the category of being; it is the first category of thought, and entirely indeterminate. But, unless these two are to fall entirely outside the process of experience, they must contain movement within themselves. The potential is a kind of actuality; otherwise, it would have no power to become actualized and would remain cut off from actuality. Similarly, the "immediate" must contain mediation if it is to have any relation to ordinary kinds of experience. We must regard it as an approximation to a limit of sheer immediacy which is never attained. Pure immediacy is only an abstraction. In his desire to avoid assumptions, Hegel made the easy mistake of confusing an unreflective attitude toward experience with an immediate content of experience. This was an inadvertent desertion of his own method. As a matter of fact, the two forms of immediacy that he singled out for analysis are not the only possible ones. He chose them because thinkers happened to be particularly interested in sensation and thought in his day. There is no reason, apart from this historical accident, why he should not also have considered immediacy of action, for instance. The very fact that dialectic distinguishes two different forms of immediacy is suspicious; it suggests that they are not pure but relative to some mediated content.

So far as experience is immediate, the distinctions which it contains are only implicit. It is full of qualities, processes, relations, things, interactions, values, and everything that can be experienced; but these have not been separated out. Consequently, it has no specific character and is describable only by approximation, analogy, or negation. It is neither intellectual nor emotional—these are specific categories. And if it is described as feeling or emotion, these terms cannot have their usual limited meanings. It is neither particular nor universal; it is not even characterized by the qualities of immediacy and indeterminateness, for it is without any specific qualities whatever. We often experience objects which are predominantly immediate or given in this sense. We may be walking down the street, thinking about some problem, and be vaguely aware of passing someone—not any specific individual, not a man or a woman, and not humanity in the abstract, but "someone." In such an experience the contrast between particular and universal has not been explicitly made. Or we are aware that "something" is going on, in the sense that there is movement, change, disturbance, not further specified. It is true, of course, that these words are themselves characterizations; that is inevitable. We can only point in the direction of the immediate; we cannot describe it directly. But we can point, because it is always present in a more or less describable context.

Taken literally, then, dialectic converts the immediate aspect of experience into a kind of experience which it makes the starting-point of inquiry. But this literal meaning is not essential to the theory.

Dialectical immediacy is not the sensuous given of contemporary philosophy. It is not an aggregate, sequence, or flow of sense data; for by reflection we discover terms and relations in the immediate; but the examination of sense data can lead nowhere, for they are—

DIALECTIC

or should be, if they really are sense data—just what they appear, nothing more and nothing less. In them appearance and reality coincide. I am aware of certain sounds, colors, feelings of uneasiness or satisfaction, and that is all that is given; any interpretation I may make is added. That this sound is louder and less pleasant than that one may be given as a datum, perhaps; but the relations that define those elaborate constructions which we call "truck" and "bird" and which we identify as the sources of the two sounds are certainly not given. The whole function of "the given" is to provide something absolute in experience which cannot be doubted or questioned. It offers a foundation of hard data for the softer superstructure of knowledge and reality. But for dialectic the absolute lies at the other end of the process of inquiry; this method is opposed to the whole set of assumptions and the entire way of thinking associated with the concept of the given. Dialectical immediacy is much closer to custom and tradition, which in many respects are also unreflectively and directly given. Customary behavior and attitudes contain implicit meanings that can be brought out by reflection. Dialectic is a deeply historical way of thinking and is keenly aware of the historical meanings latent in the present world and in present experience. The difference is that, while custom and tradition are local and selective, always having conceivable alternatives, the content of dialectical immediacy claims to be true, not for this or that group, time, and place, but universally. The absolute truth is implicit in it because the reason which it contains is universal as well as historical reason.

For dialectic, all experience in its endless forms falls somewhere between two ideal limits—pure immediacy at one end, complete mediation at the other. As we shall see, the position, when consistently developed, implies that no experience reaches either limit and that each has something of both qualities in it. But the limits are not alike; for, while relatively immediate experiences contain little mediation, highly mediated experiences do not contain little immediacy. As an experience is more immediate, it is less mediated;

but as it is more completely mediated, it is not less immediate. Immediacy is a constant factor, but mediation is variable.

The construction of the dialectical system of knowledge is the organization of the forms of experience into a unity; for each of the beliefs, concepts, and attitudes which, taken together, make up the total of human experience contains some truth, and so has a place. Provisionally, we may think of them as arranged in a series between the two extremes, though the analogy breaks down eventually. Some of the forms, such as sense-perception, fall nearer the immediacy end of the scale; others, such as morality and art, are nearer the other end. Also, the same object may be experienced in different ways, just as music may be heard either so that the emotional experience almost entirely excludes understanding or so that it includes a grasp of the structure of the composition. A physical object may be experienced through simple sense-perception, or scientifically, or aesthetically. But with these changes the object is itself modified, since it is correlative to the experiences.

The place of a form of experience in the series and the degree of truth which it contains depend on two factors. The first is the amount of mediation that it exemplifies, in terms of opposites and their relations; the experience which is more fully mediated is the truer. The experience of music which distinguishes between form and content and makes some analysis of the musical form is superior to that which fails to distinguish. The man who realizes that the political state is made up of citizens, government, and laws thinks more truly than the one who regards the state as an abstract entity, existing independently of him and his fellows. The concept of actuality, which involves the contrast between inner essence and its outer appearances, is truer than the bare, undeveloped concept of being. Moreover, the experience or concept which not only distinguishes but relates is truer and more completely mediated than the one which only distinguishes. The experience of art which relates form and content is superior to that which finds them mutually other and more or less mechanically juxtaposed—just as the work of art itself that closely unites them is better than the one in which the content is a blatant symbol for some abstract idea, while the form that it takes is relatively accidental. The man who sees that the state is the citizens in certain relationships understands politics better than the one who only knows that two factors—laws and citizens—are involved. To see a thing as both identical and different is to see it less adequately than is the case when one knows the ground which unites the two aspects.

Second, the place of a form of experience is determined by its degree of activity and self-determination; that experience is more completely mediated and truer which contains more self-activity. And, similarly, that concept is truer the object of which contains a greater degree of independence and activity (according to dialectic, the concept itself contains activity, too). This is a difficult idea; what it means is best seen through examples. Reciprocity is a truer concept than either substance or causality, for a system of material particles or other entities in mutual interaction is more autonomous in its changes than is a single particle, whose motions and even existence depend on the existence of, motions of, and force exerted by other particles on it. The concept of a thing is relatively static; even if the thing is conceived as moving or changing, it cannot be thought of as changing itself, because the concept of thing does not contain the idea of a source of change.

Again, the moral experience of a particular isolated individual is less true than the moral life of the community. The actions of the isolated individual, so far as they are "good," are determined by a moral law. But the moral law, formulated by his reason and known by his private conscience, is a pale abstraction; being subjective, it has no intrinsic connection with concrete reality, even in his own behavior. It is universal but does not afford guidance in particular acts; the meaning of honesty, for example, in concrete terms, will depend more or less on individual interpretation. The moral experience of the individual is subjective, for this element is all that is within the control of his will. He is passive in the face of events, which, consequently, he must consider neither good nor bad—terms reserved for his own moral will. At best, he can only say feebly that the world "ought" to be good. The life of the community, on the other hand, is concrete, structured, and self-sufficing. It has a body of beliefs, practices, and objective institutions which make up its ethos. By seeing that identity with it is true morality and freedom, the individual himself becomes active and self-determined. The contradictions between universal law and particular act, subjective and objective, moral will and overt consequences, have disappeared. In their place we have the identical moral community, differentiating itself in the lives of its members. The truest concept of all is that of absolute spirit, which alone is completely active. And the truest experience is the philosophical understanding of the absolute and the act by which the individual identifies himself with it. Here is the rationalism of the dialectic.

The two notions of structure and activity are themselves parts of one single notion, for activity is impossible without structure; and, conversely, structure does not belong in a separate world of essences but is the structure of the process of spirit in the real world, which is the only one there is.

The movement of inquiry, which gives rise to the series of experiences, is not from simple to complex or from part to whole; for the immediate is neither simple nor a part. It might, in a peculiar sense, be described as an advance from abstract to concrete, since the immediate is experienced in isolation, and so abstractly. But it is best described as the progress from confused to clear ideas, since the immediate has a content that is not yet analyzed out and articulated. Now there is ultimately only one given for dialectic, and that is reality, which presents itself existentially in diverse ways. So far as it is immediately given, its content is latent; the structure is undeveloped. In clearing up our ideas of the given, we develop its content. This implies that reality can be given but that things are more than they appear to be on the surface; that our primitive experience is neither of the surface alone nor of things in their full nature but a partial experience of the total thing. This means that the existential categories of potential and actual apply also to experience. Our first ideas of reality are potentially clear, though actually confused; and progress in knowledge consists in clearing them up. Since all our ideas are about the same reality, they must share in the identity of their object. How could ideas that were simply different be about the same object, since true ideas must conform to their objects and the object is the same?

We must go beyond the concept of a series of experiences to their integration. Since relatively immediate experiences contain the potentiality of the predominantly mediate, while the latter are the actualization of the former, their relations are not adequately described by setting them out in a row, like notes on a musical scale or colors in the spectrum. The basic idea is growth or development, not succession; and this implies not only change but identity. The mediated is the developed stage of the immediate, just as the plant and the flower are the developed seed. They are not different things but different stages of the same thing. The immediate is conserved in the mediate. The course of dialectical inquiry is the gradual construction of a single truth—the absolute idea, known by philosophy, which corresponds to absolute spirit, the single reality.

Every philosophy which holds that all is one must have a way of saying it. And the form of the statement must also account for the many; for, as Plato pointed out, even though we ignore the diversity of existence, the simple statement that all is one is itself many. Thinkers have dealt with the contrast in many ways. Some have said that the many individual things are illusory and only the one is real. Others have contrasted the intelligible world and the world of sense, substance and modes, true being and becoming, reality and appearance. No two have ever formulated the relation in exactly the same way, and the variations are endless. But the same problem is always there: how far to stress the contrast between the extremes and how far to draw them together. The solution of dialectic is clear: there are not two worlds but only one. What others have called two worlds are present in every particular fact, simple or complex, important or trivial, in the form of the opposites that constitute them. Of these, one is like reality, the other like appearance; one like substance, the other like mode; one like intellect, the other like sense. And the opposites are always more or less bound together, though never perfectly, by the fact. The assumption on which this solution is based is that being is an inclusive, rather than an exclusive, notion; all the variety and all the levels of existence must be taken together if it is to be understood. It includes all the conceptual distinctions, all the particulars, and all the forms of experience that are possible.

Kant spoke of the knowledge of appearances, but Hegel described the appearances of knowledge. For Kant, the two worlds were pretty sharply distinguished, and we can have knowledge of only one. He would have liked to unite them, but his intellectual conscience would not allow it. For Hegel, just as reality assumes endless forms in its process of development, so experience also appears in various forms. This latter series of forms constitutes the phenomenology of spirit. Taken together, its members make up concrete truth; and the concepts imbedded in them make up abstract truth, or metaphysics, which is the logic of reality. The complete system of philosophy includes both. The difference between any one form of knowledge or experience and the single truth is that the truth consists of the various forms seen together as graded appearances, while none of them alone sees itself as appearance.

But this system of philosophy can never be finished; it is a continued story that goes on forever, for any statement we may make is limited and must be supplemented by another; and no series of statements will ever make up the deficit, for two reasons. First, the world is both one and many, and, according to dialectic, any given statement will stress one aspect at the expense of the other. This can be seen in simple propositions, such as "The grass is green," which asserts the unity of grass and green but fails to point out that, although united, they are not identical, leaving their relationship unexplained. In other words, every proposition must be either affirmative, stating an identity, or negative, stating a difference; but the truth is both at once. This is also the case in the abstract propositions of philosophy. We can come closer and closer to a statement that will do justice to both elements. But we can never arrive at a formulation that is quite satisfactory, though Hegel ostensibly claims to have done so in the concept of absolute spirit. It will always be possible to raise the same kind of objection against any term we may choose that dialectic itself has raised against so many others, such as "becoming," "ground," "actuality," and "idea"—namely, that it is one-sided. For instance, we may say that reality is the unity (identity) of identity and difference. But this proposition stresses the identity at the expense of the difference; an adequate statement would have to add that reality is also the difference of identity and difference, even though the difference is subordinate to the identity. This process can have no end.

The other reason why a satisfactory statement is impossible is that, since reality includes appearance, the true and complete idea of reality must include an account of the appearances; but such an account cannot be given, since the manifestations appear in history and history is never completed. Not only is reality actually both one and many, but it is a one that is continually becoming many. For this reason the dialectical view of reality contains a contradiction; it implies that reality is a completed, yet continuing, process, an eternal or timeless becoming. The process must be complete, for, if it were not, spirit would be subject to the limitations of time and so not absolute; but the very meaning of "becoming" involves incompleteness. Hegel did not clearly see the contradiction because he looked upon historical individuals as merely accidental, in the sense of individually unimportant, in spite of what he had said about including both the particular and the universal in a true concept of reality. Nevertheless, it is there. Thus the essence of reality cannot be rationally stated, since it is self-contradictory; and the system describing it cannot be completed, because reality is an unfinished process.

There persists in the Hegelian dialectic the same element which made system an impossible goal for Fichte, namely, the idea of an infinite creative energy. In the philosophy of the latter it took the form of will, while in Hegel it is reason. Now "reason" is a word which suggests finality and completeness. We feel that reason means authoritative knowledge, and it suggests that complete knowledge would be an all-inclusive and finished system of truth. But, for dialectic, reason is not primarily knowledge. Neither is it primarily order, which was the meaning it had for the Greeks. It is creative energy, and an energy that is never spent because it is infinite and therefore has endless manifestations.

To understand why "system" is such an important goal for dialectic and failure to attain it such a serious fault, we need to keep in mind that it involves the relation between thought and reality and therefore the nature of knowledge and the concept of truth itself. It is an axiom of dialectic that knowledge must be like its object, that thought must reflect being. The interpretation of the axiom is bound up with the dialectical conception of the relation between subject and object. It seems to follow that, if reality is a process, knowledge must be a process, too, in the sense not only that there is a psychological process of thinking but also that logic itself, which states the structure of being, must somehow be a process. Also, since spirit is a completed process of self-realization, knowledge must also be a completed process or a system. Thus the characteristics of dialectical metaphysics also appear in its methodology. This suggests that the dialectical theory of inquiry may be mistaken in some important respect and that the error may involve the relation between knowledge and reality. But, before considering this problem, it will be helpful to glance briefly at the historical movement, to see why philosophy was driven to this predicament.

4. Idealism, Materialism, and Process

Dialectic was the result of the insight, new to modern thought, that reality is process, together with the realization that older modes of thought were inadequate to describe its character. On the assumption that true thinking must conform to reality, such an in-

DIALECTIC

sight was bound to affect logic. And, in fact, the new concept of reality gave rise to a new logic.

The discovery of process was first made by philosophy chiefly in the spheres of mind and society. Mind, which once had been associated with logical and mathematical apprehension, had gradually come to be interpreted in terms of sense data, which almost automatically fall into patterns according to the laws of association. This concept assigned a certain place in mind to time, since the psychology of association stressed the importance of habit formation. But habit was a mechanical concept, and the temporal dimension was superficial; its significance was restricted to repetition, in which the important factor was not the process of re-enactment but the number of times it occurred. Becoming entered psychology, rather, with the newer theory of Kant that the mind is a continuous activity of synthesis of sense materials. While it would be going too far to say that he regarded this activity as creative, since the forms it followed were fixed, he was closer to this idea than to the mechanism of habit described by Hume. The difference, though perhaps one of emphasis, is very important. The pattern of habit, as understood at this time, is intelligible as a finished product at any moment, for its essence is its present strength, which theoretically can be measured. The degree of synthesis which the mind has achieved, on the other hand, is never merely the result of previous activity but always continues as a present act. Also, the concept of a synthesizing activity is distinguished from the forms which it assumes. And, unlike an association, the present stage of synthesis cannot be understood apart from its direction and goal.

At least equally important was the discovery of social process. In addition to the motions studied by physics and the activities described by psychology, there is historical change. The idea of history, too, was at first superficial and framed largely in terms of the concept of custom, which shared the weaknesses of habit. Customs were often interpreted simply as illustrations of changeless factors in human nature—of folly, superstition, and selfishness or of benevolence, magnanimity, and wisdom. Nevertheless, a genuine sense of history was developing through investigations in many directions—the study of the arts and languages of the past, the attempt to find a better foundation for politics than the social-contract theory, the description of the moral and religious customs of various peoples, and, perhaps most important of all, the renewed appreciation of the ancient culture of Greece, with its many and varied expressions. To the new views of mind and society must also be added the expanding study of biology and early gropings toward a theory of biological evolution.

These new views of change called for a new kind of thinking, for the analytic methods already developed under the influence of physical science were not adequate. Their defect did not lie where it was often thought to be, namely, in atomism, a term which is applicable to the psychology of the eighteenth century, not to the logic of the seventeenth. The real failure of analysis was its inability to give an adequate account of becoming, and its restriction to the dimension of structure in reality. It had little to say about any change except physical motion. It threw no light on the nature of becoming in history, mental and spiritual development, or even biology.

While attempting to develop the new type of thinking, dialectic was also protesting against the extension by philosophers of certain scientific concepts beyond their proper sphere. It was confronted by the picture of a dead, mechanical nature; and it denied that the kinds of becoming which it described could be explained on mechanical principles. Consequently, it turned, instead, to spirit and the self for its clues. This was natural, if not historically inevitable. And yet, in doing so, it was simply continuing the Cartesian dualism in a new form, for it was asserting that the world is divided into two parts, spirit and nature, the spheres of freedom and necessity. Moreover, it identified philosophy with the first and science with the second and thus gave rise to that unfortunate opposition which has played such a disastrous part in the thought of the last hundred years. On this matter, all that can be said is that both sides were to blame. Romanticism was simply the answer to a superficial materialism. Since nature is so different from spirit, there can be no more interaction between them than was possible between the mind and the body of Descartes. And, since nature is "dead," all activity proceeds in one direction; process is essentially creation and emanation rather than interaction.

It was the intention of dialectic in this way to unite all the oppositions and eliminate all the bifurcations that had been created by modern thought and so to start out on a new and more fruitful line of development. But, instead of relating the opposites, it explained them away. To see how this happened, we need to turn from the basic opposites, subject and object, to another important pair very closely associated with them, namely, form and content. It is the subject which contributes the form or structure to experience. The laws of nature are the laws of mind, and only a formless sense content remains over to confront the subject as a datum. These laws are, of course, a priori; as for empirical laws, nothing is said about them from a philosophical point of view. There is one other pair of opposites to be considered: form and function or, better, structure and process. Since nature is dead and inert, whatever functioning, activity, or process exists in the world must also belong to mind. The result is that nothing at all is left over for nature, which shrinks to the bare other of spirit. In the course of explanation, one of the original opposites has disappeared, while the other has been inflated to include everything.

This account is confused. If nature is dead and mechanical, it must have intrinsic form, namely, the laws which give it the name of "mechanism," though it will not then contain process. If it has no form, on the other hand, it is not mechanical, for it does not have the intrinsic properties of a mechanism. In that case it will perhaps be a disorderly flux or formless activity of some sort. But a nature that contains neither form nor activity is inconceivable. It is a nothing, not even possessed of potentialities, for only actual things have potentialities. Moreover, why should the other of spirit be either mechanical or formless? The manifestations of spirit should be at least feeble imitations of its intrinsic character; there is no explanation of why, in nature, that character should suddenly disappear and give place to something entirely different. Nature should be dialectical, not mechanical, and it should be historical. There is a complete failure to explain the existence of nature, in the character that is attributed to it.

The assertion that the idealist dialectic failed to account for nature on its own terms and accepted the mechanical theory calls for some explanation. The key idea of the period was totality—it is sometimes even described as organism—and it is impossible that this idea should not have affected the concept of nature. But what happened was that, with one important exception, the philosophers made a sharp distinction between scientific and philosophical concepts and placed such ideas as "totality" among the second. This was true even of Kant, who attempted to justify science philosophically. He maintained that science, to be science, requires philosophical presuppositions, and he tried to show what these are. But he also described certain ideas of reason, including totality, which, although they have a regulative or methodological value, are not part of the meaning of nature. Their objects, unlike those of scientific concepts, can never be perceived.

Hegel, instead of justifying science, interprets it. He criticizes Kant for developing the concepts of attractive and repulsive forces unphilosophically in his philosophy of nature.[6] As Kant interprets them, they cannot belong to science, of which he professes to be expounding the pure or a priori part, for they are more than formulas describing physical behavior, which is their only proper scientific meaning. Yet, while they are too philosophical for science, they are too scientific for philosophy, being undialectical. Instead of dialectical moments, apart from which matter has no meaning, they appear simply as properties of a presupposed substratum. Hegel holds that physics proceeds by a combination of mathematical reasoning and experience. It develops formulas and then verifies them empirically; the formulas are ideal, while experience

---

6. Logik, I. Buch, 1. Abschn., 3. Kap., C, c, Anm.

DIALECTIC

supplies the material content. But these methods will not yield a real "proof" of the basic principles—space, time, motion, force, and matter; experience just happens to conform to the concepts. The proof belongs to philosophy, which must deduce them dialectically.[7] The point here is the kind of distinction that Hegel is urging between science and philosophy. His conception is that science should be descriptive and should not allow metaphysical interpretations to slip in. That is all to the good. But he holds that the dialectical method is not only different from, but opposed to, science. The two are so utterly unlike that they can have nothing to say to each other. The only connection is that, after concepts have been developed dialectically, their existential denotation is to be discovered empirically in the material of the sciences. So far as there is a road, it runs only one way. As a philosopher he rejects the idea of mechanism completely; there are no mechanical facts for philosophy. But he holds that the concept is perfectly suitable for science.

To Fichte, nature was a negative notion, as we have seen. It was Schelling who made it positive and introduced into it the ideas of freedom and totality. He holds that the absolute appears in two forms—mind and nature. Each is both subject and object at once. The difference between them is that, in nature (or being in the form of object), object is quantitatively greater than subject, while, in mind (or being in the form of subject), subject is quantitatively greater than object. Hence he can say: "Between subject and object none other than a quantitative difference is possible."[8] Or, as he says elsewhere, nature is visible spirit, spirit invisible nature. Though different, they are not opposed. On the other hand, there is no real development; Schelling succeeded in making nature positive only by sacrificing dialectic. Hegel could never accept such statements. To him, only the idea of nature is positive and dialectical; its physical embodiment is negative, determined, and static.

The materialistic theory of nature was inadequate, and idealism

---

7. Enzyklopädie, ¶¶ 267–70, 276.
8. *Darstellung meines Systems der Philosophie*, 23.

had no theory at all. The solution was to extend the idea of process from spirit to nature, where it was more and more urgently demanded by the course of empirical discoveries and, at the same time, to apply the new logic to the interpretation of natural processes. This transformation was the achievement of dialectical materialism. The error of idealism lay in regarding nature as the alienation of spirit, instead of seeing that mind itself is the product of natural forces; the relation must be reversed. At the same time, dialectic must be generalized to apply to nature, as well as to history and human thought, which are kinds of natural process. As Engels says: "Dialectics is nothing more than the science of the general laws of motion and development of Nature, human society, and thought."[9] In this definition, motion has the general sense of change, as it sometimes does in Aristotle. With the aid of dialectic, man can change the face of society and nature more effectively than he has ever done in the past.

It is important to see the relation which this philosophy bears to dialectical idealism. Briefly, the two are alternative interpretations of the single concept of process. Both hold that reality is process, and they describe it in terms of opposites; both maintain that reality is historical; and both, in reaction against atomistic modes of thinking, stress the importance of relations. But beyond these general agreements they differ widely. It is obvious that, if, as the dialectical materialists say, the great basic question of philosophy is the relation between spirit and nature, between thinking and being, two philosophies which give rival and opposed answers to this question must disagree on every specific issue. Their concepts of reason are as different as are their concepts of reality. Any notion that dialectical materialism took over the method of idealism, while rejecting the system, is therefore mistaken. Such an idea would, in fact, itself be mechanical—as though dialectic were like a physical tool, which could be used by different people in different ways. Systematic concepts in philosophy are insep-

---

9. *Anti-Dühring,* trans. Émile Burns (New York, 1939), chap. xiii.

DIALECTIC

arable from the thinking by which they are reached. And certainly this is true of idealism, for which "the truth is the whole" and the result simply the process of philosophizing taken as a totality. The difference between the philosophies appears at its sharpest in their respective attitudes toward science. In contrast to idealism, which opposes science and philosophy in the way we have just seen, materialism wishes to unite them. It claims itself to be scientific and to have ended philosophy in the old sense. Its scientific orientation appears in its conceptions of both nature and dialectic.

It views nature as a series of processes, in which matter and energy manifest certain forms and in which the forms change, owing to the way in which the processes develop. This is to be seen in that series of processes which constitute the history of mankind. Economic production holds a central place in history because it is the means by which men more or less successfully satisfy their needs. Man is primarily a laborer and producer, and the form which his production takes at any given time is conditioned by the stage of technological development which has been attained in his society. In the economic life of society there is a distinction to be made between the productive forces and the institutional forms or relations of production which they assume. As economic life develops at a certain technological level and under a certain mode of production, the forms which it assumes become increasingly less adequate for the satisfaction of the needs of men. This is seen in the case of capitalism. Here production is highly social and involves the co-operation of many individuals in a system where the division of labor and specialization of function are highly developed. The basis of the institutional structure, on the other hand, is private enterprise and private property. As the era of capitalism advances and the means of production are increasingly concentrated in the hands of a few, the discrepancy between the productive forces of society and the capitalist mode of production becomes greater and greater. There is an increasing conflict between the forces and the forms which restrict them. The forms, however, are rigid and resist modification because they are artificially preserved beyond the point where they are economically useful by the ruling class, whose interests they represent. Gradual evolution, therefore, is impossible; and when the discrepancy becomes sufficiently great, society must undergo violent change or perish.

There are important resemblances between this theory of history and the theory of biological evolution advanced at about the same time, though slightly later, by Darwin. Central to the doctrine of Darwin, also, was a contrast between the form of the living organism and its life-processes or modes of functioning. The life-processes are carried on so that the organism may satisfy its wants; and to satisfy them, it must adapt itself to its environment. In the course of its adaptive activity it develops a form or structure corresponding to its way of life, and this form is a kind of crystallization or deposit of the past history of the species and provides the means by which the struggle for existence is carried on. If the structure ceases to be well adapted to the preservation and activities of the living being, that being will become more or less unfit for the struggle of life and will be eliminated if the discrepancy between organism and environmental conditions becomes too great.

Marx and Darwin hold in common that nature is in process of evolution, that the forms of nature are changing, and that these forms are determined by the modes of activity or behavior of natural entities in interaction with other entities and environmental conditions in general. They apply the same basic idea to two different sets of problems and bodies of data. This revolutionary idea was perhaps the greatest intellectual discovery of the century. To the Greeks, natural function was dependent on form; to these thinkers, on the other hand, form is the result of functioning—although, when acquired, it, of course, determines a correlative mode of behavior in turn. To the former, form and function were always in harmony; to the latter, not only may they be in conflict, but more or less conflict is the rule of nature, for harmony is a state but nature is a process of change and development. The Greeks had regarded form as inherently good; these thinkers, on the other hand, maintain that form is good only when it is suited to the needs of life and that when it ceases to be so it becomes bad—good and bad being defined by them in terms of natural need and satisfaction.

But dialectical materialism holds that there are also fundamental differences between biology and social history. In the case of the biological organism, changes take place with relative ease through variation and inheritance; there is nothing to correspond to the interests of the ruling class, which preserve a form beyond the limit of usefulness, unless it is the natural inertia of inheritance. Social change differs from biological in the tremendously greater importance of the internal conditions of society—technology, the existence of classes, the rational behavior of men—as compared with the external physical or social environment, a contrast which rests on underlying differences between man and the other animals. Although it is organic, society is not an "organism," in spite of the high degree of unity which a culture exhibits at any given time under the dominant influence of its economic life. Its members are not cells, nor are their relations those of cells; and society is often torn by internal conflicts in a way that no living organism ever could be. Nor does dialectical materialism accept the same biological theory as Darwin did. According to Marx, the error of the bourgeois Darwin was to miss the dialectical leaps in nature, to see evolution only in terms of gradual change. Under the influence of the mechanistic science and individualistic competition of capitalist society, he failed to see that something radically new and different may suddenly appear from time to time.

Thus dialectical materialism was formulating a new philosophy of nature in terms of the concept of development, a concept which recognized discontinuities as well as continuities in nature; qualitative leaps as well as gradual quantitative changes; and internal contradictions as well as uniformity, order, and harmony. The processes of nature are everywhere developing new forms as well as destroying old ones, and this is true not only in the spheres of life and society but in the inorganic world as well. The underlying conception of nature is the same in each case, and it is stated in the principles of the dialectical method. This materialist theory of dialectic, formulated as the basis of a naturalistic philosophy, differs in two important respects from the dialectic of idealism.

In the first place, dialectical materialism never develops its basic concepts in the abstract but always discusses them in connection with concrete processes of natural change. Since they simply state the most general features of nature, they are to be understood through an analysis of typical natural processes, in which they are most clearly to be seen. Just as science does not examine systematically the abstract idea of change but rather investigates and describes specific changes, so dialectical materialism does not analyze its concepts by themselves but, instead, interprets concrete processes in terms of them. Nowhere does it examine the concepts of contradiction, identity, opposites and their interpenetration, negation, and self-movement as idealism does. Its theory must be inferred from the concrete analyses. The reason, however, is not that it takes over its concepts from idealism and therefore considers further discussion of them unnecessary. On the contrary, these concepts all take on a new meaning. The reason for the omission is that the materialist conception of philosophy does not call for such a discussion.

Its dialectic is based on the concept of nature as a system of interacting forces ("force," here, is simply a descriptive term). It interprets process in terms of reciprocal action between opposites, and the opposites are concrete natural entities, not abstract ideas. There is an interaction between them, in which each is the cause of changes in the other. Man acts on nature, and nature on man, in the process of production. Our practice gives rise to theory, which, in turn, changes our practice. In biology, morphology and physiology mutually determine each other. Throughout nature, quantity and quality are transformed into each other. In each case there is reciprocal action. Such action between opposites is not always directly present: mathematics is a system of abstractions, not of natural processes. But, even here, the abstractions are derived from reality and used to interpret it; and their dialectical character cannot be understood if this derivation is forgotten. This interpretation of the relation between opposites is very different from that of idealism. It makes the opposites co-ordinate, and it employs the concept of causality, which idealism considers undialectical. At the same time, it differs from the mechanical theory of physical causation and the positivism of Hume in which this finally eventuated. These are atomistic and fail to see that an element exists only in a causal process which itself occurs only in relation to its complementary one within a total developing situation. But dialectical materialism does not develop a concept of reciprocal action and interpenetration, any more than it does the other basic concepts of dialectic.

In the second place, dialectical materialism formulates three laws of dialectic, which dialectical materialists say were developed in idealist form by Hegel.[10] This, however, is not the case. The notion of laws of dialectic is scientific and entirely foreign to idealism. Here "law" does not signify a formula for prediction of the sort found in the various sciences but rather a form for interpreting their data, concepts, and predictive statements. A dialectically understood science, it is said, will predict better than a nondialectical science, because it is truer. The laws or principles of dialectic define the meaning of the dialectical view of nature and therefore also the character which scientific thinking must have if we are to understand nature. To return to the comparison with evolution, they are analogous to such Darwinian principles as overpopulation, variability and inheritance, and natural selection, which define the evolutionary concept of biological change.

The first is the law of the transformation of quantity into quality, and the converse. Quantity increases or decreases gradually; but qualitative changes occur suddenly, by a leap, when a certain quantitative limit has been reached. Water, cooled gradually, suddenly changes its state and turns to ice when its temperature reaches the

---

10. Cf. Engels, *Dialectics of Nature,* trans. Clemens Dutt (New York, 1940), chap. ii.

freezing-point. In chemistry the increase of the number of atoms of a given element or elements in a molecule results in a qualitatively different compound. The accumulated savings of the craftsman turn into capital and the craftsman into a capitalist when the savings reach the point where they can be used to employ laborers and allow the budding capitalist to supervise and control production and to appropriate the surplus value created. Materialism naturally emphasizes the transformation of quantity into quality much more than it does the converse, for it regards matter as primarily quantitative in its simpler forms and motions. The qualitative potentialities and latent contradictions which it contains develop only gradually and, through successive cycles of development, give rise to chemical, biological, and social forms of matter, with their own characteristic quantitative and qualitative aspects. The law expresses a dialectical theory of emergent evolution. But to idealism quality comes first and is then externalized into a quantitative many through the extensiveness of nature, expressed in number, plurality, and magnitude. Idealism, like materialism, asserts the double transformation of quality into quantity and vice versa; but the entire process is subordinated to that of negation. And, while quantity is the negation of quality, we cannot say that quality is, in the same way, the negation of quantity, for the two are not co-ordinate. Quantity, having negated quality, is then itself negated—first in the concept of measure, which unites the two, and then finally in the passage beyond the whole sphere of quality and quantity, to the sphere of essence, which appears in both qualitative and quantitative forms.

The second law is that of the interpenetration, unity, or identity of opposites. This law might with some justification be considered the most basic of the three, for in it we perhaps see best that nature is a dialectical process of growth through conflict. Every unity contains latent opposites which, when they develop, come into dynamic contradiction and interaction. Illustrations are to be found everywhere in nature. Identity and difference, for instance, are always together and in reciprocal action. Natural differences are always destroying any supposed abstract identity, for nothing in nature remains permanent, everything is subject to continual change and modification; on the other hand, real identity is always overcoming and including differences within itself. In biology, heredity and adaptation are conflicting factors within the evolutionary process. In thinking, the law means the relativity and mutual limitation of concepts, so that, instead of "either-or," the clash of theories which are apparently irreconcilable gives rise in the end to a "both-and" of a novel character. But, above all, the law is illustrated in the relations of theory and practice, which interact not in an external and mechanical way but through their mutual penetration and modification. We have already noted that materialism regards nature in terms of the interaction of co-ordinate opposites and have seen how this position differs from idealism. It is clear that the relation between opposites must be differently conceived in the two philosophies, since the opposites themselves are not the same. In the present context the difference is not, as is sometimes said, that idealism conceives the relation statically, with the contradictions submerged in an identity, while materialism is dynamic. It lies rather in divergent conceptions of the process and its outcome.

Third, there is the law of the negation of the negation. The second law stressed the factor of difference in change; it is the third, really, that stresses the unity or identity. The second stated the nature of motion at any moment; the third states the sequential relation. There are cycles of change in nature, which proceeds not in straight lines but in spirals, returning on itself. The beginning of a process is preserved in the end, but with a difference. The original quality is modified by the process that it has undergone. Private property is negated by capitalism, which is, in turn, negated by communism. Communism brings back private property to the worker, but in the form of consumer goods, for land and the means of production are now socially owned, not individually as at first. The seed is negated in the plant. But the plant flowers and is itself negated in the fruit, which is the seed again. But the fruit is not the same as the original seed, for it contains many seeds, not just one; and these may also differ qualitatively from the original, since the species is part of the evolutionary process. But the relation between beginning and end is not the same for the two philosophies. In materialism we have to do with a process which is describable essentially in terms of causal interactions and ends in a resultant different from the interactions which produced it, although it contains elements which were already there at the beginning. For idealism, on the other hand, the elements of the process are *aufgehoben* in its outcome. This word stands for a kind of identity in difference which cannot be described as the resultant of a process which has taken place in simply sequential stages. The concept which it expresses is a repudiation of the notion that nature can be finally understood as a serial temporal process. For idealism, the second negation is ultimately the subject recognizing itself in the objects set over against it.

Thus idealism and materialism interpret the same words in different ways. The general differences of materialism from idealism, already partly indicated, can be summarized briefly. In dialectical materialism time wins out over eternity; becoming is unfinished, nature an endless historical process. For it, also, opposites are coordinate; contradiction is between equal elements, and neither can be described as the "other"; there is real interaction. Finally, there is decay as well as growth, death as well as birth, passing out of existence as well as origination of the new.

Dialectic arose, then, as an attempt to think reality in terms of becoming; and it is interpreted in one way by idealism, in another by materialism, because they have different theories of becoming. The problem of inquiry is the same for both: How can we grasp process? Both reply that we can do so only if the logic of inquiry itself shares the nature of process. But here again their interpretations of the principle differ. If we can understand the principle and its interpretations, we shall be able to evaluate dialectic.

DIALECTIC

5. Logic and Process

Dialectic holds that knowledge is participation in reality, as well as contemplation of it. To know is not merely to apprehend an object which is simply other than the subject and act of knowing; for if the object were simply other, according to dialectic, a gap would exist which could never be bridged. To say that knowledge participates in its object is to say that it is fundamentally like the object. Then, if reality is process, knowledge will also be processive. The idea of process must be the process of the idea. This is precisely the nature of reason in dialectical idealism; it is able to grasp becoming just because it shares in becoming, unlike the static thought of the "understanding." This doctrine is carried over into dialectical materialism which, however, has its own distinctive theory of the relation between logic and process. That theory is the concept of ideology, which holds that, since man is by nature historical, his concepts and presuppositions, as well as any body of knowledge which follows from them, are also parts of the process of history and are valid only in relation to their historical setting.

The claim of dialectic that knowledge participates in process is not the obvious assertion, accepted by everyone, that there is a psychological and epistemological process of inquiring. Nor is it the assertion that knowing is an act which comes at the end of inquiry or forms its last phase. The characteristic claim of dialectic is rather that concepts themselves share in process. "The Idea is essentially process," says Hegel.[11] In this sense we may say that dialectic presents itself not only as a logic of process but as a logical process.

The assertion that concepts or ideas are in process is an extraordinary one, for they have usually been considered to be or to have structure; they are "forms," and the term has been taken to imply fixity. Whether "ideas" have been assigned a kind of ontological independence and timelessness or, at the other extreme, have been considered verbal definitions reached by stipulation, or

---

11. *Enzyklopädie*, ¶ 215.

whether some intermediate position has been taken, in any case they have been considered unchanging. There is change of ideas, as when we discover new ones and forget or reject old ones; there is no change in ideas, for a modified idea is, strictly speaking, another idea.

The position which we are considering is the consequence of taking "idea" in two different senses, in such expressions as "idea of reality," and identifying them. The idea of reality may be either (*a*) the essence of reality or (*b*) knowledge of reality. Now if reality is a process, it does not follow that its essence is, too; for the essence might be a set of timeless ideas, while reality might be the process of their gradual embodiment in some concrete form. Nor does it follow that, because there is a process of knowing, its content is also a process; for the true idea or concept of things might be a timeless essence. However, dialectical idealism is not guilty of confusion on this matter. It is aware of the distinction but deliberately identifies the two meanings of "idea," because it holds that reality is essentially a process of knowing. Therefore, idea is for it both knowledge and essence. Reality is the process by which absolute spirit becomes aware of itself, becomes self-conscious, reflects on itself; and it attains this knowledge by making itself its own object or creating its own other. This doctrine is the reason why, according to dialectic, process and result, method and system, and the act of knowing and the idea which is its content cannot be separated without distortion of the truth.

But there is appearance as well as reality and being as well as becoming. On the principle that knowledge must be like its object, it follows that we need a second logic to think appearance. Becoming is unified, but beings are many and isolated. The logic of appearance, then, is a logic of atomic being; that of reality, a logic of unified becoming.

It has often been held that reason and logic, its tool, are concerned with form or structure and that the structure of thought conforms to the structure of reality, or that reality conforms to the laws of logic. Now the theory of two logics arises from the belief

DIALECTIC

that everything can be stated rationally, together with the discovery that reality is more than structure. It is not enough to describe the formal aspect of things; all aspects must receive logical expression. But whatever is not structure escapes ordinary logic; therefore, another is required to deal with it. This theory is an expression of extreme rationalism: the belief that reason can comprehend everything. But for such rationalism one must pay a price. If there are two logics, the question of their relation immediately arises. If they have different laws, why are they both called "logic"? It seems necessary to make a choice or else confess that logic itself is illogical because it is equivocal. We cannot take refuge in a pragmatic criterion and say that each works in its own sphere, for we are assuming that the value of logic is to help us describe reality and not merely to provide a tool for the achievement of relative human purposes. On the other hand, if they have something in common, it would seem that it is the common element that should be called "logic," so that the two would be one after all. The possible alternatives are clear. We can either insist that there really are two logics and stop there; or we can choose one as the standard and either reject the other entirely or try to make it somehow an auxiliary.

First, it may be said that there are two logics and that their laws are simply different. For the logic of being, everything is identical with itself; for that of becoming, nothing is ever simply identical with itself, but, instead, everything is continually becoming different. For formal logic and the understanding, the law of contradiction holds; for dialectical logic and the reason, opposites are identical, in spite of, or even because of, the fact that they are contradictory. But if this were so, what is true for one logic would be false for the other. And, as there would be two ways of thinking, not reducible to any common denominator, philosophy, which claims to provide the unity lacking elsewhere in experience, would lose its chief claim to existence. That is just the charge that dialectic levels against common sense—the failure to be consistent with itself and unified. This is certainly not the right alternative.

Second, we may hold that there is only one logic and that its basis is the law of contradiction, which is as absolute for dialectic as for formal logic. The crime of dialectic, on this interpretation, is not to have thrown out the law of contradiction (or, rather, of noncontradiction) but to have recognized that contradictions exist. This had for a long time been denied; men had said that the objective world is consistent and that contradiction is only "subjective." But contradictions do exist, and we are forced to think just because they are continually being presented to us in experience. Instead of two logics, we have to deal with logic, on the one hand, and existence, on the other; and they do not agree. The law of noncontradiction is the driving power of thought; it is because contradictions are inacceptable to reason that we go on from thesis to antithesis to synthesis, and then start over again. We are moving toward an inclusive truth, which is consistent. If we could reach it, we would stop thinking and simply contemplate, but we never can. Only the absolute is free from contradictions, and there is nothing consistent in our experience, for the only consistency is an inclusive one. The traditional laws of thought hold; everything is identical with itself, and contradictories cannot both be true. But the laws have only one instance.

This is no closer to the answer than is the first alternative, for it implies a sharp split between appearance and reality. Everything we experience is contradictory, false, and illusory—mere appearance; reality is something different and lies beyond it. But dialectic, far from rejecting appearance, holds that reality is the whole system of its appearances. There is no reality that does not appear. Moreover, this theory implies that we can use logic only negatively, not positively. It is an instrument to purge false opinions, but it does not help us to formulate a set of true ones. We must live pragmatically, by whatever theories work best; but we can never claim that we are living by logic. We reject beliefs by logic, but we cannot say that we accept them on the same grounds—not even one, let alone a whole system of them. There may be degrees of truth, but there are none of contradiction, and every concept is damned. Far from being rationalistic, this theory ends in skepticism.

The remaining alternative is the actual position of dialectic. The logic of reality is the logic of becoming; but the logic of being is not to be rejected entirely. It is a useful auxiliary and is contained in dialectic, from which it can be obtained by abstraction. If we ignore the process by which opposites are generated and identified, we are left with them as independent terms, having relations to one another; for most purposes they can be understood well enough as they stand. The study of these terms and relations, taken as data, is formal logic. The relationship between the two logics is that of whole and part. Just as reality is process with structure, so truth is the dialectical movement, which contains a corresponding logical structure. But the truth is the whole; so the logic of being has only a limited degree of truth because of what it omits. That, however, does not mean that it is entirely false.

But this is too easy a solution, for dialectic accepts contradiction, while formal logic rejects it; the two are incompatible. We appear to be back at the first alternative, with two different logics on our hands. And there is another difficulty. If the truth is the whole, we are caught in a dilemma. We know too much to be satisfied with the logic of the finite but, since we do not have the whole, not enough to use the logic of the infinite. We seem forced into skepticism, the second alternative. We must revise this interpretation of dialectic.

The absolute is not contradictory in the way that finite things are. Everything finite contains opposites that are given as ultimate constituents in it, which yet cannot be united; if the absolute were contradictory in this sense, it would be finite itself. But the opposites which it contains are not ultimate data, for we can get beyond them to the process in which they are generated and united. And the process is consistent, in that it is unified. It contains implicit contradictions, which become explicit when the terms are separated from their context; but it does not contain unresolved contradictions because the terms, in fact, are in and depend on the context. Also, while the absolute has identity, it is not the identity of formal logic, which is that of static "things," but rather the identity of growth and development. So the dialectical statements that we make about the absolute cannot be understood in the same sense as can statements made about finite things. "Reality is contradictory" does not have the same kind of meaning as "This blade of grass is contradictory"; and the same is true of statements about the respective identities. Statements are true of the absolute only analogically, not literally. But we can apply them, so we need not fall into skepticism. We can even assert statements of formal logic, such as "The absolute is identical with itself," though they will have only a partial degree of truth. So there are not two utterly different logics, having different spheres of application.

The position may be summarized as follows: There are two logics, one of appearance, the other of reality; and the first is contained in the second. We understand reality most adequately when we think in terms of its logic, dialectic. But, because we are parts of reality, our thinking cannot be literally true; for knowledge must be like its object, but our thinking is finite, while its object is infinite. Therefore, dialectic can give only an analogical, not a literal, account of reality.

The doctrine of the two logics has appeared repeatedly in Western thought. The origins of the second logic are in the ancient Greek concept of analogy or proportion. The doctrine was accepted by Christian scholasticism, which added a logic of analogy to the traditional syllogistic reasoning. The syllogism and its presuppositions are suitable for dealing with the facts of the sensible world, but they cannot be applied to the divine nature; for our concepts are drawn from experience and are therefore tinged with matter and finitude, but God is infinite and immaterial. Each concept applies to only a limited kind of being and hence has its corresponding negative: for man there is not-man, for animal there is not-animal, for substance there is not-substance, and so on in every case. But being is unlimited and has no negate. Man can think God only by analogy with his creatures, each of which bears traces

DIALECTIC

of its creator. The creatures both are and are not like God. They are like him because they participate in his perfection; they are not like him because their natures are limited and their existence dependent. The only way to express this double relationship is by analogy, for ordinary logic would either attribute finite predicates to God, which would be false; or it would refrain from applying any predicates at all, on the mistaken supposition that no positive knowledge of his nature is possible.

The doctrine of two logics has been asserted again more recently, though less clearly and consistently, by Bergson, who has said that the concepts of science and the intellect are too rigid to grasp change and that another kind is needed: static concepts for being, fluid ones for becoming. One way of thinking is suitable for knowing the material, another for knowing the psychical; one for quantity and another for quality; one for the practical needs of life and another for insight. The notion of fluid concepts is based on the same belief that knowledge must be like its objects in the essential respects. But Bergson does not explain how concepts can be fluid; and if the metaphors are pressed, the admission is likely to come out that insight into reality is a matter of intuition, not of conceptual knowledge at all.

The intellect falsifies—that is the charge behind the doctrine. There is only one truth, anything less is false, and the intellect always has less. Or, to take one form of the charge, abstraction is falsification. A great deal of ink has been expended to explain the meaning of this proposition, but it is really not very difficult. Consider the familiar example of motion. To understand the motion of a projectile through the air, we trace its path, which is an aspect of it. But the path is not the motion, and in considering it we lose the motion. Is this true? Certainly there is a tendency in our minds to do so, or people would not have found the discussion of Achilles and the tortoise so fascinating. We become absorbed in describing how Achilles must cover half the distance to the tortoise before he covers it all, and half of the remaining half after that, and so on; and we tend to forget that these relationships are abstractions from the event. But is it impossible for us to remember? It may be, from a purely rational point of view; there is a sense in which reason tends to claim, in its concepts, the sole avenue to truth. But what this doctrine forgets is that man is emotional and moral as well as rational. And our emotional experience and moral sense give us humility and an awareness of the extent of our ignorance, if we do not deny their relevance.

Every great philosophy has recognized the limitations of logic, in one way or another. And this is the real significance of dialectic: it is a revolt against rationalism. But if our logic is inadequate, is the remedy to invent another to make good the deficiencies of the first? Is it not more likely that, if the intellect absolutizes, the second will prove as dogmatic as the first? Philosophy will never escape the limits of reason in this way. It will do better to recognize other forms of experience, such as poetry, faith, and moral choice. The failure of dialectic is that, having brilliantly criticized reason, it tried to construct a superlogic and so fell back into rationalism again, more hopelessly than ever. But here its own truth is illustrated; for, by claiming everything for reason, it lost the restricted territory that really does belong to it. Reason turns into its opposite, and dialectical logic is irrational, for it fails to account for structure, the true subject of logic.

It was suggested above that, for dialectic, reality is "process with structure." But this is not quite accurate; for, when dialectic holds that becoming includes being, it means by "being," first, "thing" or substance and, second, quantity. But neither of these nor the two of them together are structure. The omission is explained by the attitude of dialectical idealism toward science and scientific reasoning. It considers the pattern of formal reasoning to be mathematics; mathematics is identified with the thinking of physical science; science is associated with materialism; and materialism is defined as atomism, the atom being the prototype of the thing. Now, for an extreme atomism, all complexity is to be explained quantitatively, by addition, composition, or aggregation. To idealism, consequently, mathematics is the science of quantity; and, in fact, it regards all formal reasoning as "quantitative," combining separate, isolated terms in a mechanical way. It is interesting to note that for Plato and Descartes, on the contrary, mathematics held a high place because they associated it closely with form. The absence of the concept of structure makes inevitable certain deficiencies in the philosophy of idealism.

For example, structure is an essential part of what we mean by a "finite thing." Without it, we cannot explain how a house differs from a factory, a cabbage, or an atom. Lack of a theory of structure is one reason why idealism is not concerned with individual things, except to urge their unreality. It was pointed out earlier that for idealism all relations are asymmetrical. Its inability to account for symmetrical relations is part of the same lack. Failure to explain how we can say "The tree is not the stone and the stone is not the tree" might not seem a very important defect in a philosophy. But its implications are tremendous; for, without symmetrical relations, we cannot talk about finite existents either, since these must be related by at least one symmetrical relation, namely, otherness. To accept form, of course, is not to accept any specific theory of the nature of particulars; nor is it necessarily to accept particular finite existents at all, as irreducible factors in the world. But a theory of form is a necessary condition for any doctrine of finite existents.

Again, dialectical idealism is often called an "organic" philosophy. But this is not correct; for an organism, on any reasonable definition, includes a structure and corresponding ways of behaving; without the first component, we do not have a concept of organism at all.

Finally, negation itself has two forms—internal analysis and external delimitation. The first is illustrated when I say, "This stone is not gray"; the second when I say, "It is not that tree." But for dialectic all negation is the distinction of opposites within a single thing or process or within reality itself. Therefore, the second form of negation is inadmissible, since it presupposes things in relation, and it reduces to the first. Apart from opposites, dialectic has no place for structure and relation; it can see only quantity.

The stress on quantity is continued by dialectical materialism, in the law of the transformation of quantity into quality; and it is open to the same criticism as before. Quantity is not enough to explain quality; by increasing the first, we do not bring about the second. A mob of people, no matter how large it grows, does not turn into a legislature, a union, or a community. For such transitions a definite order is necessary. This is always the case; a large aggregate remains an aggregate. It is true that a quantitative change will bring about a qualitative one under proper conditions, as when change of temperature results in change of state in a body. But this is not the only change involved; different relations between the parts of the body are also essential. Without specific relations, elements of any kind form a mere aggregate—that is, a collection in which the elements have arrangement but in which the arrangement is indifferent and can be altered without the collection's ceasing to be a collection of that specific sort of elements. Quality and quantity tell us something significant about change only if structure is implicitly included in the meaning of one or both. But so to include it is arbitrary and misleading. It is different from both, and at least as important a category as either.

The first law of dialectic reflects the shortcomings of the period in which it was formulated. But to grasp its significance we must see that it is one part of an attempt to eliminate the dualism of two logics. This is to be done by abolishing the traditional distinction between science and philosophy. Both deal with the laws of motion, the various sciences in their detailed formulas and propositions, philosophy in the general laws of dialectic. Since both are expressions of the scientific attitude, there is only one logic—that of scientific thinking about change. And yet the old distinction has not entirely disappeared. Materialism makes a sharp distinction between metaphysical and dialectical thinking and between formal logic and dialectic. These distinctions largely correspond to those

DIALECTIC

already made between the logics of being and becoming. Then is there one logic or two?

In answering this question, dialectical materialism distinguishes between the propositions of science and its presuppositions. There is the body of scientific knowledge, on the one hand, and the concepts and postulates which form its foundation, on the other. The propositions of science are established and universally accepted. Two and two are four, bodies fall according to the law of gravity, chemical elements combine in definite proportions, biological evolution occurs, and so on. There is no room for difference of opinion here, except on the frontiers of science. But this body of knowledge can be interpreted in different ways. If by "logic" we understand a general way of thinking, the results of science can be interpreted in terms of two logics. That two and two equal four will have one meaning to the metaphysical, mechanistic thinker, who considers arithmetical operations to be entirely different from one another. It will have another meaning for the dialectician, who sees the close relation between addition and multiplication and understands why four is both a sum and a product. Evolution will mean one thing to the thinker who interprets it predominantly in terms of overpopulation and the struggle for existence; it will mean something else to the man who sees the connection between life and death, between heredity and adaptation, and who analyzes the evolutionary process in terms of opposites such as these. Also, the presuppositions affect the course of investigation. They partly determine the kind of question that the investigator will ask, which problems will occur to him and which he will consider important, how many interconnections he will see between different fields, and what kind of theories he will develop. Yet the presuppositions are different from both facts and methods of proof.

There are, then, still two logics, in the sense of two ways of thinking—the metaphysical and the dialectical. And we must again ask, What is the relation between them? Dialectical materialism gives two different answers. According to the first, metaphysical thinking and formal logic, which accept the law of noncontradiction, are a narrow and limited way of thinking; dialectic is the comprehensive view. The first sees things in comparative isolation, the second in their relations—but they are the same things. The first is contained within the second; and one can advance from the first, as an elementary stage of thought, to the second. The difficulty in this point of view is the same as before: the first kind of thinking accepts structure and the law of noncontradiction, the second rejects it. But you cannot logically both accept and reject.

The second answer is that metaphysical and dialectical thinking are expressions of two different ideologies. There is one body of scientific knowledge, acquired and tested by universally accepted methods of investigation. But it can be interpreted in either of two different ways, which are mutually exclusive. If you see things dialectically, you do not see them metaphysically and mechanistically, and vice versa. The difficulty in this answer is that it represents a halfway position between holding that, since there is one body of scientific knowledge, there is a single logic and concept of truth, and denying it, since that body of knowledge can be interpreted in different ways. The concept of ideology, if carried through to the end, implies that a single body of knowledge, universally recognized, cannot exist, for the distinction between knowledge and its interpretation breaks down. If this implication is accepted, we have a third possibility: ideologies are relative to the historical needs and circumstances of the men who hold them. But, before examining this possibility, something must be said about the concept of ideology.

The ontological basis of ideology is the relation between form and process. We have seen that dialectical materialism views all existence, including human existence, in terms of these categories. Since man always lives in a given historical and social situation, his thinking, too, will assume a corresponding logical form, which is a function of the economic forces and antagonisms of society. Such a historically conditioned way of thinking is an ideology. This concept was implicit in the philosophy of Hegel, who saw that thinking has taken different forms through history. But the implications escaped him, and it remained for Marx and Engels to develop them and the new idea of man as the historical animal.

An ideology is a more or less closely knit system of beliefs, determined by economic forces, and reflecting the position of the thinker who holds it in the historical process. It presents itself to him as a logical system, having its own internal justification; the real objective forces and subjective motives which led to its adoption are unknown to him. It includes more or less articulated beliefs on all the subjects about which men reflect, such as law, politics, morality, religion, philosophy, science, and art. It is the man's view of the world and himself and his place in it. It need not all be consciously formulated, by any means; but it will be more effective practically when it is formulated.

We may distinguish three elements in its foundations. First, there is a set of theoretical presuppositions and concepts about the nature of existence and knowledge. In a developed ideology these will include views on such subjects as change and permanence, the stuff of nature, the forces at work in the world, the nature of man, and also a theory of what truth is and how it is to be found. Second, there are beliefs on practical subjects, about what is good and bad, desirable and undesirable; there is a theory of ends or ideals. Finally, there is some conception of the relation between these two, describing how the end is to be attained. For instance, as in bourgeois liberalism, the theoretical beliefs may be largely scientific in character; the practical beliefs may center around a conception of human happiness and unhappiness; and the relation may be a belief that science should be used for the control of nature, to increase happiness and eliminate suffering, and be made effective by popular education and enlightenment. The body of detailed beliefs follows from the interpretation of events in terms of the presuppositions. The first, theoretical, part of the presuppositions may be called a "logic," since it comprises the intellectual basis for the interpretation of existence. It is in this sense of the term that we have spoken of metaphysical and dialectical logics.

If science is the study of nature and man is a part of nature, it follows that human activities can be studied and understood scientifically, through the causes and forces which give rise to them. Human thinking is no exception. Philosophies and religions are as legitimate data for scientific investigation as anything else is. They are natural phenomena and have natural explanations. This was not entirely a new idea. Hume, for instance, had already made a beginning by writing a natural history of religions, in which he interpreted religion and its historical forms psychologically. Such a study will be a historical analysis, considering each system of beliefs in its own context, examining the society in which it appears, to see why it arose and what function it performs; for thought does not have its own history and inner dialectic, or, rather, the inner development is subordinate to outer events. Its determining conditions are external to it and are primarily economic; they lie in the needs of life, the mode of production, and the struggle for existence.

Since the way in which a man thinks depends on his social and economic situation, significant ideological differences will correspond to important differences of economic function. The broad divisions are laid down in the class structure of society. So far as one class represents or incorporates in itself the needs of the time, its ideology will be that of the whole society, for it will express the interests of all important groups. But with the development of a given mode of production, there comes an increasing differentiation of classes and conflict of interests, and the development of corresponding ideological differences. As history is a record of class struggles, the class is the characteristic bearer of an ideology.

The theories which men produce are expressions of what they are and of their historical situation. Religion arose, for instance, according to Marxism, because of primitive man's awareness of and awe in the face of the forces of nature, which he could not understand but which he tried to explain by formulating a nature religion. The theories evolved at any later time are equally expressions of what men are and of the economic and social situations in which they have developed. But man has a double nature, practical and theoretical; and the second is subordinate to the first. He wishes to understand himself and nature so that he may foresee the consequences of his actions and of natural events, in order to gain in mastery over nature and himself. And so far as he is in conflict with his fellows, he desires to gain power over them, too. An ideology, therefore, is a means for the realization and the protection of economic interests. Law and religion, for instance, are means which the ruling classes uses to safeguard its position. And they are not only weapons in the class struggle but also disguises, lending to the interests of a limited group the appearance of universal validity.

The illusions which men hold, as well as the beliefs which have an objective basis, have a sociological explanation. It may be that the state of society as a whole is such as to produce some belief which is simply a product of human imagination, as in the case of primitive nature religion. But, more often, ideological illusions have their source in the division of labor, which produces the separation of mental from physical activity and of production from consumption. In a class which is cut off and insulated from the realities of material existence and labor, thinking will in the long run also get cut off. So Marxism explains the existence and persistence of illusions in human thinking economically and socially, through the condition of man and the persistence of classes. It does not resort to a specifically psychological explanation, as did Nietzsche, and say that the mass of men need to live according to fictions and illusions because without these they would feel so insecure that life would no longer be possible. Not only is this cynical doctrine an affront to human dignity, but it involves a complacent fatalism, which accepts the state of the people under exploitation as inevitable. Instead of justifying it as a psychological necessity, Marxism condemns the persistent resort to illusory ideologies as a reactionary flight from reality into the realm of subjective fantasy and an evasion of responsibility.

This brings us to the question of evaluation. How is the validity of an ideology to be determined? In considering this question, we must keep in mind that every ideology is to be considered from two points of view, which are related. It is a natural phenomenon, having causes and effects. As such, it is not to be evaluated but explained. But it is also a product of thinking, belonging to the ideal world. As such, its relation to the real world—in other words, its validity—needs to be investigated. Now the term "validity" in this context no longer has the meaning it once had. To ask of an ideology in the old sense, Is it true? Is the way of life it holds up as the ideal, good? are meaningless questions; for it is the expression of social needs which are historically conditioned, and in the absence of those needs it is not merely false but unintelligible.

Its validity lies in its relation to those needs and is therefore primarily a practical matter. Specific ideologies arise because they perform a function in the life-process of the men who develop them; and they may perform that function well or ill or cease to perform it at all. The question to ask about an ideology, then, is: Does it adequately express and effectively further the interests of the class which produced it? Is it timely? This sounds as though it is usefulness, not truth, that is important or that an ideology is true if it works and that its truth is its working. But dialectical materialism is not pragmatic in this sense. An ideology will not work unless it conforms to historical and natural necessities. The outlook of the bourgeois era, for instance, met the social needs of the middle class in its extreme individualism and the demand for freedom from interference; but individual enterprise was also favorable for a time to the development of modern society as a whole—it was called for by the historical situation. Again, mechanistic and atomistic thinking in the physical sciences worked well during the same period, not only because it was part of the ideology of the dominant class but because there really is a quantitative aspect to nature and units which can be added together; its limitation was its failure to see the qualitative discontinuities as well and their dialectical relation to quantity. An illusory ideology fails to work precisely because it does not conform to the objective necessities of the historical situation; and it seems to work only because its adherents may be able for a time, ultimately through a favorable economic position, to stand aside from the course of events or to hamper historical tendencies.

Practical utility and theoretical validity cannot be separated; and

DIALECTIC

neither can the real and the ideal character of ideologies. This is the real meaning of Marxism. The notion that ideas are weapons is superficial and mechanical because it implies the separations. An idea is not the same kind of weapon as a knife or gun. It is not a useful tool, with a certain power, which can be picked up and employed for whatever purpose we choose and then laid aside. Ideas are effective weapons, but they are not subject to our voluntary control. They can be used only as we use ourselves. They are inalienably part of the men who believe them, and their conscious use as propaganda is built on the foundation of their prior status and effectiveness as beliefs. They have a theoretical quality of truth which is compulsive. It is words and things that are "weapons," not ideas. If the scheming propagandist understood the meaning of the words which he used, he would not act as he does. He would then have ideas to believe in, not words to use.

On this matter, dialectical materialism differs from liberalism, which, in effect, stresses the ideal, theoretical character of ideas to the exclusion of their practical properties as natural social phenomena. Liberalism holds that, though interests may be limited, conflicting, and historically conditioned, logic and knowledge are inherently universal and can be shared by everyone. They can, therefore, be used to bring about agreement or compromise between conflicting groups, for we can, after all, understand one another, even though we disagree. In spite of their instrumentalism, liberals regard ideas not as natural weapons but rather as ideal truths having a validity independent of the economic and social situations in which they arise. This would be possible only if logic was not, like interest, bound by its historical context. But such a supposition is untenable, for it implies either that man is only half historical in his essence, while the other half is free from the effects of historical events, or else that there are two separate historical processes going along in essential independence of each other. Either alternative introduces an impossible dualism into human nature and history. The theoretical and practical aspects of man, his ideas and his interests, are inseparable; they are both aspects of the historical situations in which they arise.

Man, then, participates essentially in the historical process, and his understanding of the world will be that which is possible from a specific perspective. But both the objective situation and he himself are limited and determinate in character. The world which he experiences is a specific historical situation, not the whole sweep of history; and he is not man in the abstract but that unique man who is the outcome of a long development. His knowledge, then, will be cast in the mold of the ideology peculiar to that historical situation and of the logic which is its foundation. Rather than two logics, there are many, a different one for every age and class. This is the third possible interpretation of dialectical materialism, mentioned above. Different "logics" are not parts of one inclusive logic, as idealism holds. Neither are they alternative interpretations of an identical body of knowledge, for there is no single body of knowledge. But logic, ideology, and knowledge are relative to the historical needs and circumstances of the men who hold them.

The whole problem of historical and cultural relativism is thus implicit in the concept of ideology. It was formulated by Marx and Engels in economic terms, but it is independent of this formulation and cannot be evaded by simply rejecting an economic interpretation of history. The question is not the nature of historical forces but the nature of knowledge for historical beings, and this is as inescapable as history itself. It is not limited to the relation between economic classes or periods in the history of the West. It arises in connection with the biography of an individual, the perspective of a class or other social group, the outlook of a historical era, the presuppositions of a culture, or any other mode of historical existence for men.

At first glance, the statement that knowledge contains an ideological element seems to be refuted by the facts. East and West, for instance, use the same technology, which is founded on the same scientific study of nature. They carry on commerce with the same means of transportation and communication and fight with the

DIALECTIC

same weapons. And not only East and West, but worker and capitalist, Communist and Fascist, primitive and modern civilized man—define the categories as you will—all share at least to some extent in the possession of a common body of scientific and technological knowledge. But this argument is specious, for people can use and deal with the same things, yet think in different ways. One group can appropriate the results of the thinking of another group without assimilating the thinking itself, although in the long run it will prove impossible to continue using the things and techniques successfully without also learning to understand them. But using and thinking are not identical, and it follows from the concept of ideology that different ideologies mean different bodies of knowledge. However, in periods of profound social conflict and change there will be conflicting ideologies present in the same individuals and groups, even in an entire nation or culture. But this does not prove that the same body of knowledge is present in different men bearing different ideologies. Rather, it indicates that there are different bodies of knowledge present in the same man, but in a confused and unresolved state.

The difficulty in this solution of the problem is that dialectical materialism does, after all, claim to understand reality. On the one hand, the theory implies that an ideology is a function of historical conditions, valid and meaningful only in relation to them. But, on the other, dialectical materialism presents itself as the true interpretation of history. It is not merely the way things appear to have happened, from the perspective of the proletariat in modern society; it is the way they actually did happen, regardless of what may be said from one or another perspective. On the one hand, there are bourgeois and proletarian ideologies, giving alternative interpretations of man, history, and nature, each valid for the class that holds it. On the other hand, dialectical materialism presents itself not as one ideology among others but as true, because in becoming scientific it has transcended the conditions which have limited the validity of all ideologies in the past. The crucial question, clearly, is: What are these conditions?

EXISTENCE AND INQUIRY

There are two different answers. The one given by dialectical materialism is that ideologies are, in the last analysis, the result of the operation of two factors—the existence of classes and the domination of man by nature. Their immediate cause is diversity and conflict of interest. Class interests reflect the division of labor, which gives men different roles in production. And the division of labor, in turn, together with private property, is responsible for the warping and cramping of human nature to fit the limitations of class existence. Because of this, man is unable to understand historical and natural forces as he could if classes were abolished, and therefore he is subject to them instead of controlling them. He is the slave not only of nature but of his own creations. But the lack of knowledge of nature is also a direct source of ideologies. Ever since man began to reflect, he has tended to invent fanciful explanations for natural events which he could not understand. Supernatural and idealistic theories are the results of his ignorance—attempts to explain nature in terms of man's ideas instead of explaining thinking man as the product of nature.

But man has at last reached the stage of development at which he can abolish both classes and his subjection to nature. Classes will be abolished by the revolution of the proletariat, which, while still a class, no longer counts as a class because it represents the interests of all future humanity and the overwhelming majority of present humanity. It is the vehicle through which the final dissolution of classes will take place, not primarily because of its moral superiority over other classes, but because of the impersonal dialectic of history. The proletariat is also the representative of the scientific philosophy of the future. The class which puts an end to classes will also, and for the same reasons, put an end to ideologies. The leap out of the realm of necessity into the realm of freedom is also the leap from ideology into science. And through scientific knowledge man will be able increasingly to control not only nature but his own actions, through the knowledge of their social consequences. In the past, needs have determined ideas; but, in the future, ideas will not only direct the satisfaction of needs but even control their occurrence in

DIALECTIC

many respects, through the scientific understanding of man and his relation to nature and society. Thus, while it is true that man essentially participates in process, he is at last able to understand it and to state its laws.

The other explanation of the existence of ideologies places their origin in the historical nature of man himself. To say that man is historical is to say that he develops in interaction with circumstances; he both changes and is changed by nature. But, if this is true, he will continue to be historical after classes have disappeared and been forgotten. How, then, can his needs and his ways of thinking be exempt from this process? There could be a finally "true" ideology only if there were permanent needs of a permanent human nature which that ideology could satisfy. But dialectical materialism, like scientific forms of liberalism, denies this in any sense that is relevant to the question. It follows that science and scientific philosophy are themselves parts of an ideology—the ideology of the modern world of industry and technology and of future society so far as it is built around them. This ideology is suited, more or less, to the needs of that society; but it cannot claim absolute validity beyond the conditions and needs of such a society. No matter how long the culture lasts, how powerful it may be, and how successful in mastering nature, its view of the world will still be simply one more point of view. It is a very important perspective on reality and in certain respects contrasts sharply with all others that we know; but it is, nevertheless, only one perspective.

Thus we have two explanations of ideologies. First, there is the theory that they arise from ignorance and the conditions of class existence, both of which are now being finally abolished; second, there is the theory that they are inherent in the historical nature of man. It may be argued that these two explanations are compatible, because science, the basis of our cultural outlook, has the unique quality of being self-corrective; it does not claim absoluteness, as all past ideologies have done, but claims validity only as far as it succeeds in predicting events, thus enabling us to control them better. Therefore, neither is it relative as past ideologies have been, nor does it claim a dogmatic finality; but it is capable of and demands endless transformation and improvement through the course of history. It is the final form of human thinking and, at the same time, the supremely historical form. This position is, in effect, a fourth answer to the question which we raised concerning the relation of the two logics in dialectical materialism. It denies that there really are two logics and holds, instead, that there is a single, historically developing logic of empiricism. But this logic at every stage of history is found in combination with nonlogical factors which are relative to historical circumstances. This is the position taken by all reflective adherents of scientific philosophy, including both dialectical materialists and those liberals who adopt a scientific humanism.

This theory may be true of some ideal notion of inquiry. It certainly is not true of science as it is understood in actual discussions of these questions. On the contrary, adherents of scientific philosophy always define knowledge in such a way as to make it the exclusive possession of contemporary science, interpreted in terms of such contemporary ideas as the ability to predict. Knowledge is carefully defined on the basis of methods, kinds of evidence, criteria of validation, the very concept of validation itself. And not only is existent scientific knowledge, interpreted in this way, asserted to be superior in cognitive value to every other form of experience; it is asserted to be the only form of experience that yields any knowledge at all. In comparison with other forms and modes, its claims are true without restriction. Here dialectical materialism is in agreement with liberalism. All knowledge is scientific knowledge. The beliefs of all men at all times can be divided into common sense and skills, which are crude forms of scientific empiricism, on the one hand, and superstition and fantasy, on the other. Dialectical materialism incorporates a critique of liberal rationalism in its outlook, but the rationalism that it rejects is of action, not of thought. Like liberalism, it claims a unique position for science, which places it above the historical plane of ideological thinking.

The relation between the two logics, then, according to dialectical materialism, is not that of part and whole, the narrow and the inclusive. Neither is it that of mutually exclusive historical alternatives, whether two or many. It is, rather, the relation between ideology and science, the conditioned and the unconditioned; for science is not historically conditioned, as the ideologies of other ages and cultures have been, in such a way that it may eventually give way to another kind of thinking. Its present achievements are limited and may be progressively increased and improved through the whole future of man, as long as that future lasts; but it will still remain science. Thus we come to a position not so far removed from that with which we began. Instead of a contrast between the logics of appearance and reality, we have the contrast between ideology and science; and, in place of a single logic of appearance, we now have many ideologies, giving the many varied appearances of knowledge. The appearances are many, the reality one, so to speak. This is the doctrine of the two logics, based on an interpretation of science and transformed through an increased understanding of the cultural differences of history.

But this position has not seriously considered the implications for science of the concept of ideology. It is one thing to hold that all knowledge is empirical. It is a very different thing to identify empiricism with a set of highly specialized concepts and methods, elaborated quite recently in the history of Western culture and highly characteristic of it. This solution of the problem, which is implicit in the existence of a multiplicity of cultural perspectives, is based on the idea of progress. But the argument is circular in the invidious sense. Progress is defined in terms of the undoubted accumulation and refinement of predictive knowledge. But all that this proves is that there is progress in predictive knowledge. And this is not enough, for there are other possible criteria of progress (if we are to speak in these terms), and there are other criteria of knowledge, for example, self-evidence or inclusiveness. This is not the solution to the problem of cultural relativism.

The questions which arise in the present context are two. First, is the version of empiricism which we are considering suited to the discovery of all types of structure in nature and society; or is it, on the contrary, limited to certain types, such as causal uniformities? Second, does it really recognize the existence of nonformal elements in nature, apart from sense data? I think the answers to both questions are negative. At any rate, the answer to the second is negative. Contemporary logical or scientific empiricism avoids the problem of logic and existence by simply ignoring the nonformal aspects of reality with which dialectical logic originally attempted to deal.

Thus, to sum up, neither dialectical idealism nor dialectical materialism has solved the problem of how man can understand reality when he participates in its process. Idealism develops the concept of analogical thinking; but it fails to relate this to formal logic or to show how the two are compatible. Materialism, on the other hand, fails to apply the notion of historical perspectives to itself or to offer any useful principle for dealing with the whole problem of ideology. Both versions of dialectic are limited by the special form in which they conceived the original problem.

6. Dialectic and Empiricism

The degeneration of the concept of reason and the superficiality of the concept of nature, against which dialectic was a protest, belong essentially to the eighteenth century. The analytic ideal of reason characteristic of the century that preceded it was not atomistic; it was concerned with structure as well as elements and, far from being opposed to synthesis, naturally led on to it as a complementary process. Nor was the reality envisaged by the great thinkers of the earlier period either static or mechanical; these adjectives would have been rejected by nearly every one of the men who thought in terms of substance, essence, attribute, and mode. Except for Hobbes, they did not attempt to apply the concept of mechanism at all beyond material nature; and they did not regard mechanism as a complete or final explanation for anything.

Dialectic is directed very largely against the later, eighteenth-century view and the concept of the "thing," which is its common-sense expression. Hegel assumes that this notion is natural to untutored modern man. Marx makes the same assumption, though his reasons are different. Hegel understands by a "thing" what is separate, static, and complete; the thing is discrete, different from and indifferent to every other thing. He considers relationship to be its negation—having already defined it in such a way that relationship is excluded from its nature. All along, he identifies the finite with a thing in this sense. The pattern of his thinking is the same, whether he is discussing the object of sense-perception, the self, freedom, logical concepts, individual moral conscience, or the God of popular religion. They all claim to be things and make impossible pretensions to absoluteness.

Similarly, relations do not enter into the internal nature of a thing. Its internal nature excludes properties, though it can be itself only by having properties, which give it a definite character. And in the problem of properties the concept of the thing in all its forms, and hence the finite as well, goes to ruin. In general, Hegel rejects relatedness as a fundamental datum of experience. Immediate experience is continuous, but for him continuity is a negative idea, meaning homogeneity and lack of differentiation; and so it must be developed into its implications, that is, into its opposite. Therefore, in thinking about finite existence, the relatively developed concept of discontinuity is truer than the more primitive notion of continuity. Also, the argument seems to run, since nature is essentially "other," the elements of natural existence must share this characteristic and must themslves be mutually other and indifferent. And finite spirit is tainted by the defects of finite nature. This is the rationalism of the dialectic.

Again, the long idealist criticisms of quantity and the eulogies of quantity by materialism are characteristic of the period. Admiration of the previous century for the infinite had given place to a more critical examination of the notion and a realization of the difficulties inherent in the concepts of the infinitely large and the infinitely small. These problems were a central theme of the Kantian antinomies. Whether we proceed by division or by aggregation, it seems impossible to understand nature in quantitative terms. There appear to be but two alternatives. We can conclude that whatever is quantitative is appearance, because it is contradictory: idealism. Or we can say that everything in nature develops by contradiction; quantity is only one side and continually passes over into quality, and vice versa: materialism.

If we regard things as discrete and discontinuous, then motion, change, and relation—and even such concepts as atom and point—are contradictions. If we begin by postulating only one side of the facts, then we shall have somehow to "deduce" the other; and, now having two incompatible accounts, an either-or, we shall have the problem of synthesizing them. The paradoxes of Zeno, the antinomies of Kant, the dialectic of Bradley, are the only possible outcome. Motion implies that a thing both is and is not in a certain place. A point is a something which is spatially nothing. Since an atom is defined so as to exclude relations, it follows that relations contradict its nature. And an aggregate of such entities can never produce anything new, except by turning into its opposite. But why make these assumptions?

To be empirical is to recognize that both continuity and discreteness are given in experience. We find that things have both intrinsic and relational natures. Motion and rest are both facts. Subject and object are given, both different from and in relation to each other. Nature contains both structure and process. Such statements are not a philosophy, for they explain neither the terms nor the relations between them; they are only the starting-point. But they are a starting-point. Opposites are together in the concrete; we do not have to put them together. If we do not begin by supposing that they represent rigid distinctions and contradictory concepts but take them as we find them, knowing that we do not yet understand their relations to each other or clearly what they are, then all the elaborate apparatus of dialectic is unnecessary.

And this is the real meaning of dialectic. It is an empirical philosophy, which holds that these distinctions really are given, that they are not rigid and absolute but are possessed of only a relative validity. That is why they allow of and demand both recognition and synthesis. Here materialism is more empirical than idealism, though idealism is more philosophical in its analysis of categories. There is more than rational form, law, order, structure, and quality in reality; and what remains over cannot be dismissed in vague or negative terms, as matter, content, or a manifold of sense data. Reality contains nonformal elements—that is the lesson of dialectic. Process, development, destruction, contradiction, negation—such things cannot be described in the old language. But the attempt of dialectic to formulate a new one was not entirely successful, and its statement was confused, because of a failure to distinguish between the essential problem and its accidental historical setting. The criticisms made by dialectic were sound, but it was misled by the necessity of making them into misstating the problem.

Opposites exist together in the concrete, and their synthesis is the process of existence itself. Reason must describe them and their relations as completely as it can, and there is only one reason. But reason is not outside the process; and how can we understand it when we are at the same time in it? This is the problem which dialectic willed to posterity.

Subsequent philosophy is still attempting to solve the problem. So far as knowledge is concerned, the conclusion to which we are driven by the discovery is that man exists in a perspective. The philosophical problem of knowledge will lie in man's relation to his perspective. The problem of the two logics can be solved only by shifting the discussion from knowledge to reality. And, so far as reality is concerned, structure is the proper sphere of logic; process, so far as it is more than structure, must be dealt with not by a second logic but in other terms.

Pragmatism is one attempt to deal with the problem. It conceives man as becoming, though it has little use for the concept of opposites. Like dialectical materialism, pragmatism holds that practice is the final measure of theory; that man is, first of all, an agent; and that contemplation must take its place in relation to action. Unlike dialectical materialism, however, pragmatism is unhistorical, and its concept of ontology is weak. With idealism, it holds that the true criticism of ideas is internal, in that they are not to be rejected from the standpoint of any dogmatic philosophy but to be taken without preconceptions. Unlike idealism, however, it holds that the criterion is external as well as internal, since the standard is not the internal consistency of the idea but its effectiveness in mediating other experiences or achieving purposes. We may regard pragmatism as an attempt to combine the logical clarity of analysis with the recognition that reality is a process. Pragmatism is, therefore, closer to dialectic in its theory of existence than in its doctrine of inquiry. Yet its conception of inquiry is new, being affected by the dialectical concept of thinking. And its concept of reality is also new, being affected by its concept of inquiry.

PART III
Pragmatism

1. The Origins of Pragmatism

EVERY significant intellectual movement is both old and new. Its adherents can always point for confirmation or illustration of their views to early history, where either facts bear them out or perhaps even analogous beliefs are to be found, explicitly held by individuals or groups. At the same time, they can claim to have discovered a truth or to possess an insight which no one has ever had before. Thus they are at once radical and conservative. This feat is not possible through deliberate effort. It can be accomplished only inadvertently, when historical circumstances are favorable to a peculiar combination of intellectual continuity and novelty.

In the case of pragmatism, antecedents are easily found, for the appeal to practice is very old. It is a dimension, rather than an era, in the history of man. Moreover, the early history of Western thought contains well-known instances of philosophers who made the appeal, including Protagoras, who advanced the claim that one idea may be better than another, though none possesses superior truth. But pragmatism as a separate doctrine, with a specific character and a continuous history, does not antedate the modern era, though its roots extend far back in modern thought.

At the time when men held that only logically clear and distinct ideas and what is derived from them are true, they observed that some unclear ideas which, accordingly, did not deserve to be called true are useful. Confused or obscure ideas may perform important functions in experience, as we have seen. They may serve as clues to what is beneficial or harmful to life, as when the pangs of hunger warn us to eat or an agreeable taste suggests nourishing food. Or they may enable us crudely to predict the future, on the basis of what our senses tell us more or less directly. This eventually suggested that the concept of truth might need revision, so as to make a place for the rejected elements of experience. Later, the development of the idea of process brought with it a conviction that new intellectual means were needed to deal with a world of change. The result was dialectical logic, which attempted to describe both change and the unclear elements in existence. But this logic is unacceptable to pragmatism, which is affiliated with experimental science as interpreted by the British tradition in philosophy. Dialectical idealism had attempted to fit science into a framework, the outlines of which were determined by other factors; the orientation of pragmatism, on the other hand, was, at the beginning, largely determined by science, and other elements of experience were interpreted accordingly. Pragmatism, therefore, made a fresh attempt to define truth and to formulate a logic of process.

Every intellectual movement has two sides. It is both a criticism of the past and a construction of something novel. The critical element in pragmatism is the claim that many human beliefs have been without a bearing on experience, so that, whether they are considered true or false, they make no difference to men, and the demand that we accept for logical consideration only ideas whose truth or falsity would make a difference. This line of criticism continues an effort that has been carried on by a long line of thinkers ever since the beginning of the modern era; it is part of the old demand that all ideas be subjected to the tests of observation and experiment. It is a continuation of empiricism. The novel, constructive element is the contention that all beliefs and knowledge are bound up with action—in a wider sense, that man is, first of all, an active being and that the other sides of his manifold nature, including reason, can be understood only in relation to this. In a word, pragmatism is an active empiricism. Here again are concepts long known to philosophy; for Socrates sought to define ethical concepts by induction from experience, and the appeal has been made from mere thought to action whenever philosophy has been considered a way of life. But the two terms now acquire new meanings.

Pragmatism aims to be an active empiricism: it is the combination that is new in modern thought, and through it the component elements are modified. Knowledge, which was once regarded as an essentially nontemporal contemplation of an object presented to the mind, had gradually become temporalized. But temporalized rationalism, though active, became unempirical through attributing everything positive in knowledge to the mind, while temporalized empiricism, based on associationist psychology, was passive. Yet the clearest lesson of the whole period seemed to be that human knowledge is derived from experience by patient and sustained activity, which is itself inseparable from the knowing. Active empiricism rejects the contemplative ideal and holds that human knowledge is a participation in existence. Knowing is an interaction in which the mind, or rather the inquiring individual, is active and, through this activity, learns from the environing world. And not only is knowledge inseparable from process, but the temporal emphasis of empiricism is shifted from past origins to future consequences, since action is directed toward the future.

It is the aim of pragmatism to eliminate dualism from inquiry. Many traditional theories, it holds, which were closely associated with traditional practice, involved a separation between logical and psychological meaning; this was based on a separation between thought and action, which, in many cases, was, in turn, rooted in the dualism of mind and body. The aim of active empiricism is the reunion of these elements. To understand the method of attack, we must have in mind the situation in theory of knowledge at the time when pragmatic ideas were first becoming crystallized. The "problem of knowledge," as it came to be called, had arisen through the separation of sensory experiences as effects from the objects which were their supposed causes. This separation soon spread from sensations to concepts and gave rise to the question of how the subjective forms of the mind can be valid for the real world.

At the same time there developed another separation, between patterns in nature and natural processes. Observation shows us sequences in nature. But if we ask whether an observed sequence is likely to recur, there is no answer because no reason can be found why it either should or should not do so. The sequence is simply a separate fact, capable of correlation with other facts but in itself isolated and supplying no clue to further relations. It is a pattern which has no discoverable function or effective role in the general course of events; in fact, the theory in question does not include the notions of effectiveness and function. This is the source of the problem of induction—the twin to the problem of knowledge.

The solution of pragmatism is to recognize the fact that man is a part of nature and in constant interaction with it. When we do this, the artificial character of these problems becomes apparent. The forms of knowledge have a function, which is to enable man to deal effectively with the problems of his natural environment. Since they are elaborated to serve this purpose and undergo a process of natural selection in the course of inquiry, it is no miracle that they are valid for the real world. And, since nature exhibits both order and disorder, continuity and novelty, in its processes, we find, in analyzing observed sequences, reasons for believing that they either will or will not recur. The logical forms which we elaborate by reasoning and apply to specific situations form the starting-point for habits; and we use the habits derived from past experience as guides for future action. But we are not isolated inquirers. As individuals, we are members of a community of inquirers; and the community has roots in the past. We have at our disposal the results of science, which are the outcome of the past thinking of the entire race. The continuity between past and future goes beyond the individual. The import of pragmatism is a naturalistic and social logic.

This logic not only is a reaction against certain earlier tendencies, however; it also has origins in others, the most obvious of which, perhaps, lie in the sciences. Here pragmatism unifies ideas which had previously been unrelated. We have, for example, noted a contrast between logical and psychological meaning. It was largely mathematics and the physical sciences which suggested to philosophy a logical, in the sense of a formal, theory of meaning. But in philosophy, unlike the sciences, this theory was for a time relatively divorced from any notion of action. The psychological theories of meaning, on the other hand, owe their inspiration primarily to biology, building on earlier philosophical psychology; in fact, "psychological" could almost equally well be called "biological" meaning, since its root is the utility of thinking to the organism. In some philosophies these two views of meaning remain unrelated, or perhaps one is even ignored. Logical meaning is concerned with what an idea is; psychological meaning with what it does. The first is based on formal reasoning and necessary truths; the second begins with induction and the contingent truths of fact. But pragmatism pointed out that the two are not in reality different kinds of meaning; rather, they are two aspects of the single process of inquiry and so are integrally related. Again, pragmatism has affiliations with the early, analytic period of modern thought, both philosophic and scientific; for experimental logic is analytic, in that it attempts to abstract from data the structure of nature. On the other hand, it is also affiliated with the later period which conceived nature in terms of change. Through formal meaning and analysis it has some kinship with rationalism. Through psychological meaning and its interest in change, development, and the genesis of ideas and beliefs, it has a more obvious kinship with empiricism.

But, while the new concept of knowledge and inquiry is based on a philosophy of change, the latter has not been elaborated by pragmatism in any characteristic way. The emphasis, rather, has been on problems of methodology; and, in spite of important contributions in other directions, pragmatism still remains primarily a methodology. The criterion of consequences is the one important doctrine shared by all pragmatists, and the divergent lines of investigation which have been followed out by those who hold this doctrine basic for philosophy bear witness to their inability so far to find further common ground.

The reason is that pragmatism has been shaped by both the naturalistic and the idealistic traditions in modern philosophy and has been unable to throw off the influence of either one or to combine the two in any satisfactory way. This double inheritance is easily overlooked because of the close association of pragmatism with issues bearing more directly on knowledge and method, but it is of fundamental importance. We need not consider it in detail here or note which elements are stressed in different formulations of pragmatic doctrine. The relevant features will receive attention later. It is enough to note the climate of ideas which forms the background of the theory of inquiry. These ideas are in part explicitly stated, in part implicitly assumed, and in some respects unconsciously presupposed.

The naturalistic component has already been indicated. It is mainly the theory of evolution, which differs from older materialistic theories, among other respects, in its stress on novelty and contingency. The aspect of it which has exerted most influence on pragmatism is the picture of the evolving organism, adapting itself to a changing environment, with which it is partly in conflict, in order to survive and satisfy its needs. This notion forms the basis for a dynamic psychology, which interprets man in terms of action and action in terms of needs and of the means, including thinking, by which they are satisfied. It transforms the older empiricism, which was based on the association psychology. Biology substitutes a process of conditioning for the mental process of association. The change can be expressed in a simple formula: association psychology *plus* evolutionary biology *equals* behaviorism. Both versions attribute the acquisition of knowledge in overwhelming measure to experience, subject theoretically, but scarcely otherwise, to the limitation of the inherent tendencies of the organism, in the one case, and original human nature, in the other. Hume said that objects are associations of ideas turned inside out; Dewey and the behaviorists say that objects are habits turned inside out; while Mead says that objects are social habits turned outside in, so to speak, in the individual. The identity of theme is unmistakable.

The concept of evolution also has an application to society. Man is social in his language and thinking, in his activities and purposes, in his enjoyments and sentiments; and all these are constantly undergoing modification. However, in spite of its social and evolutionary view of man, pragmatism retains much of the flavor of individualism and is, on the whole, unhistorical. An unhistorical evolution sounds like a contradiction in terms. But in these matters pragmatism still has something of the abstract character of traditional empiricism and liberalism. Empiricism had been influenced in its earlier development by the physical sciences, which were then unhistorical in outlook. And the reformist interest of British empiricism in social change was founded not so much on a study of society and of the past, in which it had little interest, as on adherence to certain abstract moral and social principles. Its liberal individualism was well suited to a reformulation in terms of the organism and its environment—a biological version of individual enterprise but with a stress on co-operation in place of the Darwinian emphasis on competitive struggle among the members of the species. Recent recognition of cultural factors, such as language, has not erased this earlier influence.

Idealism, too, has contributed ideas on the nature of man and society. It holds that mind is active and that its activity is not determined from without by environmental forces. Its influence on this point shows in the agreement of idealist and pragmatist that ideas are neither passive sense data nor the pure possibles of logic and mathematics. They are forces which work in nature wherever they appear. There is basic agreement here as to the nature of ideas; the difference arises over their relation to man. To one, idea is end, the individual only means; to the other, ideas are means, and the individual is the end. Hegel said that we are instruments of the Idea; the pragmatists say that ideas are our instruments. But, to both, thinking means carrying an idea as far as it will go; every idea is true as far as it works; and the truth of each is limited. Also, since the truth of ideas is limited, all thought is inferential or hypothetical; it involves a risk.

The emphasis on the practical in recent philosophy also goes back to idealism, at least so far as the moral form of practice is concerned;

for Kant began by insisting that morality is as valid an approach to reality as is science; and his idealistic successors went on to make it far superior as a source of knowledge. The British tradition, by contrast, was always scientific and theoretical, a psychological dissection of human nature; and when the theoretical analysis came into conflict with moral common sense, the British resorted to such devices as the pre-established harmony of virtue and self-interest rather than admit limitations on the validity of the psychological theory through a direct moral experience of the practical. On this matter, idealism and biological naturalism reinforce each other in effecting a reinterpretation of human nature in terms of action.

Idealism also developed the idea of the community, which it holds to be an irreducible reality and not an artificial aggregate of individuals, or even a voluntary association. It regards the social as a moral, and almost a religious, category. Society is objective spirit, while individual experience, so far as it is merely private, is only subjective spirit. In pragmatism the idea of the community receives a new form and is more closely related to the active character of knowing. If mind were passive, the same world might be simultaneously given to a number of independent knowers. But if their worlds are in some important respect the result of interpretation and if the knowers are practical beings with mutual relations, then their interpretive activities must also be related if there is to be a common world at all. In other words, society is not an entity but a set of interactions. The problems of communication and a common world, however, with which pragmatism has been concerned, are the result of the impact of individualism on idealism. They were not central to dialectical idealism, whose standpoint was too universal to consider them seriously.

But while these two traditions have contributed to the formulation of many ideas, there is no philosophy of nature, no theory of man, no theory of any aspect of reality, which is characteristically pragmatic. In particular, it is surprising that pragmatism, in spite of the enormous influence of evolution, biology, and scientific method, still has no clear-cut, unambiguous philosophy of nature. This failure to reach conclusions by the employment of its method betrays the conflict within pragmatism. As we shall see, it is the source of an ambiguity in the theory of inquiry itself.

However, pragmatism does hold that the world is changing and in process. The flux of events is immediately given; man is immersed in it and has direct experience of it. And, since the world is temporal, knowledge of it will have a relation to time. Things are in process of becoming, and we must see them in their genesis and becoming to understand them. So, while analysis is necessary, to describe only the properties, structures, and relations of things would be like studying morphology without going on to physiology. We can understand the form of a thing and the way it behaves only in relation to the forces and processes which have brought it about. This principle applies to the study of inquiry, too. Since thinking is a process of adaptation to reality, it must be understood in its genesis; and the forms which it assumes must be seen in relation to the forces and circumstances which produce and suggest them.

Inquiry, according to pragmatism, is a present activity, but it has a reference beyond the present. It is a process by which we deal with the future, with the aid of experience gained in the past. In existence, past and future are inseparable; and to know one is to know both. But there are respects in which they differ, and, influenced by the differences, pragmatism has adopted two methods. The first may be called the "genetic method"; it is concerned with origins and exemplifies the old principle that to know a thing is to know its causes. The second is the "experimental method," according to which knowledge is predictive and to know a thing is to know its consequences, actual or potential. The difference between them, however, as will appear presently, is not that between past and future, though this contributed to their differentiation. Both are presumably employed in everyday life and in the sciences. Whether there is any specifically philosophical method and knowledge, according to pragmatism, and, if so, what its relation is to these two methods are questions which may be deferred for the moment.

These methods, at any rate, are regarded simply as the ways of thinking which man has found successful in his efforts to understand change. They are not peculiar to philosophy, though they are employed by philosophers as well as by other people. However, they are not given an equal stress by pragmatism, for, while the experimental method has been the subject of constant study, the genetic method has, for the most part, been presupposed rather than discussed. Since they are of central importance for our inquiry, it will be well to summarize and compare them.

There is, however, as we shall see, another conception of inquiry implicit in pragmatism, which stresses the present rather than either past or future. It has not been developed, because the definitions of meaning and truth in terms of consequences have thrown the emphasis away from the present. Nevertheless, it is suggested by the doctrine that reality is present existence; for, if existence is present and if philosophy is an attempt to understand existence, does it not follow that philosophy is more concerned with an analysis of the present than with prediction of the future?

2. The Genetic and Experimental Methods

A genetic explanation, as the term is used here, accounts for a thing through its origins. It attempts to answer such questions as Where did this thing come from? How did it originate? What has been its course of development? These questions can be asked about anything that has become. Such a concept of explanation becomes a method when we add to it criteria for the discovery and evaluation of evidence; and the use of the method involves, in addition, techniques by which the evidence is collected and the criteria applied. But it also involves assumptions, and it is these, rather than criteria and techniques, that are of interest for the present discussion.

The most fundamental assumption of the genetic method may be called the "postulate of identity in development." By "identity" I mean that the same entity persists through the process of change.

The unique entity which exists at the end of the process must also have been present in some form at the beginning. A plant originates in a seed; but it is the seed of this particular plant and no other. By "development" I mean that the entity changes progressively, so that the stages of change have some kind of serial order in addition to their temporal and causal relations. It is not implied that the development is purposive, however; only that it is directional. In addition to this assumption, there is at least a tendency to postulate certain uniformities in nature to account for the uniformities in the genetic process. Some students of the history of man have spoken of the evolution of mankind and of such institutions as the family; and they have outlined the development of such concepts as "God" and "justice." Mankind, the family, and the ideas of God and of justice are each considered a single entity. Yet each has assumed various forms, and each form is to be found at different places and times in various societies. Families may be matriarchal or patriarchal, religions polytheistic or monotheistic, and cultures backward or advanced. To explain the presumed unity of the diverse historical manifestations of such an entity as the family and the recurrence of similar types, the evolutionists have assumed uniform characteristics in man and nature and uniform laws operating in different circumstances.

Explanation on a genetic basis does not imply that ultimate origins exist, though this has at times been claimed. Indeed, if existence is a single, unbroken process, there can be no ultimate origins or absolute ends of anything. All knowledge must be of a segment of the process; for inquiry proceeds extensionally through time, and time is without beginning or end. It is necessary to trace origins only as far as may be required to understand the entity or occurrence under consideration; and it is quite conceivable that we might know how a thing arose and yet not know how its origins themselves arose. Thus it might be possible to trace the roots of modern science but not to discover the first origins of human thinking; to trace the origin of man from other species but not the origins of life itself.

According to the experimental method, to know an object is to know the consequences to which it will lead, in its interactions with other things under assigned conditions, or the effects it will bring about; or, conversely, it is to know the conditions which will produce the object. In short, experimental knowledge is a knowledge of natural interactions. The possible interactions into which any natural object can enter are unlimited, and so is possible knowledge of it. But definite, limited knowledge is attained whenever we specify conditions and consequences and establish them by empirical verification. The process by which experimental knowledge is attained has sometimes been described as the sequence of observation, hypothesis, and verification. Pragmatism has shown how much these familiar words are a simplification of what really happens in inquiry and how inadequate psychologically the traditional logic was. In the first place, there must be analysis of the situation and specification of the problem which it presents, before observation in the usual sense can occur; for the orderly mind and detached attitude usually associated with this word are impossible in a situation of confusion or practical conflict. Further, to describe hypothesis simply in terms of formal reasoning suggests too purely intellectual a process and glosses over the imaginative element involved in the envisagement of alternative sets of possibilities. As for verification, the element of trial and error may be progressively reduced by the imaginative elaboration of consequences in advance, but it can never be entirely eliminated. The respective values of alternative hypotheses cannot be accurately weighed ahead of time, and verification may involve lengthy operations of great difficulty and complexity.

If experimental reasoning means the proportioning of belief to evidence, it appears to involve at least two assumptions. First, experimental knowledge is not intuitive—this is almost a tautology. Immediate knowledge of given data may or may not exist, but in any case there can be no immediate experimental knowledge of data. Moreover, experiencing a natural object and knowing it are two different things. What is given is not experimentally known, and all empirical knowledge is mediated by some kind of evidence. Second, the possibility of logically proportioning belief to evidence appears to presuppose some kind of harmony between knowledge and existence, though the proper mode of stating it is notoriously difficult. It has been stated in variations on the principle of the uniformity of nature, and it has been formulated as a principle of induction. Both have been criticized. But, whatever the best formulation may be, experimental reasoning presupposes that there is some connection between the evidence and the nature of the unobserved states of affairs concerning which we infer, such that the first provides logical ground for making assertions about the second. We have experimental knowledge when the interpretation of data is based on definite logical procedures. Knowing is an act or series of operations which establishes a relation between the datum and its interpretation, or, roughly, between percept and concept. It is a process by which belief in the future is logically grounded in the present and in past experience. Here, again, criteria and techniques must be specified, in order to determine how the method is to be applied and in order to define the meaning of logical belief. But these need not be considered here.

The place of the experimental method in the philosophy of pragmatism is too familiar to call for illustration. It is equated with empiricism and is usually described as the only possible way of acquiring knowledge of existence. The place of the genetic method is not so well known. Its principal use is in connection with the instrumentalist theory of logic.

According to this theory, thinking originated as a way of solving the problems presented by specific, environmental situations when other inherited or previously acquired modes of response proved inadequate. It presupposes that the organism has reached such a stage of complexity that its interactions with environmental circumstances are not immediate and that its environment has become sufficiently extended to permit of a distinction between the object which as end will satisfy organic needs and the means by which it can be attained. Like everything else in nature, thinking must justify its claim to continued existence by its utility. Therefore, its practical character has persisted and constitutes the element of identity which runs all through the history of thinking, or at least through all normal thinking. Thinking is problem-solving. But there has also been a progressive development of various logical habits, forms, and criteria through history as man has gradually learned to cope with existence in the hard school of experience. Men have become increasingly realistic in their dealings with situations; and, with the growth of knowledge, they have learned to gain a real security by the control of nature and to discard the devices they once used to gain a feeling of security that was only illusory.

This account of the origin and growth of logic rests on a theory of human nature according to which the need for security is inherent in man. It is as much a part of him as the fact that he is a creature living in a world of change and danger. But it can be satisfied, the theory continues, in either of two ways. One is by the slow understanding of nature through experimental intelligence and the limited but solid control that it gives. The other is through magic, dreams, ritual, authority, and all the other emotional outlets through which man expresses his hopes and fears. The second is the path men long tended, and still tend, to take, for it is easier and enables them to escape for a time from stubborn reality. And yet, though many emotionally derived ideas are not checked by facts and may superficially seem to be divorced from practice, some, at least, meet the test of utility in another way; for the dreams and fantasies which men entertain in philosophy, religion, and art constitute a world that is closer than reality to their desires, and one which they can control. And the fantasies may perform a practical function, if they are not exaggerated, through providing a satisfaction of the human need for certainty and security and so giving man confidence to face the dangers of living. This is one way of ending doubt and fixing belief; and it has been practiced not merely by scattered individuals but by entire societies.

Thus, as reflective men have observed in every age, human nature contains both rational and irrational elements. And the traditional dualisms of philosophy—between reality and appearance, mind and body, theory and practice, permanence and change, reason and sense, supernatural and natural—are really projections of this duality onto the cosmos. The problem of living is to discover how the rational can control and direct, rather than be compulsively controlled by, the irrational. And the significance of social evolution, as well as the task of pragmatism, lies precisely here; for the time has now come when it is possible for man to control not only nature but his own destiny as well. And the fantastic speculations which once had an excuse in the natural insecurity of primitive man, and perhaps gave him a courage he could not have otherwise achieved to face the dangers of his situation, are now simply escapes from reality or rationalizations of a privileged social position.

Thus the pragmatic theory of inquiry rests on propositions asserted by or implicit in the genetic method, as well as on the evidence for the validity of the experimental method. For this reason, it is important that we should be as clear as possible about their relations. They tend to be identified because both study change, and, from one point of view, this similarity sets them off from other types of inquiry. All knowledge is analytic in a broad sense, for all knowledge makes conceptual distinctions, in order to describe diverse aspects of objects. But some analyses are concerned only with structure. In contrast with them, the two methods that we are considering are concerned with natural interactions and the analysis of temporal change. Now, in determining the conditions of change, the difference between past and future is secondary, and one might easily conclude from this that the two methods are the same. For if B was conditioned by A in the past, it is reasonable to suppose that under similar circumstances A will continue to be a condition of B in the future; and we can state as an empirical generalization, "Under appropriate conditions, if A, then B."

In this respect, origins and consequences are complementary. Our logical forms and criteria are psychological and historical, both in their source and in their use. And the significant contrast in inquiry appears to be not between genetic and experimental methods but rather between logical meanings, on the one hand, and psychological origins and consequences, on the other. This is the position taken by Dewey when he speaks of "the Darwinian genetic and experimental logic."[1] Here and elsewhere he means to be giving two different names to a single method. But it is a mistake to identify the two. The identification would be correct if the difference between them lay in the fact that one is directed toward the past and the other toward the future. But this is not the important difference.

The real difference between them is that the genetic method is concerned with concrete existence, while the experimental, on the other hand, is concerned with abstract conditions. Other differences are implicit in this contrast. The genetic method arose as an attempt to explain the state of modern Western society. It was connected with the idea of progress and antedated the theory of biological evolution; but it received a fresh impetus and a new form through the application of evolutionary theory to human history. It is concerned with individual objects, whose origins it attempts to trace in unique processes of development. Its typical question is: How did this unique event or individual thing—such as modern civilization—come about? The experimental method, on the other hand, developed in the attempt to discover uniformities in nature. Its aim is to discover the conditions under which a certain type of effect will occur. It is concerned with classes of instances and with individuals only as they conform to the defining conditions of the classes involved. The genetic method seeks, and has often claimed by implication to possess, a complete explanation; for the origins out of which the object under investigation arose are as concrete as the object itself. Experiment, on the other hand, never claims to provide a complete explanation. It recognizes that the conditions which it describes are always limited in number, that other constant factors not mentioned or fully known

1. *The Influence of Darwinism on Philosophy and Other Essays*, p. 18.

are present, that additional unknown but relevant differential conditions may exist, and that there may be alternative ways of producing the same general effect. Its goal is the determination of the necessary and sufficient conditions for the occurrence of a specified result; but this is an ideal which, as it knows, can be only approximated, except for practical purposes.

The scientific study of genetics, either in biology or elsewhere, results from the application of the experimental method to the study of origins. Therefore, the genetic method, as described here, is not to be confused with the science or sciences of genetics; for as soon as the experimental method is applied to the study of origins, the investigation turns toward abstract laws and conditions of heredity, growth, or development and is no longer an attempt to explain the concrete by the concrete. Attempts to combine the two methods have been made from time to time in the social sciences, where investigators have searched for laws of social evolution, professedly by empirical methods, and at the same time have discussed the unique origins of unique entities. Whether the two methods are, in fact, compatible is, of course, a further question.

The experimental method aims at a determination of the conditions of change; it deals with causes as well as effects, conditions as well as consequences. In that sense it might also be called a "genetic" method. But this would only be renaming it, for past conditions are determined in the same way as are future consequences. And we determine conditions and consequences at the same time, in describing relational patterns that recur in similar situations. The genetic method, on the other hand, attempts to present a concrete, unique past or, rather, in most cases, a concrete, unique process which has been occurring in the past and is still going on. It actually does this by the use of abstract concepts, as when it enumerates stages of historical development; but, in effect, it aims at a total reconstruction of what has been.

When sequences of events recur, we can have experimental knowledge of the past. If we have observed events of types A and B in certain relations, then, when we observe an instance of B, we may infer that it is probably the effect of, or partly determined by, a previous A. Thus we reason from the present to the past. But in such cases the study of origins is not carried on by a distinct mode of inquiry; it is pursued by the same method and subject to the same criteria that are employed in studying consequences. In both cases we reason by analogy from observed instances to unobserved instances which are held to resemble them in significant ways. We assume in the one case that past processes, in the other that future processes, are analogous to the observed present or to the segment of existence which includes our data.

This is the case in the biological sciences, in which many members of the same species are observed and the species is asserted to be part of a general course of evolution, the outlines of which are inferred from directly observed evidence. It is assumed that the processes, tendencies, and laws which characterized the past were similar to those observed and inferred to be operative today. Here the abstractions of experimental reasoning and the uniqueness of a single, developmental process meet. But the biologist does not consider the species a real entity, as the organisms he observes and dissects are real. Nor does he, as a scientist, consider life itself to be a single entity—as the social evolutionist does in the case of civilization and mankind. He considers his theories to be the best interpretation of a unique past that has been made so far; yet they are only abstract theories, not the reality itself or a copy of it. The same holds of every historical science.

There was a unique course of past history, just as there is now a unique present. But, unlike the present, the past can no longer be given. And even if it could be given, it would not thereby be known by the experimental method, for which having and knowing are different. But the genetic method claims, in effect, to reconstruct the past and thereby enable us to know it in its concrete particularity. It does not, of course, profess to include all the details, but it does claim to give us the unique quality we should have had if we had lived through it. It also presents its account as science. If its claim is valid, it enables us to "have" and to know the past at the same time. Is this possible?

The difficulty of knowing unique objects is that scientific knowledge seems to involve assigning an object to a class and hence dealing with it in terms of its similarity to others, for scientific knowledge is verifiable and probable. But verifiability or confirmability presupposes the possibility of recurrent, similar cases; and an event may be called "probable" only if it is considered as a member of a class of events. The social evolutionists met this difficulty by basing their conclusions on the study of various societies, institutions, customs, and beliefs. They described many similar instances of each type of fact, such as polytheism, agricultural economy, and the matriarchal family—presumably comparable to the many instances of a biological species. This body of data provided the basis for inductive generalization; and, by comparing their instances, they constructed a hypothetical and typical course of development. There is another difficulty in the study of origins: in many cases they are unrecorded, and either the surviving traces are slight, or there is nothing discoverable left. The origins of the family, the processes of human thinking, and the idea of justice are simply unknown. Social evolutionists have attempted to meet this difficulty by formulating a hypothesis concerning the course of evolution and verifying it by showing that observable facts correspond to some of its implications. If history and prehistory had followed the course outlined, the result would be the present as it actually is; therefore, it is probable that the hypothesis is correct. This is usual scientific procedure. It often happens in the study of nature that an entity is not directly observable, and its existence is inferred from its effects.

But, in following this line of reasoning, the genetic method really deserts the concrete event for abstract types; for the institutions, customs, concepts, and attitudes which it describes are simply forms or patterns, abstracted from the stream of history or applied to it. Instead of studying the unique origins of a unique historical occurrence, it considers properties and complexes of properties which recur or may recur at different times and places in similar instances. And, in abstracting the properties from the concrete event, it loses the uniqueness of the latter in class concepts. In short, it adopts the procedure of the experimental method. Moreover, classifications are relative to purposes, and the same object can always be classified in many ways, from different points of view. Therefore, the typical forms and hypothetical stages of social evolution cannot claim to be so fully real as is the actual, historical process. They are merely one possible interpretation of the past. In the case of the experimental method, the purpose of the classifications of events is clear. It is the prediction of the future, and it is justified by its success. The question naturally suggests itself: What is the purpose of the kind of classification made in following the genetic method, and what is the warrant for its acceptance?

Its purpose is to demonstrate a progressive development in man, from the beginnings of his existence up to the present. To carry out this purpose, a hypothetical, imaginary scheme of development was constructed in terms of stages of culture which were ordered serially with reference to the goal of evolution. The goal was defined in various ways—as maximum human happiness, altruism, mental development, adjustment to the environment, the development of the higher powers and capacities of man. But the reality of progress seemed so clear that the definition of its goal was of only minor interest.

The older genetic theory has been discredited by the discovery of facts which contradict it. Known differences between observed cultures are incompatible with the laws of uniform social development and are evidence against the existence of similar uniformities between the observable present and the unobservable past. Nevertheless, the theory still persists. And this is not strange; for the truth is that its basis was always the optimism of the modern world rather than logical evidence. That being the case, it might reasonably have presented itself as an ideal and goal of human action; and this, of course, is what it really was. But such was the temper of the period that the ideal could gain acceptance only in the guise of a scientific description of facts.

In its account of man and his experience, as we have seen, pragmatism offers another version of origins; but it is like the old one in its general outline. On the basis of its theory of human nature and needs, it interprets history in terms of the development, spread, and application of reason in human life. The goal of the process is the control by man of nature and himself. The stages of this development are not, and need not be, described in detail; classifications are never final or of first importance. Nor has history by any means been a smooth, even advance; it has been interrupted and has had periods of regression. But the general direction, the achievements, and the over-all trend are clear. They are to be read in the history of culture, science, and the arts and in the story of man's conquest of fear, ignorance, and superstition.

This scheme of development is based on selected features of the present and past, and it is substantiated by observable facts because they were chosen to fit it. The criterion by which the stages of mankind are ordered is technological achievement and the ability to predict events. It is certainly possible to interpret history in terms of these factors; but there are also many other possible criteria, and justification must be given for choosing this one rather than some other. The justification offered is that this one explains the facts better. But this is not satisfactory, for the criterion has not been independently confirmed, since the facts were selected to fit it. The old genetic theory purported to explain the present by the past. This one reverses the procedure and explains the past by the present. The principle is the same in both cases, and the question is how far it can take us toward historical understanding. We do not gain a very complete understanding of a thing if we are told only what it came from; we do not understand contemporary institutions and beliefs when we are informed that they are the last members in a long evolutionary series of different forms. No more do we understand adequately some past set of beliefs and institutions if we are

EXISTENCE AND INQUIRY

told that they constitute an early member of a series which leads up to the present.

Every age and every culture must be understood on its own terms. The question to be asked finally is What is it?—and it is not answered by saying what something else is. The genetic method, however, evaluates history by external criteria; that is the fallacy. In postulating certain forms of human relations and thought, it abstracts institutions and beliefs from their own context and classifies them in terms of the very different context of the interpreter.

Such a charge, of course, raises a crucial question. In the last analysis, must we not interpret everything from our own historical perspective? And, if so, does not the charge imply that we can understand only ourselves, a conclusion both futile and in conflict with obvious facts? I do not think so. We can live only in our own perspective; but it does not follow that we must interpret other perspectives in terms of our own. The interpretation of history by imposed classifications is inadequate; but it does not follow that we can understand only ourselves unless all knowledge is artificial classification. And if, as I should maintain, it is not necessary to view an age merely in the light of its similarity or dissimilarity to others, it is possible to understand the past on its own terms. All knowledge involves the use of concepts, but it does not follow from this that all knowledge involves the notion of a group of similar individuals, either actual or possible. Furthermore, it is possible to abstract concepts from, as well as to apply them to, subject matter; or, rather, it is possible to abstract a structure, corresponding to which we formulate a conceptual definition. So far as classes are involved in knowledge of unique individuals, a natural classification—as contrasted with an artificial one—presupposes exactly this procedure of abstracting a significant structure.

It is obvious that men in the past did predict and control events, with varying degrees of success. But the question is whether this is what they were trying to do. The fact is that control of nature was often incidental to another goal or kind of activity; and in such cases, to describe the activity as "control" is to apply categories inappropriate and foreign to it. To take another illustration, there have always been individuals in society, with various social relations and attitudes. But it does not follow that we can understand them by applying such categories as egoism and altruism, competition and co-operation; for it may well be that the concepts, attitudes, and goals employed in such an interpretation are not parts of the way of life and experience of the men we are describing. The desire to control natural events presupposes a certain sense of separation between man and nature; altruism and co-operation are meaningful only if there are not simply individuals but also an individualism of a certain sort to overcome. Nor can it properly be said that these societies had a certain character and were tending in a certain direction, though their members were unaware of the fact; for to make men the tools of unknown forces is to rob the concept of progress of its meaning. And to impose on a culture an external criterion, which it would not understand or accept if it did understand and which has meaning only for the inquirer, is highly arbitrary. The genetic method interprets the past in terms of experimental knowledge and shows that there has been progress—in experimental knowledge.

But it is not merely the past or even other cultures that are involved. The question arises as to how far our own society and experience can be correctly interpreted in terms of the same criterion. We begin with ourselves and find that man today is the tool-making animal, the technologist and experimenter. We then apply this conception of man to other cultures and ages. Thus the genetic method abstracts experimental thinking from the present and takes it as the clue to history. But is the abstraction, important as it may be, the essence of knowledge and thinking in the present? If knowledge is defined in terms of the experimental method, it will, of course, follow that all knowledge is experimental. And since there is unquestionably more experimental knowledge today than ever before, it also follows that there has been progress in this respect. But it is not clear what further conclusions can be drawn.

There can be no quarrel with this definition of knowledge for specific purposes, nor can anyone reasonably object to the classification of historical data in the same terms, for some stated purpose. But it does not follow that, because definitions or classifications are useful for one purpose, they are valid or useful generally. The test of both is utility; but before the test can be applied, we must know for what purpose they are to be used.

The purpose of definitions, concepts, and inquiry in philosophy is philosophical understanding or the solution of philosophical problems. The crucial point is the identification of the problems. They can be defined in terms of the methods of philosophy; or they can be defined independently and the relevance of any particular method determined accordingly; or, finally, problems and method can be considered together. Since there is a sense in which definitions depend on choice or stipulation rather than upon argument, let us approach this matter by examining the consequences which follow the acceptance of the genetic and experimental methods as determining, or at least limiting, the nature and scope of philosophy. The influence of both has been toward the restriction of philosophy to criticism and the exclusion of constructive knowledge and theory from its proper activity.

In the modern world the conception of philosophy as criticism has spread with the increasing stress on empiricism, for empiricism has often been taken to imply that the function of philosophy is cathartic; it is a purging of the mind by the elimination of unempirical notions and beliefs. Thus the first task of philosophy in the age of reason was held to be the elimination of superstition and prejudice; later it became the elimination of meaningless terms and statements. This program presupposes such concepts as "superstition," "prejudice," and "meaninglessness." These have in part been supplied, of course, by the experimental method. But in part they are based on the genetic method; for, since social evolution has been progressive, according to this view, the beliefs and attitudes characteristic of the earlier stages of history are by definition superstitious and unempirical, or are likely to be so. Perhaps we can even say that these qualities tend to increase in direct proportion to our distance from the present, if we do not interpret the statement too rigidly, and remember, for instance, that the Middle Ages constituted a regression from the earlier, high state of Greek civilization. The tendency of history has been, on the whole, according to this theory, from emotional escapism to intelligent realism and from the control of man by emotion to his intelligent control and direction of his emotions.

The question I wish to raise here, without discussing it in any detail, is whether this notion of history does provide a sound basis for philosophical criticism or whether, on the contrary, it is not itself a superstition, based on untenable assumptions of the last century. We cannot compare directly the experiences of present and past men. But no one skeptically inclined can overlook in the contemporary world grounds for doubt as to whether modern man is less emotional and more rational than his ancestors were and whether these elements of his nature are in a healthier relation to one another. And, so far as the genetic method rests on such dubious psychological guesses, one can reasonably question whether it is firm enough to provide a basis for a philosophy that is really empirical. In short, philosophical criticism should be directed upon, rather than based on, the genetic method.

The spread of the experimental method has also contributed to the identification of philosophy with criticism. In a nontechnical sense we experiment in everyday life; in a more rigorous sense, experimentation is the method of the sciences of nature. The philosopher may be said to experiment in the broad sense; but he does so as a common man rather than as a philosopher, and whatever knowledge he acquires in this way can hardly be called "philosophical" knowledge. Even if philosophy is regarded as an exposition and defense of common sense, it must go beyond common-sense experiment to an analysis of a peculiar kind, in order to achieve any positive results of its own. And in the rigorous sense philosophy does not experiment at all. Therefore, when meaning and truth are defined in terms of experimental consequences, empirical knowledge is, in effect, identified with experimental knowledge of a nonphilosophical kind. Or, if philosophical inquiry does yield knowledge, it will be knowledge of a second order; it will be restricted to theories about the nature of knowledge and method, meaning and truth. It will be knowledge about knowledge. It is in this sense that pragmatism was called a new name for old ways of thinking; for the identification of knowledge with experimentation—whether under the name of pragmatism, instrumentalism, empiricism, operationalism, or something else—is the last stage in a development that reaches all through modern times.

Thus the implication of the two methods is a restriction of philosophy, largely if not entirely, to a critical and negative function. But pragmatism includes another and more positive notion of philosophical inquiry. Instead of the concept of consequences, it takes as its starting-point the principle that all categories are to be found within the act and situation. It begins with a concept of existence rather than a method and regards inquiry as an analysis of existence. The question philosophy asks is What is it? rather than How did it originate? or What are its conceivable consequences? Since existence is not a finished state of being but a becoming, the analysis will also reveal origins and consequences, but these will enter as aspects of present actuality rather than as independent factors. So conceived, philosophical inquiry has a positive, constructive function and leads to philosophical knowledge.

This aspect of pragmatism has remained subordinate and partly implicit. The reason is that it appears to lead in two different directions, which are determined by the idealistic and naturalistic components of pragmatism, respectively. Therefore, so far as these represent the basic metaphysical alternatives, it is necessary to make a choice between them. If we follow idealism, philosophy is an analysis of experience; if we follow naturalism, on the other hand, philosophy is an analysis of natural existence. It may well be that it is a mistake to formulate the problem of existence in these terms. Indeed, I think that this is the case and that the future of philosophy depends on abandoning them and the metaphysical dualism from which they arose; for, while they involve real philosophical issues, they also conceal unreal problems and dilemmas, arising from false assumptions and dead controversies; and, more often than not, the latter obscure the former. Nevertheless, they have exerted a tremendous influence on recent philosophy, including pragmatism. And in practice, though not in strict logic, they have often seemed to imply a forced choice between knowledge and existence: philosophy is either a theory of knowledge and experience or a description of existence, either epistemology or ontology, but not both. This is another false antithesis. The real significance of pragmatism lies in its attempt to escape from these dilemmas and achieve a fresh orientation for constructive philosophy. And it has achieved the fresh orientation just so far as it has succeeded in throwing off the old categories.

In accordance with this interpretation, I shall urge the following points: (1) Inquiry presupposes an antecedent object, and to account for it we must begin with real existence. This object cannot be defined by knowledge; on the contrary, knowledge is intelligible only in terms of it. There is the object of inquiry as well as the object of knowledge, and the two concepts are distinct. The experimental method describes the object of predictive knowledge; but in its philosophical form it fails to account for the object of inquiry, because it denies antecedent existence. (2) In addition to consequences, pragmatism recognizes antecedent or independent existence, for the most part in naturalistic terms. But its notion of antecedent existence is incompatible with most interpretations of the method of consequences because these two elements have been so largely shaped by rival philosophical traditions. And its concept of existence as process is vitiated by untenable assumptions derived from Darwinism and the genetic method. (3) The chief significance of pragmatism lies in its emphasis on the present rather than in the method of consequences. (4) There is need for a new concept of philosophical inquiry, as an analysis or description of existence, based squarely on the principle that present existence as the object of inquiry is given not merely for feeling but for knowing.

The notion that there is some kind of opposition between having and knowing, given and interpretation, or concrete existence and conceptual knowledge is mistaken.

I shall not attempt to develop the last two points but shall merely indicate their relevance to the explicit pragmatic concept of inquiry, defined in terms of consequences.

3. The Notion of Consequences

The rule for the determination of clear meaning was stated by Peirce in these words: "Consider what effects, that might conceivably have practical bearings, we conceive the object of our conception to have. Then, our conception of these effects is the whole of our conception of the object."[2] The idea of an object is the idea of its effects, of what it will do and of what will happen to it under various conditions. The idea or conception is a definition or a set of properties and relationships. In a more extended sense, it is also the set of implications which, as we say, follow from its definition.

But we can also treat the idea itself as an object and ask what effects it will have under the condition that someone believes or entertains it. The idea, like the object, will have effects, for, as a habit of acting, it is a natural object.

Let us use the neutral word "consequences" to refer to either the logical implications or the natural effects of an idea, or to both together. The two classes—implications and effects—are mutually exclusive. Implication is a formal notion, having to do with the content of a concept or a proposition or with what "follows" from them. On any theory, these are not subject to change. We may accept or reject, make or discover, use or define, concepts; but a given concept has a changeless identity and does not alter, for if it did, it would no longer be the same concept. The same holds of a proposition. Effects, on the other hand, fall within the sphere of events. It is the difference between being and becoming. But, al-

---

2. *Collected Papers,* ed. Hartshorne and Weiss (Cambridge, 1931-35), Vol. V, ¶ 402 ("How To Make Our Ideas Clear").

though they are different, logical implications and natural events may meet in a single locus; for behavior, which has causes and effects, may also be logical. In view of this fact, let us divide the various possible consequences of ideas along different lines into the logical and the psychological.

By the first we shall understand the implications of ideas or their formal structure, together with their embodiment in acts and habits. It is logical consequences in this sense which are intended when it is said that ideas are "plans of action." By "psychological consequences" we shall understand all the differences, both logical and nonlogical, that an idea makes in the existence of the individual who holds it. They might also be called "existential" or "human" consequences. These two classes, unlike the others, are not mutually exclusive. The second includes the first, for logical consequences are also psychological, since we trace implications by mental processes and sometimes act in accordance with them as suggested by circumstances. But not all the psychological effects of an idea are logical. A concept may arouse hope or fear, pleasure or pain, in us; but these effects are not logical in the sense of being part of the consequences stipulated by the concept. Logical consequences are one division of psychological ones. Let us examine the two more closely.

The logical consequences of an idea comprise its implications and the habits of action to which it gives rise. These are not the same but are closely related, according to pragmatism; they are distinguishable but not separable. The implications of a concept are what follows from the definition. We may define an oak tree by such characteristics as type of bark, kind and shape of leaves, and their arrangement on the branch. Such a definition is neither true nor false, we say. That is, it is not a statement about nature but the analysis of a concept. If we wished, the word "oak" might be made to refer to some other concept instead of the one we have chosen—to a larger or smaller or otherwise different set of characteristics. To call a tree an oak is to imply that it has the characteristics stated or contained in the definition; and the implications may be made explicit in propositions. If this is an oak, its leaves will have such and such a shape: thus we apply the concept. The characteristics are part of the effects, in the sense of the rule which says that our idea of a thing is our idea of its "sensible effects," of which leaf shape is one. How much we include in a concept is a matter determined by explicit definition, tacit usage, and practical utility. Our concept of an oak may include the fact that it will make good firewood; on the other hand, we may consider firewood a second concept. But leaf shape is also "another" concept. How much we include in the relational structure of concepts that we associate with the word "oak" depends on choice and on usage.

A definition is not a habit, but its use leads to a habit. Indeed, to have a concept at all is to acquire at least the beginning of a habit, even though it be only a tendency to picture in our minds and classify the tree we saw yesterday. Without such beginnings, we have a verbal formula rather than a concept. But habits are of many different kinds, and practical bearings in the restricted sense may arise only under special circumstances. The fact that hardwood burns well may lead us to set to work at once, chop down the oak, and saw it up; but the rule does not say we will do so. It only says **that we would tend to do so under suitable circumstances.**

The notion of logical consequences is embodied in several familiar statements. An idea is a plan of action; all distinctions of meaning are possible differences of practice; concepts are instruments by which we adapt ourselves to reality and pursue our goals. These statements suggest that, for pragmatism, formal concept and psychological embodiment are somehow two sides of a single fact. The relationship can be expressed in several ways. The ideal intensional implications of an empirical concept are endless, just as the effects of the empirical object in its natural interactions are endless. The same is true of the corresponding habit, which applies to an endless number of possible situations. But the concepts which men entertain and use are, in fact, always limited, and in two ways. They are general: they cover only certain types of condition and leave the details beyond these indeterminate. They are vague: there are instances concerning which they are undecided—there will be cases in which our criteria do not enable us to say whether a tree is an oak or not. Habits share the same or analogous limitations; that is why we cannot live by habit alone. This close relation between concept and habit might be stated in terms of the traditional distinction between form and matter. An empirical concept is a form or relational pattern; a habit is its material embodiment. We find conceptual form embodied in matter, and biological matter exemplifying form in its behavior.

The contrast between form and matter distinguishes concept from habit. Their connection may be illustrated by the old distinction between what an idea is and what it means. The idea is a relational, conceptual pattern and also a psychological behavior pattern; it means or refers to sensible phenomena. The double pattern might be called, by an extension of meaning, the "connotation" of the idea; the sensible phenomena, its "denotation." The double pattern points to, or is a sign of, or terminates in, sensible data; and it must include some criterion for determining to which of the many sense presentations of experience it does refer. Conversely, the data are, or, rather, become, signs of the pattern when they are interpreted. Thus we say, "That looks like a plane," interpreting the speck in the sky in terms of a certain structural and behavioral pattern; and we act accordingly. A pragmatist may stress the general pattern, or he may stress the particular actions and sensible effects which it denotes in a given situation. He may regard form as more important than matter, or conversely. He may be primarily interested in connotation or, on the other hand, in denotation. Here there is room for difference of opinion. But if he accepts the notion of consequences, he must hold that the two are inseparable in the last analysis.

The psychological consequences of an idea are of various sorts. Suppose that an economist anticipates a social catastrophe, such as a world-wide depression. He will form a more or less clear and detailed picture of the probable state of affairs which the predicted event will bring about. But, being human, he will also be affected with feelings of melancholy, pain, and insecurity, to a degree which depends on the breadth of his human sympathies and the vividness of his imagination. He will also be moved to act in a direction and with a skill and vigor which are dependent on his abilities and personality. These are consequences of the believed idea on the man. Suppose, on the contrary, that he expects an era of peace and prosperity. He will be equally affected, but in an opposite way. Instead of pain, he will experience contentment and a feeling of security. Instead of warning the public of what is to come and exerting his energies to ward off the disaster, he will make plans of a different sort and begin to carry them out. If ideas are doubted or contemplated rather than believed, their general effects may be much less; but they will still be present; for, just as we draw on past experience in predicting the future, so is, for instance, the expectation of good fortune or disaster tinged with emotional qualities derived from experiences already undergone. And the same is probably true, to a degree, of all ideas in their relations to all sides of our natures. How far these consequences extend and how intense they may be are not important for the argument.

James pointed out that there is a sentiment of rationality in us, a sense of the intelligibility of the situation and the sufficiency of the present, marked by subjective feelings of peace, rest, and the absence of need for anything further in the way of explanation. To experience this sentiment is to believe, to cease doubting and questioning. He argued also that any philosophic idea which arouses this sentiment in, and is accepted by, many people must make appeal to all the important aspects of our natures—emotional, volitional, moral, and religious, as well as logical and narrowly practical. He was speaking of philosophies, but what he said may be extended to all ideas. And whether he was correct about the conditions for acceptance or not, it is clearly true that ideas do affect us in many ways. All these ways together make up the significance which the idea has for us.

No classification of psychological consequences can claim finality. It must depend on a distinction of the various aspects of experience, and no enumeration of these can be complete, or perhaps even satisfactory as far as it goes. However, we can formulate a triple classification which will be adequate for the present purpose. The conceived consequences of an idea may be divided into (*a*) logical or intellectual predictions of what will occur under assigned conditions—ideas are hypotheses or signs; (*b*) purposes entertained—this is suggested by the descriptions of ideas as tools and instruments, demands, claims, intentions, and plans of action; (*c*) satisfactions emotionally felt or anticipated. These kinds of consequences are obviously related in experience. For example, the occurrence of a predicted event is accompanied by a feeling of satisfaction or intellectual fulfilment; and both the prediction and its positive or negative verification may be related to practical purposes. In terms of our earlier division, of these three classes, the first, *a,* is the logical consequences, while all three taken together are the psychological consequences.

Again, *a* might be called the "theoretical" consequences of the idea, while *b* and *c* together constitute its practical meaning. The theoretical or logical meaning of fire, for example, might include the conditions that rapid oxidation occur, that a certain temperature be attained, and that the process be characterized by flame, not merely glowing heat. Its practical meaning, on the other hand, might consist partly in the fact that it enables us to boil water, cook our food, and warm ourselves. We do not define fire in these terms, but it is satisfying to our active natures; we experience it as an adequate means to the fulfilment of ends. Its practical meaning lies, further, in the feelings of security, contentment, pleasure, pain, and terror which it arouses. The idea is the set of conceived theoretical consequences, but it also has practical ones.

The notion of consequences also provides the basis for a theory of truth. If meaning is conceived consequences, truth is actual ones. An idea, or the proposition which explicates it, may be called true when its verifiability has been established by the observation of enough of the conceived consequences to make the occurrence of any of the others under assigned conditions probable to the degree

EXISTENCE AND INQUIRY

specified in the notion of truth. Theoretical truth will depend on the occurrence of logical consequences, and practical truth will depend on the occurrence of practical consequences.

The question may be raised as to whether a concept is ever completely or definitively verified. The answer depends on how we interpret the relation between the general pattern and particular, sensible effects. If verification depends on the former, it can never be complete, for the pattern of the concept constitutes an intension or connotation, whose extension or denotation stretches away endlessly into possible future experience. If, however, it depends only on specified, particular consequences, then complete verification is possible and takes place if the particular consequences occur. But can the general rule and the particular consequences be separated to the degree that this would imply? There is pretty general agreement that they are inseparable in theoretical, empirical knowledge and that certain knowledge is not attainable within a limited series of confirming situations. The difficulty chiefly, though not entirely, concerns what we have called "practical consequences" and truth.

Let us suppose that a man is driving to New York and finds the road blocked at a certain point, with a sign stating that a bridge is out. He remembers seeing a side road to the right some distance back and, from topographical and other indications, infers that it will eventually take him to a junction with the highway again. He turns his car around, drives back, and tries the detour. He finds the highway. The problem, it may be said, is solved, and the idea completely verified.

But whether it is completely verified depends on an important problem, the solution of which is by no means obvious. Thinking, it is often said, is concerned with specific, problematic situations. Its origin is practical, in such efforts as those of the organism to find food; and it never entirely loses this character. Therefore, when the highway is reached, the problem is solved. But to say this is to imply that there is a fundamental difference between theoretical and practical judgments and that, although the former have endless implications, those of the latter are finite and exhaustible. This is a possible position, certainly; but one should be clear, before adopting it, that it involves the acceptance of two different meanings for empirical knowledge. We may know something practically, or we may know it theoretically; and on this theory neither implies the other. The word "practical" in this context itself has two possible meanings, one of them referring to what we have called "theoretical knowledge." First, it may refer to purposive activity; and, second, it may refer to the rough knowledge associated with everyday familiarity and use, as distinguished from the knowledge of the expert or scientist. But the difficulty is the same, no matter which of the two meanings is intended: practical knowledge and theoretical knowledge, as we have been using these terms, are independent; and a proposition may be true in one sense but not in the other. One may have practical knowledge without theoretical, because the limited consequences sufficient to establish the former may be insufficient for the latter. And one may have theoretical knowledge without practical: we may know theoretically without being able to accomplish our purposes or validate our practical beliefs, and we may have an abstract knowledge without possessing the intimate familiarity of the practical worker or craftsman.

The problem of the driver, it may be said, is to reach the highway beyond the road block, and that is clearly particular. But his problem is, rather, to reach his destination. And are we sure that his destination is the city? It is certainly more than a geographical location. It may be that the man is not driving to New York at all, except in an incidental sense; his real purpose, let us say, is to meet a friend, whom he may find by chance on a wrong detour, the place of meeting being quite incidental. In other words, a purpose involves generality and is not exhausted in any one particular act—for the meeting of the friend, too, is part of something more. Purpose derives its generality from the conceptual element that it includes; and, unless it does include such an element, the word is misapplied. A purpose is accomplished rather than verified. Yet its accomplishment involves a practical judgment, and this judgment requires verification with respect to its practical consequences.

EXISTENCE AND INQUIRY

Unless these consequences are restricted to a specific sensory experience, such as a feeling of satisfaction, they will stretch out indefinitely into the future. If the purpose of the meeting is the performance of a friendly act, the meaning of friendship itself, or of a friendly act, will call for further verification, in order that the purpose may be accomplished.

Something similar is true of feeling. Let us suppose that we doubt the integrity of some individual. We say to ourselves, "This situation is the test; if he meets it, I shall feel such absolute confidence in him that it can never be shaken, no matter what happens." The test is met. But can a feeling have such finality? If the doubt exists, it cannot be removed in this way, for there is generality in feeling, too, when it contains a conceptual element. A feeling based on the empirical evidence of a class of data is inseparable from logical implications; and if the evidence constitutes a verification, these implications carry it on to further events. We may have confidence in people for years, only to be betrayed by them in the end; or consider them untrustworthy, only to find that they were worthy of trust all along.

In other words, whether theoretical or practical, verification is endless. To carry out a rational purpose involves unlimited acts, to verify a sentiment involves unlimited experiences. If the present situation presents us with problems which carry us beyond it into the future, there is no point where we can stop. Of course, we also have limited needs, ends, and desires which may be satisfied within a limited period of time—a minute, a day, a year. I now intend to open the door, and I do open it; I intend to write a letter tomorrow, and I do write it. My practical acts are completed. But it is better in such cases to speak of expectations and needs and of their fulfilment and to use terms such as "manipulation" and "habitual behavior" than to speak of complete verification of a practical idea over a period of time. Limited purposes may be achieved, consistently with this theory, only if the purpose is a specific limited experience. But a rational purpose directed on existence and reaching into the future could never be fully accomplished, for purpose, so far as it is rational, is not merely accompanied by a judgment but actually includes a conceptual factor. This much, perhaps, we can say, without attempting to deal with the difficult subject of practical judgments. And so we will say, categorically, that all experimental knowledge rests on partial verification or confirmation.

However, it is conceivable that some problems are soluble and knowledge attainable within the present and without reference to the future. Everything has effects, it is true; and all empirical statements, unless their reference is explicitly limited to a definite sense presentation, have endless implications. But it does not follow that the effects are necessary for knowledge. If they are not, verification in its usual sense will not always be essential for knowledge, either. This would, of course, mean the abandonment of the notion of consequences as definitive of all meaning and truth. And it would mean that the important contrast in knowledge, or one important contrast, would be not between theoretical and practical knowledge but between the present and what goes beyond it. But, whether such a position is accepted or not, it seems clear that to distinguish between theoretical and practical knowledge on the ground that the latter has a finality which the former lacks is to invite difficulties.

The rule for clear meaning stated above was formulated solely with reference to logical consequences. And, with the one important exception of William James, pragmatism has continued to define both meaning and truth in these terms. But if pragmatism is identified with logical consequences, its philosophical significance will be rather narrowly restricted, for it will in effect be identified with the experimental method. Because he accepted the restriction, Peirce went so far as to say that pragmatism solves no real problems but only enables us to eliminate unreal ones. Its purpose is the clarification of meaning. This is certainly one central function of philosophy. But it may be questioned whether it is the only one, or even the primary one; and Peirce himself did not so regard it. Traditionally, philosophy has aimed at breadth as well as clarity, and the attainment of the latter has been regarded by the great figures as the preliminary to a constructive interpretation or synthesis.

The breadth was introduced into pragmatism by James, when he widened the notion of consequences to include all the aspects of experience. A similar extension of meaning had occurred earlier when romanticism revolted against the limitation of the term "experience" in the eulogistic sense to the spheres of science and reason; and the causes of the revolt were very largely the same in the two cases. The effect of the change, in James, is to shift the emphasis from the future consequences of an idea to its present effects on the believer. The function of ideas is to harmonize conflicting tendencies and opinions, with a minimum of disturbance to the individual. Consequently, the idea which gains acceptance is the one which provides the greatest present satisfaction. However, in the attempt to formulate the notion of truth psychologically, in human terms, James at times notoriously confused logical implications and practical effects. There are historical causes which explain why the confusion arose; but that does not make it any the less serious.

Instrumentalism may be described as an attempt to remove the confusion and the conflict without sacrificing the breadth. Dewey clearly and consistently adheres to the earlier definition of consequences; yet his conception of pragmatism is, in a fundamental and inclusive way, humanistic. The conceived logical consequences of a concept, as a hypothesis about existence, constitute its theoretical meaning. But if it yields knowledge, it also has a wider human significance in the practical effects that it may bring about in human lives and experience. In instrumentalism, too, the ultimate significance of ideas lies in the contribution which they make to the organization and harmony of the present; for ideas refer to the present situation. The solution of a theoretical problem involves the resolution of conflicting elements in the immediate problematic situation; and an analogous resolution occurs when the problem and solution are practical. However, although instrumentalism avoids the confusion of theoretical and practical consequences, there is another difficulty implicit in it. Not all problems, either theoretical or practical, are actually soluble in the present. And, so far as thinking is instrumental, present intelligent action will in some respect be a means to future ends. But there are present ends, as well as future ones; and this fact will sometimes result in a conflict between the competing demands of the future and the present.

The contrast of theoretical and practical consequences has played a large part in the development of pragmatism. It reflects in part the duality of the experimental and the genetic methods; for the concept of theoretical consequences is really an interpretation of the experimental method; while the notion of practical consequences—and, in fact, the whole program of interpreting ideas in terms of human needs, satisfactions, and acts—stems from the evolutionary naturalism which also finds expression in the genetic method. The contrast also reflects the difference between pragmatism as an experimental logic, on the one hand, and as a naturalistic theory of human existence, on the other. Finally, it also explains to some extent the two conflicting tendencies to interpret experience sometimes in terms of the future and at others in terms of the present.

All these distinctions are, of course, valid and important. The problem is to describe them in such a way that their partial character is made clear, so that they do not harden into the kind of antitheses which create specious but serious difficulties for philosophy. The importance of the concept of the situation lies precisely here. It provides a core, around which the various distinctions group themselves and in terms of which they are related. But to recognize the central place of this concept is, of course, to relegate the notion of consequences to a secondary position.

Let us consider the phases of the problem in the order indicated: (a) logical consequences; (b) total psychological consequences; (c) instrumentalism; and, finally, (d) the relevance of the concept of the situation to the subject of inquiry.

4. Logical Consequences

In discussing logical consequences, it is important to distinguish between two different interpretations of the notion, which may be called the "restricted" and the "unrestricted" or "general." In the restricted sense the concept of logical consequences is simply the theoretical formulation of the experimental method. It is entirely compatible with, although it does not imply, a realistic philosophy of nature, which holds that the objects of inquiry exist independent of, and antecedent to, inquiry. Experimentation is a natural activity, carried on by the natural individual, working in an environment, usually with the aid of some kind of apparatus or tools. But, in defining operationally the concepts employed in experiment, it is not necessary to hold that apparatus, environment, and organism must also be defined operationally. Or, if the attempt is made to do so, they may be assigned additional characteristics which are not operationally defined. Moreover, the theory only states how empirical knowledge is acquired; it says nothing positive about the nature of the knowledge that may result from the employment of the method. This, like the nature of existent objects, is simply a further question.

In the unrestricted or general sense, the theory of logical consequences defines not only a method but also the nature of empirical objects and the meaning of truth. It becomes the basis of all theoretical philosophy—theory of knowledge, philosophy of nature, metaphysics, and every branch which purports to say anything about existence. The restricted theory presupposes a distinction between the process of acquiring knowledge and the result and between inquiry and its objects, which may exist independently. The unrestricted theory denies the ultimate validity of these distinctions. It holds, on the contrary, that knowledge cannot be separated from the activities by which it is gained and tested and that cognitive objects must be defined in terms of the cognitive process. Both British sensationalism and German idealism have contributed to the abandonment of the distinctions; for both have stressed the

PRAGMATISM

mental factor or the interpretive character of knowing to the point where inquiry and knowing in the end define their own objects and the independent existent has disappeared.

The unrestricted theory of logical consequences has many forms and goes by many names in contemporary philosophy, but they all have one trait in common: they define the actual object in terms of possible experience, instead of explaining the possibility of experience by an actual object. Thus they scale down existence to the size of knowledge. At the same time, the unrestricted theory as it appears in pragmatism does, as we shall see, presuppose independent and antecedent existence because it places inquiry in both a naturalistic and a social setting. This presupposition does not accord with the demands of the theory itself.

In this section we shall be concerned with the general theory. The restricted theory is essential to the understanding of empirical knowledge. But I shall urge that the general theory is mistaken in its explicit or implicit claim to be the basis of all philosophy. The issue is partly one of definition; and, so far as that is the case, all that is possible is to point out what follows from different conceptions of philosophy. The general theory holds that existence can be only experimentally defined and known. From this it follows that the description of existence is not the proper business of philosophy but belongs to the sciences, which apply the experimental method systematically, and to everyday life, which applies it unsystematically; and it also follows that, roughly speaking, philosophy is an analysis or description of knowing rather than of the objects of knowledge. The question to be raised is whether such a division between knowledge and its objects can be consistently maintained. The alternative, which I should maintain, is that philosophy is primarily concerned with the nature of existence and that knowing is only one of its concerns, though certainly a very important one. It should be possible to begin philosophizing at either end, with either knowing or objects; and the study of either should lead eventually to the other. But a radical theory of logical consequences, if consistently adhered to, rules out such reciprocity because it holds that the interpretive and practical nature of knowledge makes impossible any apprehension of objects except in terms of experimental knowing. The question we shall consider is how successful such a theory is in getting on from knowing to real objects of knowledge. This much is clear: it does not start with them.

The general theory of logical consequences begins with the notion of a perceptual given, which is described by various terms: the given, the had, immediacy, feeling, the qualitative, ineffable, aesthetic, sensuous, or concrete. All these terms agree—and, indeed, this is their point—in taking experience as the datum of philosophy. And they are intended to denote the raw, thick experience which precedes intellectual analysis rather than the refined, thin experience which follows it. But within this thick experience inquiry discriminates data which serve as the starting-point of interpretation. These data also are described in various ways: sense data, qualities and relations, hard data, qualia, unanalyzable contents, and so on.

One basic proposition may be asserted of the given in both these senses: Real existence is never given for knowledge. The original given which precedes reflection may be considered an object of enjoyment, use, or some other practical attitude and activity. Thus, to the workman or artist the tools which he uses are immediately given. Or the original given may be regarded as the total perceptual or practical situation in which the individual finds himself. Thus, to every one of us the familiar paths which we habitually follow as we go about our business are seen within their customary setting, and the totality is given. But in neither case is such a given an object of knowledge, for knowledge can appear only after something problematic has been discriminated and has served as a stimulus to a process of inquiry. Things as they are unreflectively experienced may on this theory be real, but they must be real for feeling or use. They cannot be real for knowledge—if for no other reason, because unreflective knowledge is a contradiction in terms, since knowledge implies prediction, either deliberate or implicit.

The data which provide the starting-point of experimental

inquiry, however, presuppose some process of analysis. As Dewey says, they are not given but taken. As Lewis states the same point, the sensuous given is an element disclosed by the reflective analysis of experience. But these data are no more real for knowledge than is the given which precedes analysis. In a way, they are less real, for, in being discriminated and marked off, they have lost their former status of familiar acceptance and have become problematic. Their relations to other possible data, which may be given in the future under specified conditions and on which their classification as real or unreal, objective or subjective, depends, have not yet been ascertained. They have lost the primitive reality of feeling and use and have not yet achieved a reality for knowledge.

Everyone agrees that the perceptual given is somehow a manifestation or revelation of reality; this is true indirectly, even of illusory experiences. The problem is to define the relation. Aesthetically speaking, experience is a democratic word, and everything is unreflectively experienced as real—stars, ghosts, social institutions, values, and numbers, as well as the things, persons, and events which we perceive and deal with immediately and directly. But all these things are given as real for feeling or belief, for action or use, rather than for knowledge. As soon as the question of knowledge is raised, the primitive unity of the individual and the world is broken; and, according to the experimental method, the datum of belief, action, or use is replaced by a datum of inquiry, which remains in suspension until it has been interpreted.

The interpretation is the statement of relations between the datum and possible, future data which, it is asserted, would be given under assigned conditions. All empirical knowledge, therefore, is inferential and predictive. Knowledge is always both more and less than what is given. It is more than the analyzed given because we always add to this an interpretation; it is less than the original, unreflective given because, in knowing, we select aspects or contents of this and pass over others. The double process of addition and subtraction takes place because knowledge serves action and action is purposive. It is because the needs and purposes which we bring to experience find expression in our concepts that the concepts select, interpret, and correlate the data of knowledge. Then, in the course of inquiry, we discover whether our purposes and classifications are in conformity with reality.

The relation between datum and possible future experience is formulated in a concept. But empirical concepts, in classifying objects, do not copy them. The pragmatic logic of consequences developed its theory of classification under the influence of evolutionary theory. What evolution showed was that a species is not a natural entity in the sense once believed; for individuals can be classified in more than one way and a given organism may belong to either of two classes—or more, theoretically—depending on the criteria employed. Class concepts, therefore, are not true or acceptable because they correspond to species in nature, at least in any obvious manner. Scientists had been mistaken in supposing that their taxonomy embodied the ultimate essences of nature; they had been unconsciously guided by considerations of convenience. Pragmatism simply pointed out that men are guided in everyday life by fundamentally the same considerations as scientists are.

It is important to see what is, and what is not, implied in the statement that classifications are useful rather than true or false. Essentially, it is implied, as already pointed out, that a class is not a natural entity. The particular grouping of data or objects that we adopt is made by us for a purpose, and the group exists only relative to the purpose; it is constituted by the concept and does not exist independent of it. The natural entity is a particular, unique reality, not a class. And the concept is simply an instrument by which we are enabled to deal with the reality and achieve our aim. But it does not follow that concepts are subjective or can be chosen arbitrarily. Any one that is true or useful—any one, that is to say, which verifies itself by its effectiveness—must be based on actual characteristics of the object or situation with reference to which it is employed. Effective action depends on the conformity of our purposes to the nature of things, though the conformity is not a literal copying. The position might be fairly summarized by the statement that classifying is an objective activity, although the class is not a pre-existing natural entity, since it is the result of an interaction between knower and data. Therefore, to ask whether classes are natural entities or logical fictions is to miss the point, for it presupposes that a class is a static entity, whereas, in fact, according to experimental logic, it is both relational and an aspect of an activity. Classes are neither subjective nor objective simply; they are objective within the knowing process, in which they perform a function. They are objectively relative.

The two components of knowledge—concepts and the given—are sharply heterogeneous. Both are found in unreflective experience; but for the explanation of knowledge they have different sources and are mutually independent. The difference between them is the difference between the rational and the sensuous, the articulate and the ineffable, and, to some extent, the social and the private. Empirical concepts include references to sensous content, of course; but they are intelligible without verification in experience, since they constitute the necessary preliminary to all verification. The given, conversely, contains relational elements; but it is self-contained, and its relational aspects are no more conceptual than are the others. We describe or interpret it by concepts, but the object of these activities is not itself conceptual. There is no internal or essential relation between concepts and sensuous presentation. They constitute the form and the content of experience, respectively. But because they are so completely heterogeneous, the relation between them is instituted rather than discovered: in the act of interpretation, concepts are imposed on the given, in the manner of hypotheses.

It is because of this that all empirical knowledge is, of necessity, scientific. We are free initially to interpret a sensuous datum in any way we please; it is completely receptive, since the concepts which we hypothetically apply to it in knowing are not merely about what is presented but about the relations of this to other presentations which may follow it. But the correctness or incorrectness of the interpretations must be confirmed by empirical evidence, and we cannot be said to have empirical knowledge until such confirmation has taken place. It is in the sciences that validations are systematically undertaken. But this is really an identical statement; science means here the method of making and experimentally testing predictive hypotheses.

This exposition of the unrestricted theory of logical consequences may be summarized in five propositions: (1) Real existence is not given for knowledge. (2) All empirical knowledge is inferential and predictive. (3) The basic inferential relations in knowledge, between given and anticipated data, are formulated in concepts. (4) Concepts are imposed on the given, the two being mutually independent in reflective experience or inquiry. (5) All knowledge of existence is scientific.

To accept the theory in a rigorous sense is to accept these five propositions. But most pragmatists, although they subscribe to the theory in a general way, do not accept them all. Dewey accepts all except No. 4. This he rejects because he holds that concepts and given, logical forms and logical subject matter, ideas and facts, emerge together within the course of inquiry. Both arise from the interaction of organism and environment in the problematic situation, instead of having distinct origins. Thus they are co-ordinate, and the theory that concepts are imposed on data which are logically pre-existent is misleading because it is one-sided. Interaction is a more basic category than interpretation. Therefore, instrumentalism does not accept the theory that we are discussing; for, since it is a form of naturalism or is based on naturalism, its theory of existence is more fundamental than is its theory of knowing. The instrumentalist theory of logic is itself naturalistic: logic is the natural history of thinking.

However, the position of instrumentalism is not clear, and it exemplifies the ambiguities of pragmatism which we reviewed earlier. While instrumentalism rejects the unrestricted theory of consequences, it does not accept the restricted theory. All knowledge is scientific and predictive, existence must be described in experimental terms, and we cannot talk of existents antecedent to inquiry. Instrumentalism has not formulated a philosophic method, nor has it shown how there can be any peculiarly philosophical knowledge. Yet it is accompanied by a naturalistic metaphysics, which describes the generic traits of existence. But this metaphysics, it would seem, must be interpreted either as a series of very broad, scientific generalizations or else as a series of unsupported speculative statements, which fall within the sphere of artistic expression rather than in that of knowledge. And instrumentalism is really saved from the unrestricted theory of logical consequences not because it accepts any knowledge other than experimental but because it holds that there are other ways of access to reality, which can be deliberately and systematically related to the way of knowledge.

To some extent, Peirce exemplifies the same ambiguities. While instrumentalism holds simultaneously to naturalism and the theory of logical consequences, he holds simultaneously to his own metaphysics and the theory of logical consequences. Thus he, too, rejects the unrestricted theory as a whole; but it is not easy to say what in its various constituents he accepts. Believing in scientific philosophy, he maintains that philosophic concepts must be formulated and philosophical propositions validated in accordance with the rule of consequences. It would seem to follow that all branches of philosophy which deal with existence, including metaphysics, must be experimental and branches of science; and he sometimes asserts this. But Peirce had, in addition to the principle of consequences, a belief in common human reason which approached the old doctrine of the "natural light" without including its supposed infallibility in the face of the self-evident. Because of this belief, he could hold that philosophy "deals with positive truth, indeed, yet contents itself with observations such as come within the range of every man's normal experience, and for the most part in every waking hour of his life."[3] This suggests that philosophy abstracts its categories from the common objects of experience rather than predicts consequences. But he did not develop this notion, which would have led

3. *Collected Papers*, Vol. I, ¶ 241.

to the acceptance of a relation between philosophy and science less close than the identity which he sometimes asserted.

Among pragmatists, Lewis is the only one who consistently adheres to the unrestricted theory. It is significant that he is also the only pragmatist who consistently holds that philosophy has its own distinctive method. Its inquiry into experience is neither experimental nor genetic but follows the method of reflective analysis. Its original datum is unreflective experience, and it seeks by logical analysis to discover within this the elements which are given and those which are contributed by the mind. Having its own method, it is natural that philosophy should also arrive at distinctive results. Its business is to give an account of knowing. Philosophy is reflection on experience, in a broad sense which extends to concepts and norms of value as well as to criteria of objective, natural fact. Its special study is the criteria of interpretation which the mind brings to experience. This position defines the nature and limits of philosophy more clearly than does any other account of the pragmatic method.

However, the program involves a difficulty. Lewis holds that "philosophy is, so to speak, the mind's own study of itself in action."[4] But, if this means more than that philosophy is the study of the a priori, it would seem to imply one of two alternatives: either philosophy studies mind as an empirical object, or it postulates a transcendental mind. It is clear from the development of the argument that Lewis rejects the second alternative. Then is not the first unavoidable? And must we not conclude that philosophy, as well as science, gives us knowledge of empirical objects? The analysis of experience does not lead to the postulation of a trancendental mind behind experience, as the unknown cause or source of concepts, just because the analysis of experience is, at the same time, a partial description of mind; and the fact that the description is incomplete does not affect the issue. But if philosophy can know mind by description of its peculiar activity, namely, conceptual interpretation, why can it not know other things in the same way, by observing

4. *Mind and the World-Order* (New York, 1929), p. 18.

their modes of activity and structures? To make mind the peculiar object of philosophic description is to narrow the field of philosophy arbitrarily or else to widen it without warrant. Either an ontological point of view is appropriate to philosophy or it is not. To define philosophy as the study of mind is possible only on the basis of epistemological assumptions characteristic of a certain historical era. This statement, if true, tells us nothing about the validity of those assumptions, of course. But it is neither empty nor entirely arbitrary; for most of the other presuppositions of the era have been either rejected or basically modified in the light of later experience. And this suggests the question of whether it is possible to retain the epistemological assumptions while rejecting the general point of view of which they formed a part.

But let us proceed to consider systematically the relation between empirical knowledge and its objects. Any tenable theory of truth must interpret in its own way the conviction which we all have that a true idea conforms to reality. This task is especially important for a philosophy which has shown that a narrowly literal definition of conformity is impossible because ideas do not "copy" objects. The unrestricted theory of consequences interprets both conformity and knowledge as a relation between qualitative experiences. Neither, therefore, is to be found within a single experience. Either present qualitative experience is the fulfilment of a previous prediction, which was made on the basis of a previous sensuous presentation; or it provides the basis for a present prediction, which is held to be warranted as a result of past experiences. To know an empirical object is to have a sensuous experience of it, related by an idea or hypothesis to other sensuous experiences. And the object itself is a set of possible experiences, related by concepts, which state the conditions under which the experiences will be had.

But what does "possible" mean? In this context it means "logically probable." The term does not refer to natural potentiality; and the theory, in fact, has no concept of existential potentiality but remains in the dimension of knowledge throughout. Instead of beginning with an independent object of inquiry and conceiving knowing as a process of interaction with this object, governed by a standard of conformity, it constructs the object out of cognitive experiences. The sciences do not have this difficulty, for to them the experimental method is simply a method. They assume their objects of inquiry and consider knowledge as a series of approximations toward them. But in philosophy the method has expanded to the point where it attempts to explain what the term "object" means.

Consider a man who has lived for some time in a city. The city, as a geographical area, is known to him in terms of the familiar paths he takes to work; to his home; to the grocer, doctor, drugstore, church, theater, the homes of friends. It is a set of habits. Each habit is a sequence, the various steps in which are marked by familiar clues—a traffic light, a busy square, a sign, the post office, a vacant lot, or a modern home of striking design. One habit describes the path from A, his home, to B, where he works, by way of C and D, the railroad station and the parkway. Another path runs from E to F, and still another from M to N. This description pictures habit as routine and mechanical, whereas actual conduct will vary the sequences or, at any rate, incorporate them into flexible and complex patterns of action. But it will serve to illustrate the point. The city means to the man the possibility of getting from A to B, from E to F, and from M to N. But there are many other paths he might take from A to B, some of which he knows but most of which have never occurred to him. There is an endless number of other points he has never touched and between which he has never traveled.

Now does the man understand the city as a set of habits, or do his habits mean and refer to the city? Obviously both, but in different ways. It is the difference between the order of knowledge and the order of existence. To say that there is a real city means, for a man who knows the place, that he can confidently follow any one of a number of routes to his destination. If he turns east instead of west when he leaves home, he will come out at the same place that he could have reached by another route, starting in the opposite direction. If the city is real, he must follow a certain route, or one of a certain set of routes, to reach his destination. But, conversely, if he can reach his destination by following out a sequence of experiences, the city must be real. As an object of practical action, the city is definable with reference to a set of habits; but, as an object of exploration and inquiry, it goes beyond any such set or combination of sets in all its citizens. And, though the city as an object of knowledge may be defined with reference to habits, it cannot be defined in terms of them, for they are ways of acting on something; they refer to an existent beyond themselves.

The definition of objects in terms of actual and possible experiences confuses the order of experience with the order of existence. It implies that because experience is successive, its object must be successive, too. But it does not follow, because I cross the city by proceeding successively from A to B, that the city, either as I know it or as it exists independent of my knowledge, is also successive. This is such an obvious point that it is difficult to believe that the criticism does not rest on a misunderstanding. But the theory under discussion actually does claim to define the second order in terms of the first and, to this extent, reduces it to the first.

It might perhaps be replied that the real city is a pattern of possible experiences and that possibilities are not successive. The difference between the objective and subjective orders would then be the difference between logical implication and psychological succession, between nontemporal possibilities and actual experienced events. Or it may be said that out of the various individual experiences we can construct a public or social order of possible experiences, which is the real city. It is true that both logical and various psychological orders are involved in knowledge. But, in addition, there is a third order, that of the object itself; for empirical knowledge is here of a physical object, not of either a logical or a psychological one. And the physical object cannot be defined in psychological terms, because such habits as we have described, whether individual or social, are directed on something beyond the individual or group which embodies them. The real city, as well as the experiences of it, is temporal; but its temporal order is different from that of the experiences. The city and the experiences of its residents may, for the sake of the argument, both be considered sets of events. But the streets and buildings are one set of events, the experiences of traversing them another set. Experimental logic here inadvertently identifies the process of knowing with the process which is its object. It confuses knowledge of process with the process of knowledge.

The problem is analogous to that of knowledge of the past. It has sometimes been said that pragmatism cannot deal with the past; for, since the meaning of a concept or proposition consists of predicted consequences and consequences lie in the future, all meaning refers to the future; and not only is it impossible to know the past on such a theory, but it is meaningless even to talk about it. This objection, however, rests on a misunderstanding. The logical consequences of a proposition are its implications, but implication is not a temporal relation. Such a proposition as "This substance is common salt," according to experimental logic, implies, or can be translated into, hypothetical statements of what would happen under assigned conditions. But the constituent relations of these statements are logical, not temporal at all. At the same time, although they are not temporal, they do refer to possible temporal happenings. Some of them will refer to the future: if the substance is salt, for instance, I will experience a familiar "salty" taste when I put it on my tongue. But others will refer to the past: if it really is salt and has been exposed to a humid atmosphere for any length of time, it will have caked; and if it has been kept in a container made of certain metals, the metal will have become tarnished.

Thus, if by "psychological meaning" we understand possible experiences of things, psychological meaning all lies in, or is directed toward, the future, for it has been defined in terms of action. But the experiences we have of things may point toward the past as well as toward the future. A written document may confirm a theory about some past historical event. The reading of it is the conclusion of a process of inquiry which moved forward through time. But the handwriting in the document may be well known and may point backward in time to its probable author, who died long ago. Therefore, the significance of data may be retrospective as well as prospective, though, so far as it is practical, it will point forward into the future.

Everyone who accepts the experimental method, including the critics of pragmatism, takes it for granted that the sciences are able to investigate and know the past. Why, then, should the existence of the past constitute a special problem for pragmatism, which is a philosophical formulation of scientific method? It does not present a special difficulty precisely because, in discussing the issue, pragmatism distinguishes between the experiences by which we know and the order of past events which is known. The latter cannot be an order of possible experience, since possible experiences lie in the future. First Brutus stabbed Caesar, then Caesar died. But I may learn of the assassination before I know that Brutus was one of the perpetrators. Knowledge of the past is perfectly intelligible in terms of the concept of logical consequences if a distinction is made between the logical, psychological, and objective orders. The term "objective" here, of course, refers to the order in the object and is not intended to suggest that the psychological order is "subjective"; both are orders of events in nature.

But if this triple distinction of orders is essential to describe knowledge of the past, it is equally essential to account for all objects of empirical inquiry. The real issue is not whether pragmatism can explain how we know the past but whether it accounts for objective natural existence at all, whether past or present. The physical city is a pattern of entities which are partly successive and partly simultaneous. To know it is to apprehend something of this order. In reasoning, apprehension of the pattern of the argument is as essential to knowledge as advance from one step to the next; without it we should have only a succession of ideas without unity. Similarly, the elements of the empirical object must be grasped together in their proper relations if we are to have knowledge of it.

The logic of consequences fails to see this because it holds that the function of ideas is to lead the knower up to a sensuous presentation or qualitative experience. But what we want of ideas is primarily that they should lead us to the object itself. Here a distinction is to be drawn between practical and theoretical functions. The practical function of an idea as a plan of action is not the acquisition of knowledge but the achievement of purpose or the satisfaction of want; and the object in this case is a practical one. The theoretical function of an idea is to give us knowledge of the object, to aid us in grasping its characteristics. In both cases the performance of the function involves some conformity of the idea to the objective order of nature.

The pattern of a concept which leads us up to an experience or provides the means of achieving a purpose embodies the pattern of the route which we follow to obtain the experience or gain the end. Perhaps it extends further, to include something of the structure of the practical object itself, since we have ideas of our goals and since ends are difficult to separate from means; but this point is not important for the present argument. The concept of how to get a cool drink, let us say, does not contain anything of either cold water or the cool, pleasant trickle which we experience when we drink it; but it must contain some of the structure of the route to the kitchen if it enables us to reach our objective. The pattern of a concept which gives us theoretical knowledge, on the other hand, always embodies something of the structure of the object, though not all of it. If the concept could fully succeed in bringing us into direct relation with the object, we should no longer need it; our experience would then be cognitive but not conceptual, or only incidentally so. This is why the copy theory of knowledge is mistaken; if the concept copied the object completely, it would be superfluous. However, we rarely, if ever, can dispense with concepts in knowledge. And a concept involves selection; it defines only one pattern of relations among many possible ones. But if it is reliable, the pattern that it defines must be there in existence; the pattern must characterize the object in its relations to us. And, through our transactions with the object, we discover something of the order inherent in the object itself and in its relations to other things, independent of us. This discovery marks the difference between experience and knowledge. And it constitutes the element of truth in the copy theory.

There are two reasons why the element of conformity has been obscured in the logic of consequences. One is the stress on the practical function of ideas, as means of correlating present and future experiences; the other is the emphasis on concepts as formal patterns of interpretation, having their origin in the mind or in the imagination. But as for the first point, an idea can convey theoretical knowledge, as well as be a means to a practical end. The man in the city who follows a route to work is using his idea practically, for it gets him where he wants to go; but it also embodies something of the pattern of the city streets. And as for the second point, while concepts are formal patterns in the mind, there is no reason why they should not also be suggested by the object as it is experienced and incorporate some of its structure. Let us consider the nature of conformity in further detail. It involves the relation between concepts and the given.

We have seen that the radical logic of consequences sharply contrasts having and knowing in experience. We formulated this contrast in the statement that real existence is not given for knowledge. But, if the theory is carried through to the end, it leads to the assertion that nothing whatever is given for knowledge, for the given is always ineffable but predictive knowledge is communicable. The relation between knowledge and the given is reciprocal: the known is not given, and the given is not known; for all empirical concepts and propositions are predictive and refer to the future. None of them is ever simply descriptive of what is given. The distinction between immediate and inferential knowledge disappears. Any statement which appears to be a description is a disguised prediction. This is as true of the statement, "This patch is blue" as it is of "This wood is inflammable"; for to describe the patch as "blue" is, by implication, to predict that it will meet certain tests or be correlated in specifiable ways with future experience. Thus predictive knowledge can never lead to an apprehension of objects and objective order. The nature of existence is gradually disclosed in the course of inquiry, according to this view; but the disclosure takes the form of warranted inferences, not direct experience.

An attempt has been made by Lewis[5] to connect having and knowing more directly, through what he calls the "terminating judgment." This type of judgment is intermediate between expressive statements about the sensuous given, on the one hand, and ordinary judgments of objective fact, on the other. Like the first, which describe sensuous appearances without implying anything further, it is formulated in expressive language. Like the second, it states an order and is verifiable; it states that, something being given, under certain conditions something else will probably be given. Terminating judgments deal with possible experiences: "Given this apple-like appearance, then, if I take a bite, I shall probably experience a sharp, yet sweet, taste." Possible experiences of this sort, so far as they have significance for knowledge, presuppose more than expectation based on the past; they presuppose necessary logical connections of meaning. But the question is whether merely logical connections are enough to yield a probability that goes beyond logic and whether these connections, together with the past, are enough to give a real probability for the future. Terminating judgments are the logic of appearances. But the question is whether appearances themselves are logical or, rather, whether the logic they exemplify is not itself the logic of real existence. The question is whether the probability of empirical knowledge rests on certainties of sense presentation or whether it rests on the reality of objective existence, which is neither certain nor probable but simply is. That the latter is the case is suggested by the fact that the terminating judgment itself involves reference to an action, such as biting the apple.

The nature of this act is not easy to determine. But this much seems clear: an act is involved, and not merely the appearance of an act. The meaning here seems to be that the act itself is presented, that here appearance and reality coincide, for no inference is involved. Where the act belongs in existence is another question. If it

---

5. *An Analysis of Knowledge and Valuation* (Chicago, 1946), chap. viii.

does not fall in the sphere of physical existence, it will perhaps fall in the sphere of mental existence. But it must fall somewhere; it is more than an uninterpreted appearance. The cognitive significance of the terminating judgment depends on its relation to existence.

No proof is offered in the theory of logical consequences for the statement that real existence is never given. The statement is, in fact, analytic, for real existence, whether physical, social, or of any other sort, is defined in terms of sequential correlations between immediate, qualitative experiences. It follows that reality cannot be given for knowledge within a single experience, because that would contradict the definition of reality as knowable. We have already considered why the statement has come to be adopted by so many philosophers. The explanation is in part the persistence of certain assumptions about the nature of experience and, in particular, the assumption that form and content in experience have different origins. It is in part the fact that, on these assumptions, the statement is integral to the solution of a whole set of problems, which includes the nature of veridical and illusory perceptions, the nature and validation of synthetic propositions, probability and induction, and the existence of the external world. The set of problems, in a word, constitutes the problem of knowledge. This problem, as it is understood today, emerged in the historical context of experimental science. Therefore, we may say that the statement about real existence is valid, granted a context of ideas and assumptions which have been very influential in recent times. But the context calls for discussion.

For this point of view, the given which follows analysis is ultimate, in the sense that the logical meaning of every empirical statement must finally reduce to statements of conditions for having experiences or being presented with sense data of a certain sort; while the factual evidence of its truth consists in their actual occurrence. Everything must be explained in terms of the given, while the given itself cannot be explained in terms of anything else. Ideas also are ultimate. They can be explained neither genetically nor experimentally; on the contrary, they are presupposed in every genetic or experimental explanation. Crude experience may be more ultimate than either one in some sense. But it is not more ultimate for knowledge, which analyzes it into these two cognitive factors.

The consequence of this position is that no explanation can be given for the fact that concepts sometimes predict the course of future experience or that some are more successful in this respect than others. Indeed, if ideas and the given are ultimate and mutually independent, there can be no explanation of the fact of knowledge at all; it must always remain an agreeable surprise. The two factors are related, in that both are elements in empirical knowledge. But when they have been abstracted from knowledge by analysis, their mutual relevance, too, appears an extraordinary accident.

However, if knowing is a natural process, the two factors have relations to existence and thus to each other. And if these relations could be described, knowledge and human experience itself would appear less a special miracle than an instance of principles and processes holding throughout nature. Indications of such relations are to be found in pragmatism. To accept them, or anything like them, is to go on from the method of consequences to a theory of existence. Let us consider briefly these existential implications of the given and of concepts.

The sensuous given is an aspect of a complex interaction, and to explain it is to describe the interacting elements which are its conditions. The most obvious of these are what we call "subject" and "object"; when I look at a building, what I see is conditioned by my sense organs and the building itself. But the occurrence of the colored shape that presents itself to me depends on other aspects of the perceptual situation as well, such as distance, light, and the state of the atmosphere. All these factors constitute the present physical dimension of the situation. But the situation is also historical and social, for the subject of the experience is the whole individual, with a cultural and personal past. It is the social, historical individual who sees, not a pair of eyes. An individual with a different kind of past would see something different.

In considering sense-perception, all this must be taken into account. It is generally recognized that because of the various physiological, cultural, and psychological elements involved, the individual in perception selects from what is given and organizes the material in accordance with certain principles of interpretation. The presence of such selective activity can be discovered in his own experience by anyone who is at all reflective, though it is probably more complex than anyone suspects. But, in addition to selection from the given, there is the constitution or determination of the sensuous given itself. And this determination is prior to the selection, since it has to do with the field from which selection of items is made. Such prior determination, as has just been said, is often recognized in the case of the specific data of the various senses, which are functions of the total situation. When I look attentively at a building, I see reddish shapes, a shiny glint, and other sensory qualities. From a certain analytic point of view, these qualities and perhaps some of their relations are ultimate data of experience. But from another and existential point of view, their occurrence is due to the operation of physical, psychological, and other determinants.

But the interaction which determines the objects of experience goes deeper than this. The world as given in crude, thick experience is itself the outcome of natural interaction. Specific qualitative data are contained in and selected from the situation which includes this world. When I open my eyes, what I originally see is a brick building with its windows. I do not infer it as the cause of my sensations; I experience it directly and unreflectively. The experienced building cannot be accounted for in the same way as the experienced sense data can, for it is not the same kind of entity. Yet in a complete philosophy, some account must be given of it. According to the point of view suggested here, it may be described in terms of the perspective of the natural, historical individual. The concept of perspective is a further subject, which will not be examined here; but it involves the notion of interaction. From this point of view, the philosophical explanation of sensory qualities is to be made in terms of the situation to which they belong, not merely in terms of the causal action of physical objects on the organism.

It has sometimes been suggested by philosophers that the original determination of the given is simply selective, that there exists a plenum of unperceived sensory elements, from which the equipment of the organism and other relevant factors select certain items which then enter the field of awareness, the rest remaining inaccessible to the organism. But the notion of selection does not go far enough. It might be plausible if existence were a manifold or flow of sensuous elements, including both qualities and relations, from which the individual chose in accordance with the needs of action. But the world that is originally experienced is much more than qualities and relations. And it is experienced as modified by our own natures, not as a datum which we contemplate from without.

There is no pure given, in the sense of completely raw material that is untouched by the subject which experiences it. It is impossible that there should be, for our active natures must partly determine what is presented in our perspective. What is immediately had contains something of the natures of both ourselves and the world as it is independent of our experience. This given world may be preanalytic; but it is also, so to speak, postsynthetic. It is the outcome of a process. We are not directly aware of this process as it occurs; in the conscious subject which is aware of data it has already been broken up. But we can learn something of its nature by analysis; and in inquiry we attempt to sort out the elements which are due to objects from those contributed by the subject. Thus it is true to say that philosophy is an analysis of experience. But it is at the same time a description of existence, for in the course of the analysis we discover features in the world as it presents itself which are exemplified in processes beyond that of our own experience.

To assert that sensory data are not ultimate is not to desert philosophy for science. It is not to accept an account of the physiological conditions of consciousness as the basis of philosophy. It does not mean that biology, psychology, sociology, or any other science is an authority from which philosophy can borrow its interpretations of experience. That would be the case only if we identified the given with sense data and explained their existence or their appearance in conscious awareness by physiological or other such processes. But this is not the issue. The question is which philosophical concepts we are to take as most fundamental. And the answer I am suggesting is that perspective and interaction are more basic categories than is sensuous givenness.

Ideas are as much in need of explanation as is the given. What is the source of concepts, and why do they work in practice? Philosophers who identify thinking with the experimental method have little to tell us in reply to these questions. They say that ideas are suggested by the concrete problems of inquiry; but what the word "suggest" means in this connection is not clear.

It cannot mean that ideas are abstracted from the directly presented structure of existence; for if objective existence is not given for the processes of knowing, its characteristics are not available to be observed and abstracted or to serve as clues in any other way. The only possible origin of concepts is the mind, which then refers them to experience. Since some work in practice and others do not, there must be some kind of objective check on their relevance. But if real existence is never given for knowledge, the check must be made against an order of nature with which knowledge is somehow correlated but which is only inferred, as a kind of thing in itself.

This conclusion is very unwelcome to many empiricists. But they avoid it, I believe, only by shifting back and forth between two senses of the given. The postanalytic given has no structure which is relevant for objective, communicable knowledge (although its parts may have structures which can be directly apprehended in private experience). Such a structure would constitute a limitation on the principle that all knowledge is probable and predictive. Instead of conforming to a single "given," the ideas in knowledge state relations between different "givens." On the other hand, the preanalytic given, the world of thick experience, does have such a relevant structure. Existent objects are given in the preanalytic sense; they are given for common-sense or unreflective experience, and this experience, we have said, is cognitive. But if it is suggested that knowledge involves a correspondence between idea and given object, this is vigorously denied by empiricists, on the ground that examination of the supposed object reveals only concepts and sense data, the relation between which is not correspondence but prediction. However, if it is pointed out that this view fails to account for the objective order of nature, the skeptic is referred again to our naïve, unanalyzed experiences of things and events.

Concepts are often said to be creations of the imagination, and it is pointed out that, without imagination, no amount of observation or analysis will lead the inquirer to significant results. But why some creations of the imagination or mind should be suitable for knowledge, and others not, is not at all clear. Successful theories are supposed to be the result of testing. But, as Peirce remarked, the possible theories in relation to a problem are practically infinite in number, and the chance that man would hit upon the true one for testing is too small to be plausible. Even if this should happen once or twice, it is hard to believe that it would happen often enough to explain the accumulation of knowledge that exists.

Nevertheless, this is the explanation implicit in most discussions of the subject. Our theories work because they enable us to adapt ourselves to our natural environment. To facilitate adaptation is the function of thought, and theories which fail to perform the function disappear. This, of course, is not intended as a purposive explanation but as a statement of fact. Mind is an instrument of organic evolution, and successful theories are the result of trial and error, in the last analysis, plus such directed, intelligent behavior as the organism is able to carry out. The present question does not concern the nature of truth. Assuming that we know what truth is, the question is how men ever happened to discover true theories and embrace true beliefs. The answer proposed is: by a process of natural selection. The same principle is said to explain why some newly discovered theories work while others do not. There is enough similarity between past and future to make most old truths relevant and to enable human imagination to build on its old store of knowledge in constructing new theories to be tested.

We need not discuss the adequacy of this account. The point is that it goes beyond concepts and sense data to a theory of existence which professes to make intelligible how concepts can predict the course of experience. If the actual success of inquiry is not to remain an ultimate mystery, some such theory is essential. But its implication is that knowledge is a form of existence and is to be understood as such. It involves some active relation between knower and known environment. It is not a reference of concepts to sense presentations.

It is true in a tautological sense that concepts are a priori. It is also true tautologically that knowledge is a logical construction from sense data. Knowing is an activity, and such statements as these explicate the notion of the mental activity essential to the process. But they are misleading if they are intended as empirical descriptions of the process of knowing, for they fail to make clear that knowledge is not the sheer creation of a product from passive materials. They do not describe knowing but indicate one aspect of it in abstraction from the rest. Knowledge is conceptual interpretation, an activity in which the principles of interpretation are supplied by the mind. But to say that knowledge is interpretation is very different from saying that concepts are introduced into sensuous experience from an outside source. The second statement is erroneous because it omits the natural and historical context in which concepts occur. And this context is relevant, because it makes intelligible why some concepts are formulated rather than others and, in particular, why those are formulated which have a bearing on the situation. It throws light on the element of conformity in knowledge.

The existence of a common order which is exemplified both in knowledge and in its objects was one of the earliest philosophical discoveries. Its explanation has constituted one of the most persistent problems. The explanation offered by pragmatism is that subject and object in knowledge cannot be taken as two mutually independent entities; for when they are so taken, any relation between them is inexplicable. Instead, both must be seen as aspects of a single existence. The unit of existence, at least as far as inquiry is concerned, is the inclusive situation in the human perspective. This is the significance of the biological and cultural matrices of inquiry, as Dewey describes them. Inquiry is carried on by inquirers whose relation to existence is defined by their natures. But the situation does not consist only of the inquirers; there are also the objects of inquiry, which must be described in any exhaustive account of the situation. Pragmatism has not had enough to say about these.

The radical theory of logical consequences can afford to pass over the problem of relating concepts and the given because it assumes all along the reality of objects independent of knowing and an existent world in which human practice occurs. From the standpoint of the individual knower, society and its members, like everything else, are constructions on the basis of the given. This is the influence of the empiricist tradition and its modification in the Kantian philosophy, for both of which knowledge was essentially individual. The notion of communication was as yet without logical significance in this tradition, which understood society largely in terms of custom and regarded custom as irrational. The rational element in society was the contractual element; but contract, too, was supposed to be interpreted by each member privately in terms of his own interests and his own apprehension of human rights. But to pragmatism, building on a different conception of scientific inquiry, knowledge is a co-operative undertaking and so demands a sociological analysis to supplement the individual one that we have been considering. The categories and criteria which the individual uses are largely social in their origins; historically, he is derived from society, not conversely. Social experience or the social heritage is the point of departure. Moreover, knowledge is defined in terms of public verifiability. This entire interpretation assumes the reality of communication and therefore of other naturally existent selves, not merely other rational minds. The existence of natural communication, like that of social practice, is taken as a fact. It can, of course, be analyzed in the study of signs and language; but such analysis, no matter how much or how little epistemological in tone, presupposes it. Communication is a fact which goes beyond the method of consequences and, strictly speaking, falls outside its assumptions. Social inquiry is merely one activity in the life of society, and it is this life which is the real assumption.

The existence of natural objects is also presupposed in practical activity. We have spoken above of objects of knowledge, inquiry, and feeling. But there is also the object of use, which is different from them all; it is neither conceptual, problematic, nor immediate. A mechanic uses tools, with which he is familiar from long habituation, to locate and repair a mechanical defect. The scientist may once have constructed or learned to use his apparatus; but when he is experimenting, his attention is normally focused on some other problem. He takes his instruments for granted and can use them just because he does not need to think about them. In the same way every artist uses tools in the process of composition. The tools we use are deposits of past experience; and in a sense we may be said to know them best of all, if ideas are habits. But if we consider the actual setting of inquiry, it is more proper to say that we know and inquire by means of them than that we know them as objects. We use them to know other things in the problematic situation; they are there to be used.

Thus the unrestricted theory of consequences assumes existents antecedent to and independent of the course of inquiry. They are not experimentally defined; on the contrary, they are necessary conditions for the occurrence of experimentation. Because this empiricism defines meaning and truth in terms of possible, future experience, the natural and social setting of inquiry remains a presupposition instead of forming a part of the theory. It forms the natural basis of the experimental method and explains the practical use of theoretical knowledge. It provides the psychological basis of logic. But, as we have seen, the connection between logic and psychology is complex. Concepts are psychological facts, but they affect the individuals who hold them in various ways. Only some of their consequences are logical, yet all must be considered.

5. Psychological Consequences

Because inquiry is one human activity among others, it must be seen in its total human setting to be understood. James saw this clearly. He observed that the desire for knowledge is only one human need among others. Moreover, both the need and the activity are individual. Beliefs and the evidence supporting them may, therefore, be private. Not all theories are socially verifiable, unless the scope of the term "theory" is arbitrarily limited. So the contrast between the had and the known is not the same as that between the private and the public. Some concepts may be cognitive, although the consequences which make up the evidence for their truth are purely individual. The basic contrast here is neither public and private nor concepts and given nor known and had. Instead, it is the division between theoretical and practical consequences within the experience of the individual.

To say that man is primarily an active being is to conceive him in terms of needs and wants and his attempts to satisfy them. Some of these needs are theoretical, and some are practical, and each requires its own appropriate kind of satisfaction. A theoretical need can be satisfied only by logical or intellectual objects or evidence; the satisfaction of an emotional need calls for emotional evidence; and that of a practical need in the narrower sense requires the attainment of some objective of practical action. Thus "true" and "good" are defined with reference to satisfactions: good is what satisfies a practical need, and true is what satisfies a theoretical need. But the implication is that the theoretical is one division of the practical, if we define the practical as whatever satisfies need. It follows from this that all ideas are practical, in that their interest and ultimate significance for man lie in their relation to his needs. This was the view of James when he wrote that "truth is *one species of good,* and not, as is usually supposed, a category distinct from good, and co-ordinate with it."[6] Truth is a kind of value.

This is a protest against rationalism and an assertion that each side of human nature has a right to be heard. An adequate philosophy must satisfy the whole man, not merely his intellect. The demands of the intellect must be met; those hypotheses which most reliably lead us into the future must be sought. But the final test of an idea is the extent to which it introduces a present harmony into experience by mediating between old beliefs and new facts, harmonizing conflicting theories or desires, and, in general, reconciling and relating diverse parts of experience.

The strength of this position is the strength of a comprehensive view as against a narrow one; and, in a philosophy, this advantage is tremendous. But comprehensiveness in this case entails a weakness, for it follows that truth has only a conditional claim on the individual; yet philosophy aims unconditionally at truth. No basic need can make an absolute demand. Any priority in claim on the part of one side of human nature must rest on the assumption that it involves a greater satisfaction than others do; and if it does not, in fact, yield the satisfaction, it must give way. Moreover, it may be impossible to satisfy all needs and may be necessary to choose between them. This is the real difficulty. Our theoretical and practical natures may come into conflict; for, if truth depends on the occurrence of consequences and consequences are of two independent varieties, it may well happen that one kind occurs while the other does not. In that case the idea will be true from one point of view, doubtful or "false" or bad from the other. Suppose an idea satisfies us logically but frustrates us emotionally, or conversely. This would amount to a conflict between the true and the good. Confronted by such a choice, we should be faced by a dilemma; and the theory offers no principle by which it could be resolved.

The dilemma can easily be avoided by identifying philosophy with the experimental method and viewing all such conflicts as psychological phenomena, which will resolve themselves in due

6. *Pragmatism* (New York, 1921), pp. 75–76.

time according to the laws of human behavior. But if philosophy is to be of practical significance, it must deal with the practical elements in human experience. Thus the issue is not simply the validity of certain aspects of experience; it is the nature of philosophy. On the one hand, there is a tradition which regards philosophy as wisdom and demands the consideration of all aspects of experience in evaluating the truth claim of an idea. But, on the other hand, according to a tradition equally old, philosophy stands for clarity and consistency of thought and the critical examination of unreflective beliefs; and it forbids us to accept any theory which leads to contradictions. How can breadth and consistency be reconciled? The two traditions appear to be incompatible. And, on the presuppositions which James accepted, they really are incompatible. The attempt to secure breadth inevitably leads to a contradiction in human experience between theoretical truth and practical good; while clarity and consistency can be attained only at the cost of a narrowness which reduces philosophy to an inhuman logical exercise.

The relevant presuppositions may be summed up in the statement that there is a discrepancy between human desires and the indifferent, natural world in which they exist. There is a conflict between the outer world of blind, physical forces and the inner world of man's hopes and fears, purposes, and ideals; between scientific knowledge, on the one hand, and philosophy and religion, on the other. This is the old duality of man and nature, for which materialism and idealism had already offered rival solutions. The theory of radical empiricism offers a new solution with respect to knowledge and existence: there are not two kinds of being but a single world of pure experience. An entity in this world is in one context a part of human experience and knowledge, in another context a part of nature. But with respect to values the old duality remains and is even accentuated; for, while facts are objective, values are merely "subjective," in a new and invidious sense. The term "subjective" has come to suggest what is phenomenal and possessed of an inferior reality. The theory of psychological consequences was intended to solve the problem of values in the way that radical empiricism was to solve the problems of knowledge and existence. It fails to do so, however, because of the separation of fact and value, reflected in the ambiguity in the notion of consequences.

Theoretical and practical consequences are so different that they can hardly meet at all. There are areas of experience and belief which can neither be affected by scientific evidence nor themselves have any bearing on it. This separation is supposed to make a harmony possible, and it provides the foundation for the will to believe: within areas untouched by scientific evidence, choice may be made on the basis of practical interests. But, if beliefs about facts and about values are utterly incommensurable, how can they approach close enough either to harmonize or to conflict? The separation between man's inner feelings and the outer world, between emotional needs and experimental knowledge, seems in principle complete. It might be said that they meet in action. But in what way do they meet? Is it not the case, rather, that the active individual is split and must act according to either his scientific knowledge or his emotional needs, but not both at once? The test of practical results will not decide between them, for there are two entirely different kinds of results to consider.

And yet they cannot form two separate worlds, for both are in the experience of the same individual. Relations between them must exist. Let us suppose, for instance, that scientific knowledge indicates that "skillful propaganda, no matter what its intellectual content, modifies the actions of large masses of individuals." Suppose that it satisfies a human need to believe that "human action is determined by reason." The scientific proposition implies the contradictory of the value proposition; namely, "human action is not determined entirely by reason." The value proposition also implies the contradictory of the scientific proposition and may be stated roughly as "propaganda appeals will not be effective unless based on reason." It might be objected that all these propositions are "empirical," and so there is no problem. Facts cannot conflict, and we have only to determine what the facts really are. But what are the facts? Belief in the rationality of man takes forms that can hardly be expressed in what are usually considered empirical (i.e., "verifiable") propositions. But let us consider another kind of example, which perhaps better illustrates the problem.

One belief may involve a negation of the conditions for determining the validity of the other, and so be meaningless from the point of view of the other. From the predictive point of view a belief may be true, false, or undeterminable; and from a practical point of view, a predictive truth may have value, disvalue, or, so to speak, "unvalue." Belief in the existence of God is satisfying to many people, and it does not conflict with any known scientific facts. But it negates the conditions and procedures commonly used for determining the truth of a hypothesis; observable consequences of the sort that constitute scientific evidence do not follow from it. Thus we have an expression, "God is," which from one point of view appears to be a proposition but from the other is meaningless. Conversely, it is conceivable that such a statement as "the world consists of forms and transformations of energy" might appear to be empirically established to some people but meaningless to others from a practical point of view.

In these cases the relation between the two kinds of consequences takes the form of the occurrence of one and not merely the absence, but the impossibility, of the occurrence of the other. But here the consequences are so unlike that conflict again appears impossible, since one of the two opposing elements is always ruled out. The distinction between logical and emotive meaning has its roots in this situation, where fact and value appear to exist in different dimensions. But the conclusion that the two are incommensurable should not be drawn too hastily. "Meaningless" has several different senses. In particular, we should distinguish between self-contradiction, unverifiability, and lack of context. The expression "round square" is meaningless in the first sense, the idea of God is scientifically meaningless in the second, and an isolated sensation is meaningless in the third. But if it is assumed that an internally consistent concept of God (or of some value) is entertained by someone and influences his attitudes and behavior, then such an idea is neither self-contradictory nor lacking in context. It is a logically meaningful concept, and it is in relation to the context of experience of the individual.

There remains the second sense of "meaningless" and its opposite. Without entering into a discussion of the verifiability of values, this much can be said: the context of values in experience is not merely causal. If it were, discussion would be senseless. We eat when we are hungry and drink when we are thirsty because food and drink satisfy our needs. We often discuss the desirability of eating, but we do not dispute over the ability of food to assuage our hunger. But when we discuss such ideas as "God" and "freedom," we do not weigh the desirability of believing in them; we do not regard them as causes which will produce certain effects; we do not consider them to be stimuli, like drugs, which, if taken, will produce certain responses. Instead, we consider their context in experience and reality. Whether they are "verifiable" or not is at this point a trivial question, for it is easy to define a set of psychological consequences which will give an affirmative answer. The important point is that the question, "What is the relation of values to experience and existence?" is meaningful. It is a question which men frequently consider. And this fact shows that there is a relation between the theoretical and the practical dimensions in experience, for it implies that values have a theoretical or intellectual content. Therefore, conflict between the two dimensions is possible because there is common ground.

The common ground is, in fact, double: not only does practical need and satisfaction contain a cognitive factor, but truth carries satisfaction with it. If we are to talk the language of psychological consequences, truth and good are not two kinds of experience but two aspects of experience. There is something in good that may be true or false; there is something in knowledge that may be practically good or bad.

A purely nonrational want would directly and blindly seek its fulfilment and would exist in another world from knowledge. Wrecked sailors in an open boat, crazed by thirst, might simply drink the ocean water; if there is no element of reason in the act, they are not acting against their better judgment. But in most cases there is an element of reason and a conflict between want and knowledge. Urged on by burning thirst but not out of their minds, the sailors may persuade themselves that the water is good, although experience tells them that it is salty and will make their thirst worse. It is the idea in their desire that makes the struggle possible. And when people believe in God or in the equality of races, their belief has intellectual content and makes a claim to truth. Scientific knowledge is not confronted by a rival doctrine. Yet these ideas are not simply fantasies with purely emotional significance, unrelated to our knowledge and experience of the real world. They are believed, and this means that there is a kind of experience which is neither science nor fantasy and yet is intellectual. To deny this is to assert the paradoxical theory that there are meaningless beliefs, attitudes which do not have intellectual content, though they appear to do so. But to call beliefs "meaningless" does not explain them; it is, instead, an attempt to explain them away. Such attempts are always unsuccessful. What is believed here is that the world contains another factor beyond what is described by science and verified by its methods. The belief has cognitive significance; otherwise, it would be simply irrelevant to knowledge.

Similarly, a truth which was not satisfying could not be human truth. We recognize this when we talk about the satisfaction inherent in the pursuit of knowledge. When we admit the truth of something unpleasant to us, we experience a satisfaction which overcomes another that we might have taken in some incompatible belief. There is a satisfaction inherent in the discovery and acceptance of knowledge, and it is inseparable from them. Without this, truth would be powerless and even humanly meaningless. The disinterested interest is still an interest.

What the connection is between the two constituents in an experience is a difficult question. But, in any case, it is not simply a fusion; for, if it were, the truth and value components would not be distinguishable at all; and it is not simply a conjunction, for then the problem of conflict would break out again within each component, which would, in effect, be a separate experience. Both components are present together and operative. When conflict occurs, from the point of view of the value, the truth is negated; from that of the truth, the value is negated. The value denies a truth through its own inherent claim to positive truth; the truth denies a value through its own inherent, positive value. Some logicians have maintained that there is no merely negative judgment. That is true. But they appear not to have seen that the affirmative element contained in a negation need not be of the same kind as the negative factor. The man who asserts that "no race is inferior to any other" may be not only denying what purports to be an empirical statement but also affirming the equality of men as a value which should guide human action.

The problem that we are considering is really one of economy; it is a question of how to satisfy the most needs. But it contains a special difficulty. In ordinary cases of conflict between interests, some quantitative maxim may be of help. Thus we ask ourselves whether we have the time to form a new friendship, whether it is worth the effort to attend some social function, whether we can afford to purchase some item. And, in arriving at decisions, we try to estimate which alternative or combination of alternatives will bring the greater satisfaction. But in the case that we are considering such a rule does not apply, for the rule is a maxim of compromise and adjustment, while a basic conflict presents exclusive alternatives. James believed that there are no fundamental struggles of this kind in human life, that even the most ultimate problems are soluble by degrees, that the universe is moderately friendly to man and man at one with himself. Reality will support our deepest demands, if we act with vigor. The only sharp choice which he contemplated was between action and resignation, and he considered the latter so hopeless an admission of defeat as not to merit serious philosophical consideration. This faith, however, did not take the form of an articulate theory. Instead, he tended to assume that, with the progress of knowledge, the sphere of nonscientific belief would gradually contract and the conflict of needs would gradually solve itself. The thesis of practical belief is this: "Our passional nature not only lawfully may, but must, decide an option between propositions, whenever it is a genuine option that cannot by its nature be decided on intellectual grounds."[7] But as the argument proceeds, there are indications that it may be only for the time being that the option cannot be decided intellectually. Future knowledge may alter the case.

And there is a sense in which the intellect has a voice even in the present. In effect, the position claims scientific standing for "emotional" demands by assigning to the beliefs that satisfy them a probability value of one-half, in the absence of any evidence for or against their truth. Thus they are like ordinary empirical hypotheses in having an assigned finite probability, and so they become intellectually respectable. A rational status is given to what appeared at first intrinsically nonrational. In this way the will to believe really grants to the theoretical need final authority even in the present. But the position is not tenable. In the first place, if the value hypothesis is really unrelated to empirical evidence, it does not have a finite probability at all, certainly not that of one-half. In the second place, if the hypothesis does have such a relation, the theory is a stopgap; it makes convictions into a kind of temporary prudence. Even more, instead of explaining beliefs, it makes them unintelligible by reducing them to the very scientific terms whose supposed inadequacy it was intended to make good.

There are only two tenable alternatives. If practical belief is ultimately unwarranted, then we ought always to be governed in our beliefs by the available scientific evidence. We should suspend judgment in the absence of evidence, and, when it exists, we should adjust our beliefs to its quality and strength. On the other hand, if practical belief is warranted at all, then it cannot be positively governed by such evidence, which can act only as a negative check or

---

7. *The Will To Believe and Other Essays* (New York, 1927), p. 11.

corrective when a belief has exceeded its legitimate bounds. The theory goes too far or not far enough.

The belief in human equality will illustrate both alternatives. Let us suppose that a practical belief in equality is based on scientific evidence. Then it should be proportioned to the strength of the evidence; and, if science should tomorrow uncover adverse evidence, we ought to surrender the belief or reduce it in accordance with the newly discovered facts. This conclusion could be denied only by asserting a priori that scientific evidence against equality is impossible—a position fully as unempirical as any practical belief could be. On the other hand, if practical belief is not reducible to theoretical, it cannot be shaken by new discoveries. These can correct it where it claims equalities which demonstrably do not exist; they can do no more. Science has often argued against alleged equalities of capacity by pointing out inequalites of performance, which appear to reflect different degrees of ability. In a similar way, it has attempted to disprove alleged inequalities of capacity by showing that inequalities of performance have other possible explanations. But in both cases it deals directly with actualities and phenomena and only indirectly with potentialities. The moral belief in human equality, however, is concerned primarily with potentialities and only secondarily with performance. That is why it can never be reduced to terms of verifiability, unless the conditions of verifiability are expanded indefinitely beyond present knowledge, in which case they really lose their experimental meaning. Such a belief may be meaningless in terms of experimental procedures. But, if so, this is enough to demonstrate that it cannot be refuted experimentally.

The harmony of our natures is made possible, according to the will to believe, by the fact that there is a class of needs which can be satisfied by either real or imaginary objects. These satisfactions cannot clash with knowledge, because they do not require an objectively cognitive factor. Some practical needs, such as hunger, require real objects; their satisfaction involves interaction with the natural environment. But there is another class of nonutilitarian needs, such as the religious demand, the passion for justice, and interest in mathematics or metaphysics, for the satisfaction of which the reality of the object is irrelevant. It is irrelevant because its relation to the need is merely causal and external: anything which will produce the satisfaction is adequate, whether it be a reality or only an idea. Just as anything which cuts off the supply of oxygen will put out a fire and any lethal weapon will serve to commit a murder, so anything which gives the individual the sense of comfort, peace, or security that he needs will serve the practical purpose of satisfying him. In knowledge, on the other hand, the relation of the believer to the object is logical as well as causal, and so internal. Predictions are made, and either fulfilled or disappointed; and if the latter, the need is unsatisfied and belief withheld. It is true that anything which will satisfy the definition or serve the purpose is a real object of the sort specified in knowledge. Yet, though knowledge may fit existence loosely, it does fit. This is not the case with the needs and beliefs which we are considering.

And yet, though their status may be only subjective, belief in such entities as God and justice does not lead man away from reality into a world of fantasy. Instead, it gives him courage to face the harsh realities of life and so aids him in dealing more effectively with reality. The subjective entity has an objective function. Only a diseased imagination will lead man away from the realities of action; the proper function of ideals, on the contrary, is to serve action. The harmony of ideals and hard facts is therefore assured, so long as the individual is healthy.

In other words, the will to believe leads to a theory of fictions. We must act as if our wills are free, as if God exists, as if there is a just moral order; but whether these things are so we do not know, and it does not matter. They are necessary fictions—or, rather, as fictions they are sufficient. Truth is a kind of good; good is measured by satisfaction; and satisfaction depends on need alone, which in these cases can create its own object. But need is given; the implication is that it is an ultimate biological or psychological datum. We are born with our fundamental needs. They are as directly and simply products of evolution as is anything else. The will to believe was intended as a protest against determinism and materialism; whatever the facts and the inexorable laws of nature, man is free to maintain that there is a meaning to his own life and the events of the cosmos. But its effect is just the opposite: human life is governed by mechanical cause and effect, not by reason and choice; for, if man has imperious needs, which he can satisfy only by believing, he must believe by a psychological law, whether he will or not, projecting his wishes onto the cosmos. This is what one might expect. Theories which originate as protests bear the mark of the doctrines against which they are directed.

This theory of fictions has an individualistic basis, but it is not essentially different from others which explain ideologies as mass illusions which are the result of historical determinants. Both reduce practical truths to terms of satisfaction or success; and, if they were consistent, both would conclude that the practical relations between men are always based on the interplay of nonrational interests.

To say that man believes in fictions is not only to interpret practical beliefs in terms of theoretical. It is to make a distinction between objective and subjective which has no meaning within experience, for no one ever believed in a fiction. In experience the consequences of a belief on the believer cannot be separated from the effects of its object in the world at large; for belief is experience of an object. They are separate only for an outsider, to whom idea is one thing, belief a second, and real object a possible third. Belief involves intellectual compulsion, as well as satisfaction; and so to explain belief in an object by the satisfaction which is its result is to destroy the belief—unless, of course, it is so pathological as to be beyond reason, in which case it is an irrational compulsion rather than a belief in the proper sense. Here is a theory to justify belief which, by its nature, could never be used by anyone who felt the need for such justification. He could use it only to justify the beliefs of someone else, for whom the justification would be either false or meaningless. Thus the right to believe, based on the feelings of confidence, hope, and security which its exercise produces, is really the necessity to disbelieve instead, if it means anything at all. The theory may help to explain the causes of some beliefs, but it cannot provide reasons for any. Therefore, when confronted by conflicts between theoretical and practical needs, it offers no clue to a decision between them or a mode of combining them. It describes man as a creature with needs which he can neither satisfy nor renounce. The description may be accurate, but whether it is or not is irrelevant; it is not what was intended.

The theory of psychological consequences is humanistic in the sense of accepting the totality of human experience as the basis of philosophy. If philosophy aims at comprehensiveness, this is an important advance over the narrower theory which takes only logical consequences into account. But the execution of the program is defective, for lack of a principle to harmonize the aspects of experience. There are two different harmonies to be achieved, one within individual experience, the other between individual and outer environment; but they are not connected. They may be related in action, if fictions actually will serve as a stimulus to endeavor. But, whatever is the case in action, such a relation is not adequate for philosophy; for there are two different answers to such questions as those concerning a moral order of the universe and the freedom of the will, and there is no way of getting the answers together. One is based on the principle that good is a directly experienced harmony between need and satisfaction; the other is based on the principle that truth is an empirical agreement between idea and fact. To identify philosophy with predictive knowledge, we may say, is to choose the second harmony. The will to believe, in effect, chooses the first, instead of relating the two. It attributes simple location in the subject to the experiences with which it is primarily concerned. It interprets objective issues in subjective terms. It translates such topics as monism and pluralism, free will and determinism, idealism and materialism, into terms of individual temperament. The tough-minded are comfortable with materialism, while the tender-minded are more at home with idealism. This is an affirmation of the validity of the subjective over against the objective. It is a claim that individual experience is as important in formulating a philosophy as is impersonal, physical fact.

This last is true. But the problem is to get the two together, and here the theory has nothing to offer. To combine them is precisely the aim of instrumentalism.

6. Instrumentalism

We have already considered instrumentalism in several connections. The theory that thinking originated as an attempt to solve practical problems is instrumentalist. The specific account of the natural basis and setting of thinking in the interaction of organism and environment is also instrumentalist. It provides a link between knowing and being, experimental thinking and natural existence; and it is the explicitly developed formulation of the general pragmatic thesis that thinking serves action. We now have to see how instrumentalism conceives philosophy and how far its conception solves the problem implicit in the theory of psychological consequences. The discussion will bring us back to the subject of the genetic method.

There is a duality in experience between values and existence, and in a certain sense it is also a contrast between subjective and objective. But the duality is neither absolute nor final. It is not absolute because experience itself as an on-going process contains satisfactions, and values are concrete satisfactions. It is not final because the duality, as we find it in experience, can be progressively overcome by deliberate human effort. We can remake the natural environment and ourselves in such a way as to stabilize and increase satisfactions. For these reasons there is no fundamental conflict between theoretical and practical interests. Consequently, it is not necessary to choose between facing the world with energy and courage, but without hope of finding there any source of deep satisfaction, and retreating into a private world of fantasy and then pretending that the imaginary entities located there also exist elsewhere.

The aim of action is to bring about a harmony of real existence and ideal values, actualizing intelligent ends through the use of appropriate means. In this way, theoretical and practical interests should be united, and it is the function of philosophy to describe and make vivid their complementary relation, to connect scientific knowledge with the prophetic visions of art and religion. In place of a separation between reality and the world of the imagination, it proposes a fruitful union between knowledge of existence and insight into possibilities. Philosophy is disciplined vision, practical idealism; and its task is both critical and constructive. It must criticize the habits and dispel the inertia which hold men in the clutch of the past. And it must provide positive goals of action, by interpreting the results of science in their significance for all the aspects of human life.

In discussing the relation between different kinds of psychological consequences, we were led to make a distinction between two kinds of harmony, one within experience, the other between experience and independent fact. Instrumentalism makes an analogous distinction, but it is based on a different principle and leads to a reinterpretation of the entire problem. It contrasts a harmony that is progressively achieved through time with one that comes to be within the present situation. Each calls for a word of explanation.

The harmony of existence and values is only gradually achieved. With advances in knowledge, a greater control of nature and human nature is made possible. More means are progressively at the disposal of men for the satisfaction of their needs and the enrichment of life, and so human desires can be more and more completely realized. As the means for satisfaction increase, the reasons for satisfying desires through compensatory escapes from reality diminish. Conversely, as man comes to understand himself better, his desires become more realistic and more intelligently adapted to the means at his disposal. The search for the good must be experimental because its success depends on a close relation of means and ends. The method of intelligence must supplement and correct the vision of the poet. Values, therefore, are essentially hypotheses, to be tested like any others, and either retained or discarded in accordance with the results. The reason why values can be only progressively achieved is their dependence on knowledge, which is itself a gradual and cumulative achievement. Man learns from experience and passes on what he has learned to succeeding generations. The results of past experience are applied to future problems, and so knowledge accumulates. At the same time, old theories and ideas require continual reconstruction in the face of novel conditions. Habit is the economy of thought, but habits become outmoded and ineffective when they are applied to conditions that are too different from those on which they were originally based. Thus empiricism suggests an interpretation of both knowledge and values in terms of the relation between past and future.

But the concept of the problematic situation and its resolution suggests a criterion of knowledge and value that is immanent in the present. Its origin is in the theory of logic. Within the single logical process there is movement from the initial stage in which the difficulty is merely felt, through its analysis and the elaboration and testing of hypotheses, to the final stage, in which the situation is experienced as a unified whole of related elements. The positive verification of a hypothesis is marked by a sense of unity, organization, and resolution in the formerly confused situation; and the resolution constitutes the last stage in a single, unified process. The verified hypothesis may later be applied to other cases; but the test of its present truth is its success in effecting an internal reconstruction of the present situation.

If the result of the testing is negative, the situation remains in certain respects unintegrated and conflicting. Nevertheless, according to instrumentalist logic, it is reorganized and basically unified. The problem has been located, alternative hypotheses formulated or adumbrated, and one of them eliminated. If the problem is not solved, at any rate we know that we do not know—and, it seems, what we do not know. We understand that we do not understand.

That the resolution of a situation might be negative in a more fundamental sense than this has not been recognized by pragmatism.

In the same way as in the case of thinking, intrinsic value is to be understood in terms of the organization of the present. Good consists in the meaning and breadth of present activity and in their increase. It is realized when the present becomes an aesthetic whole, in which the separations of means and end, possibility and actuality, fact and value, knowledge and feeling, have been overcome. The good is unified, unobstructed activity. "We do not use the present to control the future. We use the foresight of the future to refine and expand present activity. In this use of desire, deliberation, and choice, freedom is actualized."[8] Thus the concept of the situation leads to an interpretation of both knowledge and value in terms of the present. This is also empiricism, but not of the traditional variety.

The difference between the two notions of unity or harmony is not that one is objective and the other subjective; on the contrary, both are objective. The gradual acquisition of knowledge and satisfaction in the one case depends on conformity to facts; while in the other the situation includes organism and environing circumstances, both of which are elements in the present, experienced harmony. Present harmony no longer has a subjective connotation, for practical satisfaction always has an objective basis, except in pathological cases. Nor is the distinction between the harmonies based on the contrast of theoretical and practical interests. Both knowledge and values are progressively realized through history and are, in fact, interdependent; the first is the condition of the second, while the second is the chief reason for the exercise of the first. On the other hand, both truth and good must in the last analysis be interpreted in terms of the present process of experience and existence, which are for pragmatism the locus of reality; the immediately felt harmony is cognitive as well as practical.

The difference is rather between present and future. One kind of

---

8. Dewey, *Human Nature and Conduct* (New York, 1922), p. 313.

harmony is experienced within the single situation; the other is progressively realized through a series of situations. The question naturally suggests itself: How does it happen that there are two different notions, and what is the relation between them?

The source of the two notions of harmony lies in the instrumentalist interpretation of the process of experience in psychological terms and at the same time in terms of both logical and biological characteristics. The two harmonies are suggested by the biological and the logical aspects of experience, respectively, and the kind of unit associated with each. The biological aspect involves the concept of the practical situation, which begins with conflict and ends with equilibrium and harmony. The logical aspect involves the notion of thinking as an endless process of inquiry carried on through successive situations, in which there is progress but in which the resolutions of problems always retain something of a tentative and partial character. But because wants are modified by intelligence, practical activity has something of the continuity of theoretical inquiry; and because thinking arose out of and is inseparable from a biological basis, it exhibits something of the nature of the latter. Consequently, both theoretical and practical experiences can be interpreted in terms either of the present or of the future, depending on the unit of experience which is defined or presupposed.

There is a general difference in span between logical and biological processes. A complete logical process, from the first experience of a problem to its final resolution, may cover a long period of time. A scientist may spend years, perhaps even his entire life, in attempts to solve a single problem. The attempts are discontinuous, yet they are parts of a single process. But the biological situation and act are of relatively short duration. The process by which the animal satisfies its need for food, from the initial tension and disequilibrium of hunger to the equilibrium which follows eating, is usually not a long one; and it has a degree of continuity that is not present in the longer and sustained search for knowledge. But a theory which interprets thinking in naturalistic terms, as arising out of animal efforts to satisfy needs, will try to relate the biological and logical processes. And, since the latter have presumably arisen out of the former by an unbroken development, it would be easy to suppose that the two are somehow the same. Both, for instance, are characterized by conflict and the effort to resolve it; there are both theoretical and practical forms of conflict.

But it is clear that they are not the same when we consider the elements of continuity and discontinuity involved. Experience is continuous, but it is also divided into discrete units. The word "activity" covers both notions, and it is therefore sometimes ambiguous. It may signify a continuous process, as when we speak of "organic activity" or the "activity of thinking"; here it refers to a kind of process. But it may refer to separate acts, as when we say of a person that his various activities during the day were logically related. When experience is considered as a series of discrete processes, the logical unit and the biological unit are not, in general, the same. The first is the act of judgment, the second the act of satisfying a need. But these also are interrelated; and the discrete units, on examination, reveal some of the traits of a continuous process.

The unit of logical experience, according to pragmatic logic, is the judgment rather than either the concept or the inference. But the distinctions tend to blur. A concept is an implicit judgment, and a judgment is a suppressed inference. The spoken word "green" often stands for a judgment (though it may also signify a question or some other form of expression); and what judgment the speaker intends to communicate by it is usually clear from the context. It may be "The green of that coat is hideous"; or it may be "The lawn is very green for this season." Judgment, in turn, is inferential, since the attribution of a property or relation is implicitly a series of predictions. When the speaker describes the color of the grass, he may imply that "if blue and yellow pigments were combined in equal amounts, the mixture would have this color"; or he may imply that "under artificial light, this surface would appear blue." On this theory the distinction between immediate and mediated knowledge tends to disappear, and the process of mediation is endless. As in idealistic logic, so here, the mind is regarded as an active process of interpretation and synthesis which is unbroken and unending. On the other hand, when thinking is considered naturalistically as problem-solving, it seems to eventuate in an immediate judgment of perception, an observation which verifies a hypothesis and terminates the act of thinking. Finally, when thinking is interpreted in terms of scientific inquiry, it seems to combine some of the characteristics of both idealistic and naturalistic interpretations; and the complete act of thinking appears to be extended and inferential, yet limited.

The unit of practical experience for pragmatism is easier to identify when it is defined in terms of the sequence from biological need to satisfaction, for these provide clearly marked initial and terminal points. But the efforts to satisfy need involve the use of means, and thinking provides the most effective means of all. If the theoretical and practical aspects of action remained separate, this would present no problem; thinking would simply constitute a link or series of links between need and satisfaction. But thinking modifies wants, and it is inseparable from language and communication, which are at the roots of culture. Thus needs become intelligent and socialized, with the result that practical experience exhibits the characteristics which appear in theoretical experience. Practical activity tends to become continuous and to extend indefinitely into the future. There is one search for satisfaction; experience cannot be atomized into separate wants and interests.

Thus experience is both continuous and divided into unitary processes; and these two characteristics, which are found in both logical and biological processes and in both theory and practice, suggest two different criteria of harmony.

The position adopted by instrumentalism on this whole question is implied by its theory of the function of knowledge. Knowledge and value are, in effect, the scientific and the aesthetic dimensions of experience, and the first is an instrument for realizing the second. Each present experience has its own immediacy and its own consummatory quality; and, so far as these have significance for the

EXISTENCE AND INQUIRY

individual, the experience and its resolution are good. But experienced values, unless they are intelligently and systematically pursued, are largely the result of chance. So the enrichment of present life depends on knowledge, which foresees the future on the basis of the past. And as knowledge increases through history, value also increases, so far as the knowledge is applied. It has been applied in the past, but it can be made much more effective. It is the contention of instrumentalism that concrete values have increased through history and that philosophy can further their continued growth in the future by showing the close dependence of ends on methods of intelligent control.

But man is primarily practical, and, when he lacks knowledge or fails to apply it, he will find his satisfactions in other ways. In the uncertainty and fear of early savagery, he was driven to develop systems of meaning which corresponded to reality only loosely, and at the points necessary for survival. He found his satisfactions largely in a world of subjective fantasy. But, with gradual improvement in the ways of knowing and with the accumulation of knowledge and skills, control over nature has increased; and, as superstitions have been discarded, the interpretations of the world by which men live have come ever closer to the actual nature of things. Thus instrumentalism accepts the account of the past given by the genetic method.

This genetic account is, of course, not peculiar to instrumentalism. It is accepted in substance by everyone, whether a pragmatist or not, who holds that predictive knowledge is the criterion of reality. But it has a special significance in the present context. By implication it abandons the thesis that the present situation is the locus of reality. It reintroduces the dualism of subjective experience and objective world; and this raises once more the problem of their relation, which the concept of the situation was to have explained. It retains the will to believe and the theory of fictions; for, after all, what reason is there to believe that human ideals can ever be realized? A philosopher once said that the mind asks questions it cannot answer. Perhaps man also desires the impossible and strives for what he can never attain. The religious and artistic imagination envisage ideals which give unity and meaning to life. But it may be that the only ideals big enough for unity are too big for existence. The suggestion cannot be lightly brushed aside by a philosophy which asserts that man has traditionally sought consolation in a world of dreams because he was unable to cope with reality. It cannot reply that human ideals must prove practicable because they are produced by an animal whose nature has been slowly shaped into conformity with his environment, for perhaps mechanisms of escape themselves may perform a realistic function. And if man has been an escapist in the past, is there any reason to think he will be less so in the future?

For the genetic method the problem is unreal only because it interprets history from the limited perspective of the nineteenth century, which contrasted the real struggle for existence and the unreal world of imagination which is a refuge from it. Our society actually embodies this contrast with many variations, in its dichotomies between business and leisure, technology and art, nature and the supernatural, thought and emotion, fact and value, practice and theory. Now these oppositions are characteristic of the modern world rather than of history as a whole; yet the genetic method has made them principles of general historical interpretation. The justification offered is that our outlook is truer than others, for it is the outcome of a long development by which imaginary explanations of events have been gradually eliminated through confrontation with fact in the struggle for existence. But how far that conclusion is acceptable depends on the criteria that we apply. Ability to predict and control events has increased enormously in the modern period, along with logical and methodological developments. But does it follow that we are closer to reality? If we apply the criterion of internal coherence and unity of meaning to present social and individual life and to the set of ideas which form the basic assumptions of the modern world, the answer is dubious at best. If present unity of meaning is the test, we might well ask whether, on the contrary, we are not farther from reality;

for the present is, to a high degree, insecure, doubtful, confused, and full of conflict. There is no valid reason for believing that we have achieved greater unity of outlook or harmony of experience than other cultures have done or than our own has done at other times.

The genetic method interprets the history of mankind as a quest for security and certainty, which may be pursued either realistically or by a flight from reality. It is true that life is insecure and that men today want security. But it does not follow that this desire is the mainspring of human action or that it can be reduced to two specific and opposite forms. Because the sense of insecurity is so dominant in our time, the desire for security has been magnified into the fundamental drive of human nature. It seems to be forgotten that, even in our society, men sometimes prefer to give up security for other things. They show by their acts that they want liberty and meaning more than they do security. And they do so because liberty and meaning in action are positive, while security is negative; it is the absence of danger. Positive ends are more powerful than negative, when man and society are in a healthy state. For this reason, the concept of security is not adequate as an explanation of human action. When man is not healthy morally, he may devote his energies to escaping from something dangerous, hostile, or unpleasant; but such a course, when successful, will result only in the removal of dissatisfaction; it will not in itself constitute positive value. It is a kind of defensive warfare against the universe.

The theory that men by nature seek security is similar to the old utilitarian doctrine, now discredited, that all human action is directed at pursuit of pleasure and avoidance of pain. Hedonism was generally rejected when it was discovered to be an unempirical abstraction. Men do not usually desire pleasure in the abstract, and it does not exist in the abstract. Men engage and are interested in concrete activities, which carry with them their own characteristic satisfactions. Security is another abstraction. Like pleasure, it explains everything and therefore explains nothing. It is not a separate end, nor is the desire for it a separate, inherent need. Men find it in their concrete activities, beliefs, institutions, and relationships, when they find it at all. But beliefs and institutions cannot be understood as so many efforts to achieve it. Like pleasure, the sense of security can be made an end, for it is possible to make abstractions and subjective feelings into goals. But preoccupation with subjective feeling is neither a usual nor a satisfying type of activity. Because security is not a separate entity and the need for it is not a separate force, both must be understood adjectivally and relationally, with reference to the total situation in which they occur.

According to instrumentalism, following the genetic method, the scientific and aesthetic elements in experience can be progressively integrated, and, so far as the integration takes place, conflict is eliminated. The integration is a comprehensive aesthetic synthesis, which, however, includes the scientific to the extent that the present is enriched by intellectual meanings. There is no doubt that such unification occurs. Indeed, the two elements always are unified in experience to a large extent; their separation in analysis is more in need of explanation than is their unity. The question is not whether they are related, but how. Their separation occurs when a distinction is made between the logical or the scientific as the criterion of reality and the aesthetic as the criterion of value. The two criteria are different, and they may conflict. Once the distinction is made, it is difficult to see how the two dimensions of experience can be brought together again in any way that will yield a real unity.

The identification of the real with the known is denied. It is said that knowledge is not the exclusive avenue to reality and that things felt, undergone, feared, or desired are as real as things known. Experimental intelligence knows reality, while art and other immediate or consummatory forms of experience have reality. But the description of the two directions in which man tries to find security shows that the denial is not consistently maintained. If all sides of experience and all kinds of objects equally deserved the name "real," the objects of poetry and metaphysics, religion and mathematics, legend and communal feeling, could claim equal consideration along with those of rational foresight. And any harmony achieved between the various needs and demands of our natures would be good. But the aim forced upon us by harsh existence is adjustment to natural, physical conditions; and this adjustment is the proof that we are in touch with reality. Thus the scientific takes precedence over the aesthetic and knowledge over experienced values. A real unity might be achieved by a genuinely reciprocal relationship, in which each element was seen as one aspect, complementing the other in the same experience. But this position is ruled out if the scientific and the aesthetic are two kinds of experience and the first is a means to the second. It has never been made clear how a knowledge of means can control ends; or why, if consequences can be predicted, such knowledge should modify wants in the direction either of a more social conception of good or of one centered in the present rather than in the opposite directions. How the scientific and the aesthetic are integrated in experience is no clearer. If they are aspects of a single experience, then aesthetic experience is rational; and, conversely, in knowing we experience reality directly. But, to maintain this position, it is necessary to break with instrumentalism.

The genetic method attempts to combine the two criteria of unity. On the one hand, each present experience forms its own unity and interprets reality on its own terms. The individual and the social group formulate ways of thinking, acting, and enjoying which are more or less appropriate forms of unifying their experiences of the world. But, on the other hand, knowing is relating, and therefore to know and evaluate any present is to place it in the evolutionary process, the stages of which constitute progress. If each present should evaluate itself, the result would be sheer anarchy, and we should have no picture of the historical process of human experience. The first criterion evaluates each historical situation on its own terms, the second evaluates all from our standpoint.

The problem is an important and difficult one. Scientific empiricism implies an objective attitude toward all data and so appears to favor the first criterion; from this standpoint it would seem that each situation has its own intrinsic meaning, relative to its own perspective. On the other hand, experimental science appears to be the most adequate and authoritative form of knowledge yet discovered and therefore to supply a standard by which to measure the degrees of validity which all other forms possess. The position most frequently adopted on this matter is a compromise: values are historically and culturally relative, and each historical present must be understood on its own terms. But scientific knowledge and method are not relative in the same way; so far as knowledge and reality are concerned, it is our own account that provides the standard for measuring the validity of all others. The basis for this distinction is the assumption that values are somehow subjective and attainable in relative independence of the nature of existence but that this is not the case with knowledge. If this is so, men can achieve values without possessing more knowledge than the minimum necessary for survival. It follows that criteria of value must be understood in relation to the situation in which they arise but that criteria of knowledge must be assessed from our own standpoint. But this distinction and the underlying assumption are invalid if the present is the locus of reality, which is the basis of both knowledge and value.

The sciences of custom have familiarized us with the idea that good is relative to time, place, and circumstance. To judge the members of one culture by a code of morals and manners which was developed in another everyone now recognizes as a form of prejudice. The standards of each society must be evaluated by their success in solving its own problems. And the most enlightened of those who assert the superiority of Western culture would do so on the ground that it is better when measured by this test. But, in this matter, are not criteria of value and of knowledge on a level? Every culture and age, perhaps every individual, is faced by theoretical problems and elaborates its own intellectual methods and standards for dealing with them. It follows that, to understand forms of inquiry, we must see them in relation to the conditions out of which they arose. They are logical habits which grow and change, like any others, in response to the needs of action and experience. If this is sometimes overlooked, it is because moral limitations have proved easier to see than intellectual ones. But limitations exist in every set of intellectual criteria; their existence is inherent in the very nature of human thinking and the historical process. It follows that the Aristotelian logic, for example, must be seen in relation to the cultural conditions of ancient Greece, if it is to be understood. The same is true of the scholastic logic of the Middle Ages, the mathematical analysis of the seventeenth century, the dialectical and inductive logics of the nineteenth century, and the logic of pragmatism. The same is also true of the logic of any other culture than that of the West, as well as of stages in the history of such a culture.

Thus the two criteria cannot be harmonized by assigning one to truth, the other to value. Truth and value must be interpreted in the same way. Either both can be understood in terms of the present, or both involve some relation between past and future. The criteria are incompatible, and it is necessary to choose between them— between the present and the future, between an immanent and an external criterion of truth and value. And if philosophy is an attempt to see things as a totality, we should look to the present, for it is only in the present that a totality is ever found. As soon as we leave it, we have started through a series of experiences which is never completed. The alternative to the interpretation of meaning, truth, and value in predictive terms is their interpretation in terms of the present situation.

7. Truth, Value, and the Present

At the beginning of our analysis, pragmatism was described as a theory of inquiry designed to deal with a world in process. We seem to have shifted gradually to a very different view. Pragmatism later appeared to be a philosophy of experience and primarily of practical experience, whose most significant thesis was the definition of value as a harmonious organization of present satisfactions. But the term "experience" when used as a substantive has often had subjectivist connotations, suggesting a contrast with fact. The repudiation of such connotations is an important part of the pragmatic theory of inquiry, which denies that experiences and facts are two classes of entities. Their integral unity in inquiry is formulated in the concept of the situation. The essence of the pragmatic method is the empirical concept of experienced consequences within the situation. Here experience appears as an adjective, and nothing further is implied about the character or status of the consequences themselves.

But, while the situation forms the existential setting of inquiry, it has implications that reach far beyond such activity. It is the existential setting of value as well as of knowledge; for "satisfaction" is no more satisfactory a term in its substantive form than is "experience." Moreover, it is not an inert fact. Any situation contains enduring and stable objects, but, taken as a whole, it is not itself such an object. It is not a thing, like a stick of wood. The notion of "situation" is closely allied to certain other notions, in particular, "act" and "perspective." But whatever else it may be, the situation is a present process. Pragmatism, to employ the phrase of Mead, is the philosophy of the present. Thus the examination of the presuppositions of experimental thinking, which is demanded by the critical nature of philosophy, carries pragmatism beyond criticism to a positive theory of existence.

We have described an arc. Beginning with inquiry into process, we found ourselves gradually drawn into a discussion of the subjective effects of ideas on believers. The distinction of theoretical and practical consequences led to a split between experiences and objective realities. But experiences, too, are natural realities; and philosophy must examine their status in nature. In this way the recognition of the natural status of experience leads to the elimination of the split, for all natural realities are related. Indeed, recent thought has more and more concerned itself with relationships, until one might almost say that the concepts of "relationship" and "interaction" rather than that of "entity" now form its starting-point. To understand experience is to see it in terms of relationships and interactions within the situation.

So the arc is completed. But its two ends are different. We began with an explicit theory of inquiry, based on a notion of process which was largely implicit. But we are ending with a comparatively explicit notion of process, which, however, suggests an idea of inquiry that is still undeveloped. The explicit theory of inquiry with which we started is suited to a prediction of the future rather than to a description of the present. We have interpreted pragmatism as a movement which has advanced from a method of inquiry to a theory of existence.

The advance is, of course, only in part a chronological one, and the chronological aspect is not its point. The significance of the movement lies in its approximation toward a statement of the relation of man to the universe. This interpretation, of course, presupposes a conception of the aim of philosophy; and the validity of the interpretation rests on the acceptance of the conception.

Neither the interpretation nor the conception will be accepted by those who define philosophy as criticism; and this group includes all those who identify pragmatism with the method of consequences and understand by it the procedure of the experimental sciences. If this point of view is accepted, it follows that philosophy does not have a subject matter of its own and will not reach any positive results; for all factual knowledge is the result of observation and experiment within a limited field; and no one has yet maintained that philosophy is an experimental science. The proper subject matter of philosophy will then be human beliefs, although their study will not be restricted to it but will also be carried on by many other disciplines. Its aim will be the analysis of the beliefs. It cannot determine their truth or falsity; this is the business of the sciences. Nor can it say what is the proper meaning of empirical beliefs; for this, too, ought to be determined experimentally, by the test of practical usefulness. It can only sort out beliefs, determining which are meaningless and which have meaning or which would belong to each class, granted some specific set of assumptions about the usage of words.

Such has been the main tendency of philosophy for two centuries.

PRAGMATISM

Much pragmatic thought continues it, in maintaining that all practical problems have experimental solutions. But it is not this phase of pragmatism that marks the beginning of a new era in philosophy. On the contrary, this is a continuation of the old era of empiricism and liberalism, which has held that all ideas are to be analyzed and confirmed or disconfirmed with reference to sense-experience. If this is the nature of philosophy, it is difficult to see how it can have any positive function, though some of its advocates hold that it does. The persons best fitted to produce hypotheses are those who are going to elaborate and use them. The scientists produce their own; they do not leave this task to philosophers. The case should be the same with values: they ought to be left to those who hold them, namely, society at large. Philosophers, if called upon, will continue to formulate ideals that are as empirically meaningless as those are said to be which they have formulated in the past. If philosophy is criticism, the positive ends of action must come entirely from other sources. With this attitude, it is natural that philosophy, in spite of its critical activity, should uncritically assume the traditional values of the modern world.

But philosophy is not an effort to forecast the future. Why, then, should it adopt methods which have this aim? The strongest argument is that this offers the only alternative to intellectual chaos. Either each experience is its own witness and gives evidence as authentic as any other, or else there must be empirical standards of evaluation and comparison. But the second alternative is ambiguous. Empirical standards are not necessarily those of predictive knowledge. Philosophy, along with the sciences, once threw off the authority of the church. Is it now to stop halfway and itself accept the authority of science? Must it not, rather, develop its own criteria? If it is criticism, the criticism should be applied in this field as well as in any other.

The real reason why philosophy cannot be identified with the experimental method is that philosophy is more than criticism. We have met recognition of this fact in certain positive and humanistic tendencies within pragmatism. But these tendencies themselves have been vitiated by failure to develop an independent point of view. Since knowledge is the province of the sciences, the positive contribution of philosophy must fall within the sphere of the imaginary. The aim of philosophy will then be to provide satisfying or inspiring ideas rather than true ones. The paradoxical theory that the past changes with the present, which Mead put forward, illustrates the same subordination of positive doctrine to method. His aim was to describe reality in terms of the present. But, instead of explaining the present reality of the past, he, in effect, reduced the past to an instrumental construct for explaining the present.

I shall not attempt to discuss the nature of truth at this point. Certainly, it is possible to define truth and knowledge in such a way that they are to be found only in the experimental sciences. It is equally possible, on the basis of a distinction between appearance and reality, to define them in such a way that they are accessible only to a transcendental philosophy. Both courses have been tried, and neither has proved very fruitful. Instead, let us consider how the separation between existence and value has affected conceptions of philosophy.

The effect of the separation has been, as was just remarked, a tendency to measure philosophies by their ability to provide human satisfaction. The function of philosophy is to satisfy either the whole man or those sides of his nature which are not primarily intellectual—his imagination, emotions, or practical needs. The separation in its implications involves a split between truth and value; and it led inevitably to a redefinition of the scope of philosophy, which had to change as the meaning of truth narrowed, in order to retain its connection with practical human beliefs. If knowledge is a statement of sequences of occurrences, it has nothing to do with good and evil, which must then be described in other terms. And, so far as philosophy has anything to do with human choices, it must be something other than knowledge. Thus the place of truth in philosophy becomes subordinate, if it has any place at all: it provides the satisfaction for one side of human nature among others. The alternative is the view that philosophy is an attempt to understand the nature of things, differing from other inquiries in its breadth and in the character of its assumptions, which are of the sort called for by its scope. In philosophy so understood, truth has the central position.

Confronted with these two conceptions, we must unhesitatingly choose the second if we believe that the expression "philosophical inquiry" has any meaning, for the first reduces it to nonsense. But if we are to describe philosophy as the pursuit of truth today, in terms that have contemporary significance, it is first necessary to recover the relationship between existence and value which has been lost; and that will not be easy. The notion, so disastrous in its implications, that truth is something to be used and, aside from the use, has nothing to do with good and evil is deeply imbedded in our thinking. Its basis is the assumption which we have been discussing, the mutual independence of objective fact and subjective value. If this is accepted, the problem of harmonizing them immediately follows; and we have been largely concerned with attempts to solve this problem. Granted the assumption, the only significant harmony is that effected by the adaptation of the living organism to its environment. A certain subjective satisfaction may be gained by ignoring and withdrawing from the real world, if conflicts within the individual can be eliminated; but such satisfactions cannot be lasting.

The contribution of philosophy to the process of natural adaptation is important. If philosophy is good for anything, it should help men in the struggle for existence. But it does not follow that it can be defined by that function or that any specific theory about the nature of the struggle is true or that the assumption just mentioned about the relation of existence and value is true. However, philosophy can reject the assumption only by rejecting the theory of consequences, which underlies it, as the measure of philosophical theories. Pragmatism has found this difficult to do because of its mixed heritage.

We have noted how pragmatism has been shaped by the naturalistic and idealistic traditions in modern philosophy. The presence of these strains has given rise to the contrast, which is really a conflict, between theory and practice. Superficially, they are united in the scientific concept of the biological organism, striving to solve its problems and satisfy its needs, but really they clash; for the theoretical account of the organism reacting to its environment takes in organism, environment, and the relation between the two in one comprehensive, detached view. It is objective and contemplative. But from the practical point of view the same environment is seen from the practical perspective of the individual, and it exists only in terms of his interests and purposes; an object of knowledge is the deposit of past experience and is relative to the experiences from which it resulted. A tree is not the same object to the woodsman, the naturalist, the casual hiker, the artist. The data selected and the habits of action formed are different in each case. Understood in these terms, pragmatism is not objective relativism; for where it is objective it is not relative and where it is relative it is not objective. The objective, theoretical point of view yields an account of the facts which constitute nature; the practical, relative point of view consists of the meaning of facts, or of the given, to some individual. The theoretical attitude of naturalism is opposed by the practical attitude derived from idealism. We must act as if things were so and so, attribute certain traits to them; but, as our attitude toward the world is practical through and through, so are these assumptions. Our interpretations of experience are relative to our purposes; none of them can claim any other status. Thus the diverse elements in pragmatism have hindered the development of a systematic theory of the nature of things.

The possibility of systematic philosophy, as well as of objective knowledge in general, depends on the fact that we can discern something of the character of things on the basis of a limited experience of them. The possible interactions of an object with the rest of nature are endless. Out of this endless number, only a limited selection occurs; and of those that do occur, we observe only a few, when we observe any at all. Yet from our restricted observations and manipulations of objects, we are sometimes able to make significant statements about their properties and powers.

We do so by abstracting those factors in the interaction which are due to the object from those which have other origins, and in particular those which originate in us. The success of our inquiries depends on our skill in abstraction and in generalization, which depends on the former. All our methods and techniques are directed at increasing our abstractive powers. And this is the meaning of objectivity, which is the ability to discount the part played in our initial, uncritical interpretations by our emotional attitudes and intellectual preconceptions, in order that we may see the object as it is. Our problem is to disengage ourselves sufficiently from the situation in which we are involved to understand it. Philosophy here is like other inquiries. But, since its aim is discovery of the completely generic aspects of things, it must strive for an even greater objectivity than inquiries whose aim is practical control in dealing with specific types of situations. The task of philosophy is to aid us in seeing the object as it is; whatever contribution it may make to human experience lies in this direction. It tries to strip off both individual purpose and social convention and any other interpretation, if there is any, which obscures the nature of existence by overlaying it with an outer coating. The aim of philosophic inquiry is not addition but subtraction. This, however, is true of every intellectual inquiry to a greater or less degree, for abstraction is a kind of subtraction.

All the properties of things have implicit reference to some type of situation, though not all are relational in the sense that weight, for example, is relational. Bravery is an inherent trait of character; but we describe it as the disposition to behave in a certain way in the face of danger. To understand a property, we must see in what kind of situation it is displayed; then we may be able to see what the property is.

Let us consider three cases. (1) An apple tastes sweet to me. The sweetness would not exist without a perceiver. Yet the apple would be sweet to any observer fulfilling certain conditions, and sweetness is one of its properties, as objective as weight or shape. (2) I find that a stick breaks when I bear down on it with a pressure of ten pounds. The property was discovered through the action of my arm upon the stick. But from the experiment I infer that the stick would have broken when the same pressure was exerted on it, no matter what its source. The property of the stick is relational; but it is not relative to my experience or to the experience of anyone like me. It exists in relation to any physical force which might operate on the stick. It is what Locke would call a "power," a power to be broken. Indeed, all empirical properties are powers in this sense—powers to do or undergo. (3) Water dissolves common salt. I observe this to happen and confirm it experimentally. But the meaning of the statement that salt dissolves in water is not possible experiences of mine; it is possible action of water on salt. Unlike the first example, the property has no necessary reference to me or to an observer like me. Unlike the second, the operation through which the property was discovered did not involve my participation in the natural interaction through which the property was displayed, but only observation of it.

In all three cases an observer performs an experiment. But his role in each is different; and to define all the properties involved in terms of possible experiences is to ignore significant differences between them. To define even the first one in this way, as a permanent possibility of sensation, is mistaken because the description calls attention to the sensation of sweetness but fails to make clear that the sweetness is a property of the apple. In other words, it fails to explain the nature of the possibility. It is true, of course, that if a property exists it will be experienced under suitable conditions. But the property cannot be defined in terms of possible experiences alone, because the possible experiences depend on an actual object—in this case the apple. It might be replied that the actual apple itself is a set of properties, each of them again consisting of possible experiences. But this is not the case; the apple and its properties are actual and not merely possible. The tasted sweetness depends on the actual chemical constitution of the apple and on other conditions, at least some of which are not experienced. That they might be experienced is not the point.

The experienced quality is not a subjective sensation but belongs to the situation. Its dependence on the situation is direct. This dependence is not merely a logical connection with other experiences, of the sort expressed in the statement that if I bake the apple its taste will alter. And it is not merely a causal connection, of the sort intended when we say that the apple was the cause of the sweet taste, implying that other agents than the apple might have caused the same taste. These kinds of connection are indirect or external, in the sense that their existence is not discoverable by an inspection of the quality connected. Both are involved in the fact that the apple tastes sweet. But, in addition, there is a direct dependence of the quality experienced on the situation. By this I mean that there is a directly experienced or experienceable difference between tasting the sweetness of the apple and merely having a sensation of sweetness. The difference is intrinsic to the situations; this is due to the fact that the apple is given in the one case but not in the other. In both cases the sensed quality depends on actual conditions. But when the perception is mistaken or illusory and the sensation is, as we say, "subjective," one of two circumstances holds. Either the conditions fail to include the object or some other factor essential to perceiving the property, or else they include a distorting element, for instance, indigestion in the taster.

However, to say that an apple is given is not to say that it is completely given. If it were not given at all, ideas of it could not be suggested by the experience of it. On the other hand, if it were given completely, and as it is in independence of the situation, ideas of it would not be suggested either; the nature of the object would be directly and concretely presented, and there would be no occasion for conceptual interpretation. Neither of these two alternatives agrees with the perceptual aspect of knowledge. Also, to say that a condition of a sensed quality is given is not to say that all its constituents are given. In my experience of the sweet apple, the apple is presented; but it does not follow that all the cells or molecules in it are presented. Furthermore, when the apple is tasted, it is not given with the same clearness as the quality. But this is not surprising, since they are different kinds of entity.

Extraordinary instances, such as the observation of distant stars, should not be taken as typical in considering the subject of perception. They differ in important respects from the kind of situation with which we are concerned here. When, for example, I have an experience which might be formulated in a statement such as "There goes John" or "That is the library," the temporal span of my perception does not succeed another span which is occupied by the transmission of the stimulus. The perception is an event, and the underlying physical and physiological conditions are series of events. But the sequences of simpler events which constitute the conditions are included within, or are phases of, the total event, which is the perceptual situation; they do not precede it. We cannot indiscriminately transfer the characteristics of events on one level to those of another level and argue that, because some events are successive, an event of another sort, which is closely related to them, also consists of a succession of units. Therefore, if there are unitary events of different types and if perception involves an interaction between human organism and object, then the existence of media and the transmission of stimuli do not imply that the relation between perceiver and object is necessarily indirect. There may be perception of a present object. The existence of the object is not necessarily an inference from past causal conditions or a construction of future possible experiences. The object may be presently given.

There will be elements that are common to the two experiences, tasting a sweet apple and merely experiencing a quality of sweetness. There is, at any rate, a quality of sweetness present in both, which is the reason why both can be described by the same word. The quality exists in a context in each case and can be abstracted from it. But it is experienced in its context, and its relations to the context are essential to the experience, so that the experience is altered when the quality is abstracted. For this reason, to say that the two experiences are the same is true only in the sense that the same quality can be abstracted from each and that, when it has been abstracted, there remains no discernible difference between the two acts of apprehending it.

Sensory qualities are objective, in the sense of characterizing a situation. However, the classical theory of primary and secondary qualities has a valid meaning. A secondary quality (or, to be precise, the idea of a secondary quality) is one for the occurrence of which some observer, rather like the individual who actually experiences it, is necessary. The apple is sweet only to organisms similar in constitution to myself. The manifestation of a primary quality, on the other hand, may take place through the action of objects of very different sorts. The stick will break because of the pressure of a human hand, an iron weight, or a strong current of water. To define things in terms of possible experiences is to follow Berkeley and regard all sensory qualities as nonobjective, in the sense of that term indicated above. This is as consistent a view of qualities as the one suggested here, but it does not explain their occurrence.

The significance of the experimental method is that it enables us to discover the relational natures of things, through which they are participants in an endless number of possible interactions. From a limited number of observations of their behavior or operations on them, we abstract some of their properties. That we can do this is the chief postulate of the position which I am suggesting. The property is not identical with its manifestations. To assert that the property exists is not to assert implicitly an endless multitude of possible experiences. To say that man is rational is not to say how he would behave in every conceivable situation. But if we understand what human rationality, or the rationality of a specific individual, is and if we are given a hypothetical set of circumstances, we shall be able to say something about how a human being, or this particular person, would behave under those circumstances. However, the nature of an object is not exhausted by its relational aspects, though it is these that the experimental method is designed to discover.

Value is to be analyzed in the same way as truth. The term

"value," like the term "truth," here refers to concrete existence. We have been discussing empirical knowledge; we are now considering empirical good and evil. The question is one of concrete facts, not abstract concepts. In place of possible experiences we have to consider possible satisfactions. We call things "good" or "bad"; that is to say, we ascribe value properties to them. But the properties are not the same as the satisfactions; and, just as things cannot be defined in terms of possible experiences, so value cannot be defined in terms of possible satisfactions, and for similar reasons.

We are not concerned here with the general topic of value. We shall consider only the question of how the notion of the present situation bears on value and what light it throws on the problems arising out of the distinction between subjective satisfaction and objective fact. This is a large restriction, for the situation is a relational concept, while value involves also the private and nonrelational aspect of individuals. And in the last analysis the restriction cannot be maintained, for the relational aspects of value are bound up with the others, just as the relational natures and properties of individuals are inseparable from the nonrelational. However, some statements can be made within the limits of the present discussion.

Value cannot be identified with a subjective, psychological satisfaction, because satisfactions are taken in objects and are relative to their objects. As in the case of sense-perception, so here the quality of the satisfaction is directly dependent on the situation. There is an intrinsic difference between the satisfaction felt in an imaginary object believed to be real and the satisfaction taken in a real object. A man of dull perceptions or perhaps even suffering from delusions may believe that he is the object of respect and affection on the part of his fellows, whereas, in fact, they regard him with amused condescension. The belief gives him a sense of well-being and security. But his feelings differ from the somewhat similar feelings an individual will have whose relations with others are closer and more direct. Here, again, identical elements may be abstracted from the two instances; but in the total situations the satisfactions differ not only in their causes but in their intrinsic characters as well.

But there is another and more important matter to consider in connection with satisfactions. Value and satisfaction are not the same, for we can ask whether a satisfaction is good or which of two satisfactions is better. The questions imply the existence of a criterion by which present satisfactions are evaluated. One point of difference between value and satisfaction is that the first is total, while the second may be partial. But there is more than one totality to consider. We are looking for a standard of value which will apply within the present; but the term "present" covers both individual and situation, and each of these is in its own way a totality. Consequently, two possible criteria of value suggest themselves. It may be said that good lies in the quality and organization of the total present situation, in contrast to some partial aspect of it. On the other hand, it may be said that the good for the individual is the realization of his total nature rather than some limited interest or capacity. The existence of the two kinds of totality makes it clear why the nature of value is not exhausted by an analysis of the situation: value involves the individual, and the existence of most individuals, at any rate, goes beyond a single situation. And so in a general discussion of value we should have to ask what an individual is and how individuals embody value. However, individual and situation are essentially related, for individuals develop and exercise their capacities in situations. Therefore, here again we can say something, if not everything, about a norm of value, in terms of the situation and within the limits of the present discussion.

So far as the good of the individual lies in the development of his capacities, the situation can serve as a criterion of individual value, and the two totalities will coincide. But if the relational nature of individuals extends to values, the good of one individual cannot be indifferent to the natures of others, for they will meet in common situations. That this is true in some cases, at least, is implied in the statement that man is social, when it is made with moral connotations. And if it is true, the good of an individual cannot be defined entirely in terms of the development of his own nature. It must have a relation to others and perhaps ultimately to the whole of existence. Starting from the other totality, then, the situation will serve, in turn, as the criterion for individual development. The good of the individual will lie in activity in the situation and in the satisfaction which it involves. And the better satisfaction will be that associated with the better and more complete activity. The value of satisfaction is relative to the situation and the action of the individual in it.

Thus the separation between value and objective existence rests on two misapprehensions: first, that satisfaction is subjective; and, second, that the good of the individual does not include a relational element but is to be defined entirely in terms of his own experiences and states.

The definition of value in terms of the total situation implies the inadequacy of certain familiar criteria. For example, it is sometimes said that the satisfaction is better which is more favorable to survival or that the one is better which tends to generate further satisfactions in the future. In our example of the delusory and healthy satisfactions, the criterion of survival would usually be said to indicate clearly that the second satisfaction is the better of the two, since delusions are dangerous. But this has not been proved. If satisfaction is one thing and adaptation to reality another, it is logically conceivable that some delusory satisfactions might promote survival. The possibility can be denied only if the delusory satisfaction is, at the same time, inherently a separation from reality and not merely contingently, through its relations to other events. An even greater doubt exists with respect to the second criterion, for it is conceivable that a person who lives on illusions will be likely to experience more feelings of satisfaction over a stated period of time than one who does not. Which is likely to live longer is another matter and again raises the question of the survival value of illusions. But both criteria carry us beyond the present and so are unsatisfactory if the present is the ultimate locus of concrete value. They are attempts to compensate quantitatively for the loss of reality involved in the notion of a subjective satisfaction. When value is located in the objective situation, they become superfluous as independent criteria.

The taste of an apple and a feeling of satisfaction may not be very important either in the experience of a person or in the world at large. Yet it is important to examine them, for they have played a prominent part in the history of philosophy, and for good reason. If philosophy is critical analysis, they will be very significant, for they are the end-products of one kind of analysis. And if the aim of philosophy is to certify beliefs or to facilitate their certification, such data will be crucial; for on critical assumptions the probability of their existence is higher than the probability of most, if not all, other entities and facts. Indeed, some would say that knowledge of them is certain. There is a tendency in critical philosophy to hold that the basis of probable, empirical knowledge lies in an experiential certainty which is found in sensory data. But when critical analysis attempts to build empirical probability on a foundation of sense certainty, its aim is to bring empirical knowledge itself as near as possible to certainty. The ideal goal is a state of knowledge concerning evidence which would enable us to say, "It is certain that so and so is probable to such and such a degree." For this reason, it is critical philosophy, rather than speculative, which today is engaged in the quest for certainty.

Although it has clarified many important issues, the critical movement has from some points of view proved disappointing. It has not led to any comprehensive theory of existence, of the sort that has often been developed by philosophy. The analysis has not led to any considerable synthesis. The reason is that the course of the analysis has seemed to indicate something like an inverse ratio between degree of probability and comprehensiveness. The more probable statements are statements about very restricted entities and events of a sensory nature. It seems to follow that either the traditional comprehensiveness for which philosophy has striven is unattainable or else the critical method is insufficient for philosophy.

The preceding interpretation of pragmatism has been made on

the assumption that the primary aim of philosophy is not the analysis of experience and the validation of belief but the description of existence and that the unit of existence is something quite different from such entities as those just mentioned. But for that very reason it is essential to give some account of these entities in terms of the situation; for they, more than any others, resist such treatment. If it can be shown that their supposed certainty is obtained only by artificially isolating them from concrete existence and process, one of the greatest obstacles to the acceptance of the position advanced here will be removed.

Pragmatism has always claimed to be empirical, and with right. But, as pragmatism itself has shown so clearly, to define empiricism adequately and to adhere to the definition in philosophical inquiry are not easy tasks. To be empirical is to follow experience and the facts. But what experience and which facts? According to our interpretation, the facts and entities which result from analysis into sensory data are not enough, because the purpose of such an analysis is other than the chief purpose of philosophy. Sooner or later, philosophy must make an analysis of another sort.

Existence and Inquiry

THE history of modern philosophy, at first glance, presents a bewildering array of competing systems. But very little examination is necessary to discover that the systems are not a haphazard collection of independent creations and that the competition has definite directions and limits. The relationships are complex, and therefore the material contains the basis for more than one interpretation. Our own analysis has brought to light two different relationships. In one respect the various philosophies are complementary, while in another they represent alternative solutions to a single problem.

Modern thought, taken as a whole, has gradually moved toward a conception of existence which is now rather generally accepted, and to which a variety of influences have contributed. We have traced certain broad aspects of the movement as it occurred in philosophy. Through one period, we saw, the world was regarded basically in terms of order and structure, while the succeeding one regarded it as process. Our outlook today combines these two aspects. Whitehead has said that recent physics substitutes for the Aristotelian notion of the procession of forms the notion of the forms of process. His remark applies, of course, to other fields, such as biology and sociology, as well as to physics. It applies to all fields; but they differ in the manner and time of the discovery and in the extent of the subsequent reconstruction. In philosophy the change has been in the nature of an expansion. Philosophy has not so much substituted one notion for the other within the modern period as it has broadened the conception with which the period opened. Early thinkers began with the notion of reality as order and law; nature for them was no longer a procession of forms but had become the steady exemplification of a single, universal order.

Later thinkers expanded the view to include becoming as well as order, process as well as forms. But the two aspects were first discovered separately, one after the other, and only subsequently were serious attempts made to combine them. Thus the contributions of the principal periods have been cumulative and complementary.

But from another point of view the philosophies present alternative attempts to explain how man can know the world in which he finds himself. The problem here is not the nature of the world but the character of knowledge. The first solution that we examined was that of analysis. To call it a "solution," however, is misleading, for it suggests that some special difficulty was felt with respect to knowledge, and this is not the case. The analytic philosophers were too directly concerned with reality to think much about themselves. Their aim was to delineate existence as completely as possible, and they set about their task without doubts. This is shown by their tendency to speak of logic and method as "tools of the mind." What later thinkers would have called the "problem of knowledge" was to them simply a matter of forging serviceable instruments; and they felt themselves familiar enough with the world to know what kind of instrument was wanted. They assumed that the objects of inquiry are real or, as some said, participate in being and that they are intelligible because of their reality. They assumed, further, that the mind can apprehend these objects under favorable conditions. Whatever was unreal or participated too feebly in being was not intelligible and could not be an object of knowledge in the proper sense. It was this kind of realism which was, above all, characteristic of the logic of analysis.

But the realism declined and, along with it, the logic. The cause of the decline most familiar to us is the theory that there are two different kinds of substance in the world, mind and matter (in addition to God, who finally came to be regarded practically as a third, co-ordinate kind). But the influence of metaphysical dualism on modern thought has been exaggerated. So long as the realism remained vigorous, the dualism was powerless. These two principles did, in fact, coexist in the thought of certain important philosophers, even though they were thereby forced into occasional inconsistencies. For this reason, to describe the age of analysis as "dualistic" is misleading. It both omits the realistic elements which saved the period from the difficulties which we associate with the term "dualism" and ignores other elements which had yet to appear, or to become predominant, before the weaknesses latent in dualism could develop. It also exaggerates the place of the notion of substance in philosophy.

If a dualism of substance had been the decisive factor in producing the familiar difficulties of modern philosophy, we should expect that, along with the doctrine, there would have appeared a belief that mind is, in principle, more knowable than anything else, since on dualistic premises mental substance is more directly accessible to the knower than is the rest of reality. But this did not happen. It is true that there was a certain disposition to discriminate in favor of mind during the seventeenth century. But there was also another disposition to say that God or being is known best of all, and both mind and matter only derivatively. These two tendencies were in conflict, and at the outset the second was the stronger. The first asserted itself only intermittently, for dualism developed under the influence of the doctrine that all existents participate in being and are knowable according to the degree of their participation, which defines their reality. This doctrine influenced even those who did not explicitly hold it and was the foundation of a realism which sharply restricted the significance of the new theory.

The realism and the dualism are themselves merely elements in two comprehensive and very different outlooks, which coexisted and conflicted for a time. The fatal split between subject and object, mind and the rest of the universe, occurred only when the second point of view conquered the first. The second point of view was complex and contained many factors. One was the causal theory of perception, which held that things cause ideas and that the thing and its ideal effect are otherwise separate and independent. This is one application of the general theory of causality associated with the mechanical view of nature. It led to the distinction between primary and secondary qualities. The new theories of nature, causality, and qualities were associated with dualism, but they are not identical with it. In addition to such concepts as these, which were derived from the new science, there were others which expressed the new point of view in politics, religion, economics, education, and other fields of experience. And it is the whole complex which led to the alienation of conscious experience from the rest of reality. What the key is to this whole set of ideas is another question, which I shall not attempt to answer here.

At another place, in the examination of analysis, we considered other changes in philosophical outlook which were associated with the decline of the earlier view. The inability either to translate all common-sense facts into terms of clear and distinct ideas or to reject the residue as unreal led to a distinction between necessary and contingent truths. Before that time, existence and possibility had been distinguished, but both had been interpreted in relation to a single, inclusive reality. Now, however, existence and possibility begin to separate. At first, necessary truths were identified with the highest and most intelligible realities, while contingent truths reported only the residual element of sheer, nonrational fact. But later, by one of those interesting reversals which history sometimes displays, the roles are exchanged. It is now contingent truths that deal with reality, for reality has come to mean contingent existence, while necessary truths are relegated to the realm of mere ideal possibility. We now have the basis for a distinction between formal validity and material truth. And logic comes increasingly to be understood as the science or art of drawing valid inferences from premises, regardless of their truth. Reason has become divorced from natural fact. This conception dealt a blow to the reputation of logic in the popular estimation, from which it has not yet recovered. And it has not recovered because the notion still persists that logic is concerned merely with ideal possibilities. The connection between logic and natural fact is now made by a new branch of philosophy—the study of scientific method. But the necessity for this discipline has diminished rather than increased the repute of logic itself.

While these changes were occurring, reality was coming increasingly to be identified with process. To keep contact with it, philosophy had to break with a logic which had become increasingly separated from facts and was occupying itself more and more with the implications of sets of premises which remained fixed, regardless of their inadequacy. The criticisms of formal logic made at this time are reminiscent of the attacks launched against scholasticism long before. The "understanding" thinks according to a logic of abstract identities; it manipulates its concepts mechanically. It can deal only with abstract universals, which are powerless in the face of concrete facts, and so is too feeble to achieve any genuine insight into reality. Another and synthetic logic is needed, with power to break the bonds of rigid premises and go beyond what is given, just as the process of existence is continually going beyond the past. Thus dialectic offers an alternative account of the nature of knowledge, driven on by the emergence of a new theory of reality and the decline of an old theory of inquiry.

In its efforts to explain knowledge of process, however, dialectic overlooked structure, which it mistakenly identified with quantity and atomism; since it associated these with a materialism of inert substance, structure seemed incompatible with process. It also failed to account for the individual in the sweep of change. The individual was either identified with the isolated, atomic thing of common sense and so condemned to unreality—a supposed substratum with predicates—or subordinated to an abstract pattern of history. But process is individuated; it is not an undifferentiated flux. This is clear from both history and evolution. It is the individual society, person, community, that becomes; evolution occurs through changes in the individual organism. Therefore, to know process is to understand the individual, in the sense of the individuated unit. Moreover, without structure, both individuals and knowledge would be impossible, and experience would be only an immediate feeling of the flux; for structure gives to the individual definiteness of character and an identifiable nature that can be known.

It is the contention of pragmatism that inquiry is an activity directed on unique situations and carried on by means of conceptual structures. Its experimental logic contains all the varied insights which have gone into the formation of modern empiricism. For instance, it has a place for inductive logic, which, like dialectic, developed as a reaction against logical formalism. Inductive logic was a second theory of synthetic reasoning, and it aimed to provide the effective tool of discovery that deduction had failed to supply. Experimental logic has absorbed the central contribution of this doctrine, in its contention that present thinking builds on past experience but is always concerned with a novel situation and so goes beyond the content of past knowledge. Unlike some theories of induction and some forms of empiricism, however, pragmatism also recognizes the distinctive character and role in inquiry of deductive reasoning. And it remedies some traditional weaknesses of empiricism by describing the setting of thinking in natural processes possessing continuity. Finally, it relates the abstract and the concrete phases of thinking—universal concepts and particular facts—by a theory of hypothetical reasoning which applies the concepts to particular existents. Its account of the concrete process of inquiry unites aspects of logical theory which had previously been unrelated, and it interprets thinking as an integral part of the process of existence, distinguished, but not separated, from it by characteristics of its own.

Knowledge of process, we have said, involves the existence of concrete, individuated entities; for, without them, process would be a continuous flux which might be experienced but could not be known because it would not contain specific objects of knowledge. To this it might be objected that philosophy is a search for universal categories; and, even though no discrete entities existed, it might still describe the generic traits of passage. But to say this is both to exaggerate the power of human intelligence and to misconceive the nature of philosophy. Assuming for the sake of the argument that the notion of a continuous process undifferentiated by limited entities and of a human mind confronting that process was intelligible, the mind could not question or even be aware of the process; for,

EXISTENCE AND INQUIRY

whatever else thinking may be, it is pretty generally agreed that it always operates on something specific and limited; it does not examine or question everything at once, even when we reflect on nature as a whole. So, while it is true that philosophy attempts to formulate the generic traits of existence, the limited existent is as essential as the traits. The traits are abstracted from existence and referred back to it; and, unless existence were such as to give mind a foothold, neither the abstraction nor the reference could take place. Thus philosophy is concerned with the individual as well as with the universal.

But pragmatism has not been much concerned with the individual and the concrete as objects of knowledge, nor has it explained what such knowledge is. The problematic situation is the locus of inquiry. But the situation and the problem, though unique, are not themselves objects of inquiry. Let us use the term "concrete entity" in a comprehensive sense, which will not restrict its application to some selected, standard class of entities. We may describe a concrete entity as any existent with a structure and component energies and powers, so related that the entity is and behaves as a unit. It is not only unique but it is unique in a certain way. It is such entities which are the objects of empirical inquiry. But the problematic situation does not answer to this description. In fact, pragmatism in general has been more concerned with the methods than with the objects of knowing. It has left the description of the latter to the sciences. And, because it has conceived knowing in terms of prediction by means of abstract concepts, it is not clear how knowledge can deal with individual existents except as members of classes. To know is not to describe a concrete existent directly but to state the conditions under which an event of a specified type will probably occur, because of its membership in a class. For this reason knowledge, in spite of its practical bearing, is of the universal, after all.

Considered as a philosophy of existence, we have said, pragmatism identifies reality with present process. But this statement is an indication of a point of view rather than the enunciation of a developed theory. Today we hear much of "events" and "process"; and it is often said, with considerable justification, that these terms are vague. They came into common use at a time when the concepts of "substance" and "being" had largely lost their empirical meaning and when positivistic theories were proving unsatisfactory because they failed to account for such aspects of existence as continuity, novelty, and development. The concept of substance ceased to be fruitful when it became separated from observable attributes and was identified with a substratum in which they were supposed to inhere but to which, in reality, they were no longer related. It would be more accurate to say that the original concept was lost, though the word was retained. The term "event," even though of recent origin in its current signification, is already undergoing a similar transformation. It is being called on to perform the same function in rendering facts intelligible as the substratum was rejected for failing to perform; it is becoming a modernized substratum. That is why it is now often used in such a way as to be vague, if not actually meaningless. In a somewhat analogous manner, process is being called on to perform the comprehensive tasks which once were assigned to the concept of being. The analogy breaks down if it is pressed. Yet the concept of being has suffered a fate not unlike that of substance, and for the same reasons: it became unempirical, deteriorated in significance, and so gradually became obsolete. Its meaning in relation to existence was not disproved; rather, its original meaning altered, and it gradually lost its relevance. Unless such terms as "process" and "duration" are kept close to familiar facts, they will repeat a similar history.

Instead of using any of these terms, we spoke of "individual" and "situation" in an earlier discussion. The link between them was found in the fact that individuals have relational natures and act in situations. But these terms are restricted in application. Whether the individual is defined in terms of enjoyment, mentality, life, or in some other way, not all natural entities can properly be called "individuals." In place of this, the more general term "concrete entity," as defined above, may be used to describe any natural existent, whether an individual or not. Such an entity is concrete in that its components are mutually determining and lose in determinateness if abstracted from it and from each other. For example, when the form is abstracted from a concrete entity, it loses in determinateness; it is no longer the individual form of that particular entity.

There are many kinds of concrete entity in nature, such as living organisms, human and nonhuman communities, molecules, and artifacts. Each of these exists and acts in its own context. A human society, for example, has its own proper environment. But the term "situation," as used above, is too restricted in application to describe all such relationships. The more general term "context" suggests a suitable correlative to "concrete entity." Every such entity has a natural context, and an understanding of the entity requires a knowledge of the context in which its properties and powers are exhibited. This is equally true of an animal, a society, a steam engine, and a molecule. The nature and extent of the context depend on the nature of the entity or entities in it.

It would be the task of a philosophical cosmology to describe various types of concrete entity and their natural contexts and the relations they have to one another. The problem with which we are concerned here is in one respect more restricted. To determine generic traits of existence, it is not necessary to survey many different kinds of existent. An intensive rather than an extensive description is required, an analysis of the situation in which we find ourselves rather than an examination of many kinds of situation and entity. In discussing concrete value, we found that it seemed necessary, at first glance, to assign to the present a chronological place in history, in order to make it intelligible. But we held that such an attempt is not really necessary and is, in fact, doomed to failure because the basic criteria of value apply directly to the immediate present. Similarly, in order to understand the nature of existence it is not necessary to survey and compare all the kinds of concrete existence—an endless task. The internal analysis of a restricted situation, if carried far enough, will disclose the traits of existence, for the situation contains indications of what lies beyond it. Although it is present, it contains forces and structures which represent the persistence of the past, and it embodies aims and tendencies that point to the future. It is connected with the rest of existence through its embodiment of laws, habits, and all that gives stability and continuity to nature. It exemplifies a perspective on existence, as well as being a unit of existence, and implicitly points beyond itself.

These considerations raise again the problems of ideology that we considered earlier. We are immersed in the historical process. Not only what we are and do and feel but what we think, as well, is the outcome of historical development and clearly bears the mark of its origins. How can man, then, living always in a limited historical situation, hope to gain an understanding of the nature of things which will have even a slight significance beyond it, not to speak of anything approaching unqualified validity? If the difficulty were simply one of social and economic bias, there might be some hope of eliminating or minimizing the factors which limit the human outlook. We might at least learn to discount them to the extent of suspecting that our opinions do not have absolute validity, and so be on the alert. Even if the difficulty were that inherent in the existence of total cultural perspectives, it might at least be mitigated through the gradual overcoming of cultural barriers. But the problem is deeper than this. The limitations imposed by class and culture are simply the instances which happen to be most striking to us of a perspectival character inherent in the nature of existence itself. That is why the problems of ideology and cultural relativism are so insistent. They are expressions in human society of an ultimate trait of reality and therefore must be numbered among the basic problems of philosophy.

The foregoing argument has indicated the direction in which I think their solution lies, so far as one may speak of a solution in such a context. By an analysis of the present from within, we must attempt to formulate concepts having general validity. There is no

EXISTENCE AND INQUIRY

other course. The suggestion that we should try to get outside the present is an impossible one and could have meaning only for a fundamentally mechanistic point of view; it has never been taken seriously by any important thinker. Such an analysis would aim at a description of the nature of the present and the categories contained within it. But to undertake it, a theory of inquiry and knowledge different from any that we have examined is needed.

Philosophic inquiry may properly be described as analytic, for all knowledge is, in a general sense, analytic; but it has a distinctive character of its own. Philosophical analysis is to be distinguished from two other processes which are essentially different, though similar to it in some respects. The aim of philosophical analysis is to discover aspects of existence which are not themselves existents, in order to further the understanding of concrete existence itself. Physical analysis, on the other hand, divides its objects into parts; and its end-product is elements which are of the same generic kind as the original object, in that they are also existents. They may be entities of another kind—chemical elements instead of a compound, cells or tissues instead of a more complex organism, individual men instead of a society (for a society, too, is capable of physical analysis, as well as of other sorts). They will be smaller in extent than the original; nevertheless, they are parts of the same generic kind as the original. The third process is logical analysis of a concept or verbal expression, which proceeds by relating the original concept or expression to others, as in definition. Thus the three processes yield, respectively, philosophical categories, physical parts, and logical relationships.

Both the first and the third types of analysis are, of course, philosophical in a broad sense. The differences between them are that the first is descriptive of existence, while the second is a clarification of ideas; the first is constructive, the second critical. The first is concerned with truth, while the second deals with meaning—except when it identifies truth with common sense, the content of which it attempts to make articulate. I have called the first "philosophical" because, if the two are to be separated, as they have unfortunately tended to be in recent times, the first has the better claim to the name because it is descriptive. It might be called "metaphysical," instead. But, in reality, it cannot be separated from logical analysis, since philosophy employs concepts the meaning of which it attempts to make clear and express in words. The interdependence of the two in philosophy has been one of our chief themes. Philosophy does not begin by clarifying meanings and then set about testing their truth. On the one hand, it is concerned with existence from the beginning; while, on the other, it never finishes with meaning. For practical purposes we may be able to give concepts a definitive statement that suffices. But when our aim is to state basic categories, we find that our concepts are never quite final. Metaphysical analysis, like physical analysis, is directed on things rather than on concepts; but, instead of dividing them, it abstracts. Form, potentiality, negation, continuity, quality, or extensiveness could never be discovered by division. However, it should be noted that the sciences of nature also abstract, and they are much more concerned with this than with division. They describe structures and forces in nature; yet these are not parts of objects and are not to be found by dividing things into smaller and smaller pieces. In this respect, physics and metaphysics are alike, though they differ in generality. The Greeks were correct in relating them.

Analysis today has come to be identified with the critical element in philosophy, and it often lacks any direct reference to existence. We have examined some of the developments which led to this point of view and some of the assumptions on which it rests. But it is difficult for philosophers to throw off old habits entirely and to hand over the description of existence to others without reservation. Consequently, there is a tendency for exponents of analysis to formulate concepts which they hope have existential significance but whose actual usefulness, they think, must be determined by others. Philosophy, they hold, provides the conceptual or semantical foundations of empirical knowledge but not the knowledge itself. This program, however, has produced a thin and meager set of categories. The ones most commonly accepted are particular, quality, and relation. We have traced something of their historical derivation from empiricism, and this helps to explain the composition of the list. But if we ask why precisely these categories are chosen, the best answer is because they are simpler than anything else to be found. They resist further analysis, while the analysis of others brings us back again to them. The underlying purpose operative in this search for basic concepts has been the discovery of simples.

In this respect contemporary analysis continues to follow a thread that runs through classical empiricism: it finds in physical analysis the pattern for logical analysis. That is why the categories tend to range themselves on one level; they all share certain traits of simples, though they differ otherwise and none is absolutely simple. The view that the generic traits of existence are the subject matter of philosophy easily leads to a similar outcome. Traits are attributes, properties, or qualities; and it is easy to think of all basic categories as so many different "qualities" of natural existence. But "quality" is itself only one category; and to think of such categories as passage, indeterminacy, and continuity simply as so many qualities of things is to conceal problems and distinctions by a word. The passage of quality is not the same as the quality of passage, if there be such a quality. From our point of view, the three categories mentioned are inadequate. A sense-particular may be an "event"; but it is nevertheless essentially a discrete entity, which is finished and complete in itself; it is not involved in relations or in the process of nature. Nor is the structure of things exhausted by relations between qualities or between particulars or between qualities and particulars. There are other kinds of relations, and there are other kinds of terms; and structure itself is as ultimate a notion as either quality or relation.

Philosophy is concerned with first principles or categories, on the one hand, and with concrete, individual existence, on the other. It employs the first to throw light on the second. Modern philosophy, however, has too often been little concerned with the second. It has stressed law, uniformity, and abstract order; and these notions are not enough to interpret concrete existence. Consequently, the explanatory power of its categories has been restricted. The stress on uniformity has appeared in various forms. It occurred in the concept of uniform laws of physical nature. It also occurred in the concepts of moral law and of specific laws or forms of thought. There are physical laws for matter; moral and logical laws for mind. The state was for a time interpreted in terms of political laws, created by a lawmaker; and economic activities, analogously, were considered to follow uniform laws of economic behavior.

The central position of the concept of abstract law or order seems paradoxical in a historical era of individualism. One might have expected the individual to be the dominant notion and law to be subordinate. But the peculiar nature of human behavior was largely identified with the ability of man to understand and control events; and the condition of control was defined as the discovery of recurrent, uniform sequences. Thus abstract law is the condition of freedom, conceived as the ability to control events—hence, the more law, the more freedom—and the paradox disappears. The power of the individual depends on a world governed by laws.

Nevertheless, a difficulty has often been felt in reconciling the autonomous, human person with a universal, natural order. Christian philosophers were faced with fundamentally the same problem of relating a free, rational, and finite creature to an infinite God. Their solution—the human faculty of free choice—was carried over into modern philosophy, which attempted to unite physical determinism and human freedom in a single cosmos. Neither solution was satisfactory. The real problem here is not the reconciliation of law and freedom but the relation between abstract order and concrete existence. Many thinkers, upon discovering the limitations of the notion of abstract order, have rushed to the other extreme and rejected order entirely. They have concluded that natural laws are only human conventions of thought, or they have said that the laws of society, instead of constituting its essence, are only expressions of arbitrary will and force. But the rejection of order will not lead to an understanding of the individual, either.

EXISTENCE AND INQUIRY

Today there is an increasing tendency to make a fresh start at the problem by commencing with concrete existence—instead of beginning with the abstract order and then trying to account for the concrete. For example, the biological and social sciences today are largely concerned with unique, concrete entities, such as a specific community, living organism, human personality, economy, or culture. I am here using the expression "concrete entity" in the comprehensive sense already indicated. Obviously, there are very important differences between these various entities, which must be explained; but the differences should not obscure the respects in which they are all alike. The characteristic of recent science is the increasingly successful attempt to describe such entities in their own terms rather than in terms of their similarities or dissimilarities to others. This knowledge is not descriptive in the sense of being a mere natural history or enumeration of traits. It is genuinely analytic, a statement of the components of the entity and their relations. It involves the use of class concepts, causal uniformities, experiment, statistics, and other tools and methods of inquiry. But it employs them as auxiliaries and not to define knowledge and the object. The intent of such knowledge is to describe the individual object as it is in itself and as it interacts with other natural entities. It is not to discover origins, except incidentally; and the predictions of behavior which are made are based on actual, present properties rather than on unrealized, hypothetical conditions.

Philosophy has been affected by these trends and has played its part in them. Its conception of knowledge has been strongly influenced by the notion of abstract law; perhaps this is why it has so often taken mathematics and physics as models. But it is now bound by ideas formulated in the early period of modern thought and physical science. The most important of these is the assumption that the object of knowledge is uniformities and that an individual is to be understood in terms of its similarity to other members of a class: similarity and uniformity are important; diversity and multiformity can be ignored, except as aids to the discovery of uniformities. Knowledge takes the form of laws which apply to classes of instances. Associated with this basic idea are the specific conceptions of causality and induction which have played such a large part in subsequent philosophical thinking. The formative period of modern thought was not so much preoccupied with uniformity as were the later ones. Classical analysis, as we have seen, had a strong sense for the reality of the concrete and of individual order. But, as time passed, philosophical thinking came more and more to be dominated by the idea of a class, and order came to be identified with uniformity. The classical concept of analysis, at least in philosophy, constituted a brief interlude between the decline of scholasticism and the rise of mechanism; and, as mechanism spread, the sense of individual reality disappeared.

A concept of philosophical inquiry is now needed which will be adapted to the analysis of present existence.

Philosophical inquiry must deal with present existence: the influence of empiricism in modern philosophy, however, has tended to lay stress on either the past or the future. Early empiricism, because of its interest in the origins of knowledge, emphasized the past. To understand the meaning of an idea was to trace it back to its source in external or internal sensory experience. Such accounts, it is true, often confused the logical order of elements and complexes with the psychological order of development; but, in either case, the effect was to lead attention away from the present object. The discovery of habit marked a shift of emphasis from past to future, since a habit is a pattern of possible future action, based on the recurrence of similar sequences. The past remained important, however, since a habit is the deposit of past experiences. But the present was reduced to the status of a sensory clue to action, selected or followed out on the basis of needs and purposes supplied by the knower. The scientific affiliations of this point of view were, on the one hand, with psychology, which was first concerned with the laws of the mind and later began to study the needs of the organism, and, on the other hand, with the physical sciences, which dealt with correlations of recurring characteristics. But to describe the present a kind of analysis is required that is different both from methods which aim at the discovery of origins and from methods which are intended to forecast future experience.

Such a theory of inquiry must include several elements. First, there is needed a concept of individual form, for to know a concrete existent is at least to know its form, in the sense of "what" it is. That the existent has a discoverable, finite form of its own is a presupposition of such knowledge. If this concept has not been an object of study in recent times, the reason is that our methods and theories of knowledge have directed attention to certain other elements of structure in nature—such as correlations of two recurring elements and certain kinds of series—and so have excluded it. But form is not everything. Existence contains active energies or forces as well. This is a matter of continual observation to anyone who is not blinded by a theory. The problem is to formulate the notion of energies in empirical terms; it is not whether such energies exist. The "force" which modern thought has ceaselessly striven to eradicate was not an independent notion. It was really only an adjunct of form. A thing was thought to exert force simply because of its form or essence. Finally, the two notions, "form" and "energies," must be seen in relation, as they exist. The point of departure in inquiry is the concrete existent. And this is also the terminus of analysis; for, when individual form is abstracted from its actual embodiment, there remains a universal which might be exemplified in any number of instances. And when energies are abstracted from their actual locus, they lose some of their determinateness and become factors which might take any one of a number of forms. The complete analysis must return to its starting-point. It is in this direction that an understanding of the concrete must be sought.

Thus general changes in intellectual outlook have a bearing on philosophical inquiry. What the bearing is remains to be seen. Certainly, the changes do not solve the older problems. Nevertheless, these will eventually come to be seen in a new light. The implications can be determined only by the attempt to make the kind of analysis suggested and to discover what aid it may afford toward a general interpretation of existence.

INDEX

Absolute, the, 94, 112
  relation of opposites to, 104 f., 165 f.
Abstraction, 26
  and analysis, 21, 26
  and falsification, 169 f.
  and the genetic method, 207 f.
  of significant structures, 210
Achilles and the tortoise, 167
Act, experience of, 244 f.
Affirmation and negation; *see* Negation
Age of reason, 72
  the task of philosophy in, 212
Aggregate, and the first law of dialectic, 170
Analogy
  concept of, in Greek thought, 166
  knowledge of God by, 166 f.
  logic of, 166 f.
  reasoning by, 205 f.
Analysis, 9 f., 20 f., 25 f., 85 f.
  abstractive, 26 f.
  and atomism, 86
  of change, 203 f.
  limitations of, 148
  logical and psychological, 10
  and synthesis, 52 f.
Antecedent existence, 215, 253
Appearance and reality, 244 f.
  in dialectic, 143 f., 164 f.
Apprehension
  and interpretation, 53
  of reality, 34
Art, as creation, 112
Association
  as a conception of experience, 73 f.
  and dynamic psychology, 194
  psychology of, 147

Bacon, Francis, 28 f., 56 f.
Beliefs, 220
  conflicts and harmony of, 258 f., 266
  and fictions, 264 f.
  "meaningless," 258 f.
  philosophy as examination of, 87 f., 132 f.
  and probability, 261 f.
  and vividness, 35 f.
Bergson, Henri, doctrine of two logics in, 167
Berkeley, George, relation between knowledge and reality in, 62
Bradley, F. H., dialectic of, 186
British tradition, 196

Capitalism, 153 f., 159
Causal conditions, 204 f.
Causality, 78 f.
  as expectation, 59
Certainty, quest for, 276 f., 295; *see also* Certitude
Certitude, as a mental state, 34
Change, as creative, 117
Christianity, 78, 104, 115
Circularity, in thinking, 14
Classes
  economic, and ideologies, 174 f.
  logical, 120
    existential status of, 232 f.
    in pragmatism, 232
Classification
  of biological species, 206, 232
  and knowledge of unique objects, 207 f., 210, 232
  natural and artificial, 210
  pragmatic theory of, 232
  of the sciences, 81 f.
Communication, presupposed by method of consequences, 252 f.
Communism, 159
Community, idea of
  in idealism, 141 f., 196
  in pragmatism, 196

315

Concepts, 79, 217 f. (*see also* Ideas)
definitions of, 216 f.
empirical, 218 f., 232
and the given, 232 f., 245 f.
as a priori, 251
Conflict
of opposites, 96, 104 f.
of theoretical and practical needs, 255 f.
Conformity of ideas to objects, 232, 237 f.
Connotation and denotation; *see* Intension and extension
Consequences
of ideas, 216 f.
logical, 217 f., 228 f.
and psychological, 216 f., 220 f.
restricted and unrestricted, 228 f., 234 f.
present, 226 f., 255
psychological, 219 f.
theoretical and practical, 221, 227
relations between, 257 f., 266
Consistency, 132
Continuity and discontinuity
in experience, according to instrumentalism, 272 f.
in nature
according to dialectical materialism, 155
according to Hegel, 185 f.
Contradiction, law of, 27, 164
dialectical concept of, 133 f.
Contradictions, 96 f., 133 f., 164 f.
Contradictories, 96 f., 134 f.
scientific and value propositions as, 257 f.
Contraries, 96 f., 116 f.
and contradictories, 117
Copy theory of knowledge, 242 f., *see also* Consequences
Critical method, 130 f.
Criticism, as the essence of philosophy, 88 f., 129 f., 212 f.
Cultural relativism, 178 f.
and science, 183 f.
Custom
and dialectical immediacy, 139
or habit, concept of, 72 f.
study of, 75

Darwin, Charles, 154 f.
Darwinism, 74
Data of inquiry, 231 f.
Definitions
of concepts, 216 f.
operational, 228
Descartes, René, 47 f., 58
concept of usefulness in, 70
doctrine of objective reality in, 34 f.
inseparability of inquiry and apprehension in, 29 f.
simple natures of reason in, 44 f., 62
Description, and explanation, 33 f.
Development, and the genetic method, 198 f.
Dewey, John
conception of pragmatism in, 226
on "the Darwinian genetic and experimental logic," 204
on data of inquiry, 231
interpretation of value in, 270
pragmatic conception of inquiry in, 252
unrestricted theory of logical consequences in, 234
Dialectic, 92
an empirical philosophy, 186 f.
idealist
a historical way of thinking, 104, 139
and process, 11 f., 128, 145 f.
premises and presuppositions of, 135 f.
a logic of process, 11 f.
materialist
theory of, 155 f.
three laws of, 157 f.
a method of inquiry and a theory of reality, 92
Dialectical materialism, 11
view of nature in, 151 f.
view of scientific knowledge in, 170 f., 179 f., 182 f.
Dogmatism, 136

INDEX

Doubt, 30 f., 129 f.
Dualism
  in contemporary society, 255 f.
  in history of modern thought, 100, 148, 191, 203, 256

Effect, 215
  participation of, in cause, 35
Empiricism, 183 f.
  and criticism, 134
  stress on activity of synthesis, 53 f.
Empiricist tradition, 123 f., 212 f.
  and pragmatism, 191, 195, 252 f.
Engels, Friedrich
  definition of dialectic, 152
  on the laws of dialectic, 157
Epistemological tradition, 87 f.
Equality, belief in, 266 f.
Essence, and appearance, 103, 106 f., 118, 134
Evolution, theory of biological, 154 f.
  dialectical interpretation of, 171
  influence of, on pragmatism, 194, 232, 250
Existence, 12 f.
  antecedent; *see* Antecedent existence
  and the given, 230, 245
  and values, 259, 268 f.
Existents, finite, 104 f., 169
Experience, 17 f., 231 f.; *see also* Immediate experience
  form and content in, 128, 283
  individual, 253 f., 266 f.
  mere and true, 17 f.
  theoretical and practical constituents in, 259 f.
  thick and thin, 17 f., 52, 230
  and time, 72 f.
Experimental method, 200 f.
  and philosophy, 212 f.
  and the sciences, 238
Experimental reasoning, 200 f.
Explanation, 22 f., 32
  and description, 33 f.
  genetic, 198 f., 204

Facts, 257
  positive and negative, 118 f.
Feeling, verification of, 224

Fichte, Johann Gottlieb, 101 f., 105
Fictions, 69 f.
  and ideologies, 265
  and the will to believe, 263 f.
Finite, the, dialectical theory of, 104 f., 108 f., 165 f.
First principles, 31 f., 47 f.
Form
  and function in nature, 154 f.
  and matter, 219
  and process, 154, 172 f., 191 f.
Freedom
  as creativeness, 111 f.
  and necessity, 115, 131, 180
  and security, 276 f.

Genetic method, the, 75 f., 198 f.
  and abstraction, 207
  compared with the experimental method, 197 f., 227
  criticism of, 207 f., 274 f.
  and development, 198 f.
  and history, 204 f., 275 f.
Given, the
  and concepts; *see* Concepts
  determination of, 247 f.
  and knowledge, 231 f., 243 f.
  preanalytic and postanalytic, 230, 243, 250 f.
  sensuous, 137, 230 f., 250
  as ultimate, 245
God, 38
  idea of, 44, 47
  knowledge of, by analogy, 166 f.
Greek thought
  as compared with modern thought, 78, 116 f., 154 f.
  concept of analogy in, 166

Habit, 74, 217 f.
  and knowledge, 238 f., 269
Harmony
  of beliefs, 258 f., 266
  within experience, 266
  of individual and environment, 266
  present, 255, 268 f.
  progressive, 268 f., 277
  of utilitarian and nonutilitarian needs, 263 f.

Hedonism, 276 f.
Hegel, G. W. F.
  continuity and discontinuity in, 185 f.
  criterion of truth in, 67
  doctrine of negation in, 115
  the finite in, 105
  immediacy in, 137
  nature and the idea of nature in, 151
  relation of subject and object in, 104
  the thing in, 185
History, 71 f., 147 f.
  and dialectic, 104, 139
  and the genetic method, 204 f., 275 f.
  importance of, 4
  and knowledge of the past, 206 f., 210 f., 241
  and the relativity of knowledge, 177 f.
  study of, 6 f.
Hobbes, Thomas, 58, 182
Human nature, 46 f., 71 f., 79
  conflict of needs in, 254
  and the need for security, 276 f.
  pragmatic theory of, 202
  rational and irrational elements in, 202 f.
Hume, David
  concepts in
    of practice, 68 f.
    of reality, 58 f., 69 f.
    of substance, 37
    of usefulness, 69 f.
  doctrines in
    of force and vivacity, 35
    of self-evidence, 45 f.
    of sensation, 31, 35, 37
  a precursor of dialectical materialism, 174
  presuppositions of, 31
  rationalistic elements in, 60 f.
  a systematic skeptic, 59 f.
  view of history of, 71 f.
Hypotheses, 200, 271
  values as, 269

Idealism
  dialectical, 11, 93 f.
  and dialectical materialism, 152 f., 159, 184
  inadequacy as a system, 144 f.

influence on pragmatism, 195 f.
time and eternity in, 145
view in
  of nature, 148 f.
  of science, 150 f.
Ideas (*see also* Concepts)
  adequate, 40 f.
  affirmation and negation of, 35
  analysis of, 39
  clear and distinct, 41 f.
  function of, 80 f., 226, 241 f., 250
  intuitive, 43
  objective reality of; *see* Reality, objective
  and objects, 63 f., 133
  as process in dialectic, 161 f.
  regulative, 150
  of sense, 35
  simple, 30 f., 35, 40 f., 44, 57
  truth of, 49
  as weapons, 76 f.
Identity, 36
  in development, 198 f.
  and difference, 145, 158 f., 165 f.
  of self-evidence, 36
Ideologies
  and fictions, 265
  nature of, 172 f.
  and scientific philosophy, 181 f.
  validity of, 175 f.
"Idols" of the mind, 28 f.
Imagination
  as an escape from reality, 203, 274 f.
  as the source of concepts, 250
Immediacy
  in dialectic, 67, 137 f., 185
  and mediation, 136 f.
  sensuous and conceptual, 137
Immediate experience, 137
  existential character of, 246 f.
  indeterminateness of, 137
Implications of ideas, 216 f.
  and temporal consequences, 240 f.
Individualism, 78, 103 f.
  and pragmatism, 195
Induction, 29
Inquiry
  course of, in idealist dialectic, 138 f.
  dialectical, 92 f.

INDEX

nature of, 1 f.
pragmatic concept of, 197 f., 200, 252
and the present, 197 f., 214 f.
Instrumentalism, 226 f., 234, 267 f.
　concept of philosophy in, 267 f.
　interpretation of experience in, 271 f., 277
　on knowledge and reality, 277 f.
　theory of logic in; see Logic
Intension and extension, 219, 222
Interaction
　of objects, 200
　in the situation, 201, 247 f.
Interests, theoretical and practical, 267 f.

James, William
　definition of "true" and "good" in, 254 f.
　the extension of meaning by, 225 f.
　optimism of, 261 f.
　and the psychological consequences of an idea, 220
Judgment, 49 f.
　instrumentalist theory of, 272 f.
　negative, 261
　practical, 223 f.
　terminating, 244

Kant, Immanuel
　antinomies of, 185 f.
　doctrine in
　　of freedom and necessity, 130 f.
　　of theoretical and practical reason, 101
　self-criticism in, 130 f.
　theory of human nature in, 131 f.
　view of science in, 150
Knowledge
　and action, 231 f.
　degrees of, 61 f., 66 f., 81 f.
　empirical, 333 f.
　experimental, 200 f.
　found in the present, 269
　and the given, 231 f., 243 f.
　and habit, 238 f., 269
　immediate and inferential, 243, 272 f.
　as interpretation, 251
　limits of, 130 f.
　as logical construction, 251 f.

origins of, 26 f.
and process, 161, 240
self-correction in, 19 f., 24 f., 181 f.
theoretical and practical, 223 f.

Language
　expressive, 244
　study of, 1 f., 252 f.
Leibniz, Gottfried Wilhelm von, 43, 58, 61
Lewis, C. I., 231, 236, 244
Liberalism
　common ground with dialectical materialism, 181 f.
　divergence from dialectical materialism, 177 f.
　on ideas and history, 177 f.
　and pragmatism, 195
Locke, John
　presuppositions of, 30
　on reality, 62
　　of knowledge, 63
　on sensation, 30, 35, 44
　simple ideas in, 30, 53, 58
　on substance, 53, 58, 62
Logic (see also Consequences, logical; Two logics, doctrine of)
　and appearance, 244
　of being and logic of becoming, 163 f.
　and existence, in idealism, 102
　limitations of, 168
　in pragmatism, 192, 244 f.
　and process, 10 f.
Logical construction, 251 f.
　knowledge as, 251 f.

Man (see also Human nature)
　an active being, 190, 254 f., 257
　conflict in, 266
　historical nature of, 177 f., 181
　relation of his ideals to existence, 274 f.
Marx, Karl, 154 f., 185
Marxism
　on the economic basis of ideologies, 174
　on religion, 174 f.
　theory of economic development, 153 f.

Meaning (*see also* Consequences)
  logical and emotive, 258 f.
  logical and psychological, 191 f., 203 f., 238 f.
  theoretical and practical, 221
  and truth, 79 f.
Meaninglessness, 212
  three senses of, 258 f.
Means and ends, instrumentalist view of, 268 f.
Mechanism, 54
Mechanistic theory of nature, 148 f.
Metaphysics
  instrumentalist, 235
  of Peirce, 235 f.
Method, 1 f., 14
  philosophic, of C. I. Lewis, 236
Mind
  as activity of synthesis, 147
  native power of the, 19
  purification of the, 20 f., 23 f.
  the source of concepts, 249 f.
Morality
  and the absolute, 114 f.
  idealistic view of, 141 f.
Motion, paradoxes of, 167 f., 186

Natural selection, of ideas, 250 f.
Nature, 14
  mechanistic view of, 147 f.
  order of events in, 241 f.
  teleological view of, 16 f.
Necessity, 38
  and freedom; *see* Freedom
Needs
  biological, and instrumentalism, 271 f.
  theoretical and practical, 254
  utilitarian and nonutilitarian, 263 f.
Negation
  as actualization, 113 f.
  and affirmation, 35, 113 f., 144 f., 261
  aspects of, 110
  double, 120
  first and second, 112 f., 159 f.
  and limitation, 115 f., 121 f.
  as a relation, 119 f.
  two forms of, 122, 169
Nietzsche, Friedrich, 175

Nonbeing, 114 f.
Not-being, 111, 115, 118 f.

Objectification of spirit, 112, 118
Objects
  evident and nonevident, 54 f., 65
  of knowledge and of inquiry, 3, 215, 239
  of use, 253
Ontology, 89
Opposites, 91 f., 94 f.
  relation between
    in idealism, 105 f.
    in materialism, 156 f.
  relation of, to the Absolute, 104 f., 165 f.
  synthesis of, in idealism, 109 f., 143 f., 149
Order
  of knowledge and order of existence, 239 f., 251 f.
  logical and psychological, 238 f.
  objective, 238 f.
Origins
  and consequences, 203 f.
  study of, 197, 205 f.
Otherness, 108, 121

Particulars, 44 f., 103 f.; *see also* Existents, finite
Past
  genetic account of the, 205 f.
  knowledge of the, 205, 240 f.
  and present, 4 f.
  study of the, 6 f.
Peirce, Charles, 216, 225 f., 235 f., 250
Perception, 248
Philosophy, 33
  breadth and consistency in, 256, 266
  contemporary, 13
  as criticism, 87 f., 129 f.; *see also* Criticism
  as examination of beliefs, 87 f., 132
  and the experimental method, 212 f., 225 f., 238 f., 256 f.
  instrumentalist conception of, 267 f.
  system of, 52

INDEX

Philosophy and the sciences, 14, 90
  and the description of existence, 229
  view of
    in idealism, 150
    in materialism, 154, 170 f.
    in pragmatism, 234 f.
Plato, 143
Plenitude, theory of, 116
Possibility, and existence, 50 f., 115
Possible experience, 222, 229, 240 f., 244
  and actual experience, 231 f., 239 f.
  and objects, 237 f.
Practical function of ideas, 241 f.
Practical, the, 70
Pragmatism, 13 f.
  and dialectic, 187 f.
  existential presuppositions of its method, 251 f.
  influence of the sciences on, 193
  and knowledge
    of existence, 241 f.
    of the past, 240 f.
  origins of, 189 f.
Prediction, and knowledge, 237 f., 243 f.
Present, the
  as locus
    of existence, 215
    of value, 270
  as the object of inquiry, 214 f.
Presuppositions
  of dialectic, 133 f.
  of experimental reasoning, 200 f.
  of the logic of consequences, 252 f.
  of science, 171, 183
Primary truths, 44 f. (*see also* First principles)
  search for, 23, 26 f.
Principle of internal criticism, 8, 132
Probability, of beliefs, 262 f.
Problematic situation, 201 f., 222
Process
  dialectic, a logic of, 11 f.
  discovery of, 11, 146 f.
  and form, 154, 172 f., 191 f.
  and idealist dialectic, 111 f., 128, 145 f.
  ideas as, in dialectic, 161 f.
  and knowledge, 161, 240
  and logic, 10 f.
  and spirit, 118
Progress, ideas of, 73, 183, 208, 212, 273
Properties, intrinsic and relational, 125 f.
Property, private, 153, 159
Propositions
  predicative and relational, 123 f.
  scientific and value, 257 f., 260 f.
  truth of, 49
Protagoras, 189
Purpose, 223 f.
  and concepts, 231 f.

Qualities, sense, 36 f., 57 f.
Quality and quantity, 70 f.
  transformation of, 157 f., 170 f.
Quantity, 168 f.
  attitudes of idealism and materialism to, 185 f.

Radical empiricism, 256 f.
Rationalism, and empiricism, 15
Realism, 69
Reality, 14, 83 f.
  appearance and, 143 f., 164 f., 244 f.
  apprehension of, 34, 51, 85
  degrees of, 61 f.
  and the given, 85, 87, 231, 245
  and knowledge, 62 f.
  objective, 48, 87, 34 f.
Reason, 24 f.
  contemplative, 76
  in dialectic, 45 f.
  as habitual association of ideas, 73 f.
  natural light of, 24, 29
  and sense, 71
  synthetic, 77, 147
Relatedness, 185
Relations
  asymmetrical, 119 f.
  and terms, 54, 119 f., 126 f.
  theory
    ef external, 125 f.
    of internal, 122 f., 124 f., 127 f.
Russell, Bertrand, 124

Satisfactions, 221
  subjectivity of, 263 f.
  theoretical and practical, 254
Schelling, Friedrich Wilhelm Joseph von, 151
Science
  idealistic interpretation of, 150 f.
  as self-corrective, 181
  and values, 262 f.
Sciences, the
  classification of, 81 f.
  and the experimental method, 238
  influence on pragmatism of, 193
  and knowledge of the past, 241
Security
  alternative ways of seeking, 202, 274
  need for, 202, 264
  evaluation of, 276 f.
Self, the, contradictions in, 101
Self-evidence, 33 f.
  actuality of, 37 f.
  of axioms, 45 f.
  of complexes, 45
  identity of, 36
  intelligibility of, 36 f.
  of simples, 44
  truth of, 39 f.
  what kinds of ideas possess, 40 f.
Self-evident, the, 18
  nature of, 36 f.
Sensationalism, 69
Sense-data
  and concepts, 127 f., 219
  and the perceptual situation, 246 f.
Simple natures, 10, 44, 57
Situation, concept of, 227
  perceptual, 246 f.
Skepticism
  contemporary, 84
  methodological, 20 f., 23 f.
    and systematic, 59 f.
  rise of, in modern thought, 129 f.
  systematic, 21
Social evolution
  criticism of, 209 f.
  in pragmatism, 209
  theory of, 198 f., 203, 207 f.
  uniformity of nature and, 208

Socrates, 190
Space, idea of, 42 f.
Species, biological, 206
  and classification, 206, 232
Spinoza, Baruch
  on affirmation and negation, 35
  on history, 71 f.
  on imagination, 61
  on negation, 35, 121 f.
  optimism of, 72
  presuppositions of, 31
  on reason, 61
  on religion, 71 f.
  on self-evidence, 31, 35, 48
Spirit
  and nature, 112, 151
  and process, 118
Structure, 168 f.; *see also* Form
  of concepts and of objects, 242
Subject
  category of, 112
  limited and unlimited, 100 f.
  and object, 99 f.
    in pragmatism, 246 f.
Subjectivism, 103 f.
Substance, 57 f.
  in dialectic, 99
  the self-evident as, 37
Syllogism, 166
Synthesis, 20
  and analysis; *see* Analysis

Technology, as a criterion of progress, 209
Theory and practice, 68, 159; *see also* Consequences; Needs; Satisfactions; Truth
  relation of ideas to, 175, 241 f.
Thing, dialectical concept of, 104 f., 123, 141
Thinking, as problem-solving, 201 f., 222 f.
Totality, idea of, 150
Truth, 39 f., 48 f.
  and consequences, 221 f.
  in ideologies, 175
  and reality, degrees of, 48 f.

INDEX

and satisfaction, 260 f.
theoretical and practical, 222, 255
and utility, 68 f.
and value, 254 f.
Truths
formal and material, 46 f.
necessary and contingent, 51, 55
primary; *see* Primary truths
Two logics, doctrine of, 162 f., 170, 182 f.

Understanding, 18
Uniformity of nature, 199
and the theory of social evolution, 208
Universals, 45
Useful, the, 65 f., 68 f.
and the true, 68 f., 176

Value
and the present, 270
and truth, 254 f.
Values
and existence, 259, 268 f.
as hypotheses, 269
and verifiability, 259, 262 f.
Verifiability, 221 f.
and values; *see* Values
Verification, 82 f., 200, 222 f.
complete and incomplete, 221 f.

Will to believe, 261 f.
criticism of, 264 f.
and fictions, 263 f.

Zeno, 186

M.